Women, Sexuality and the Changing Social Order

INTERNATIONAL STUDIES IN GLOBAL CHANGE

edited by **Tom R. Burns**, Uppsala University, Sweden and George Mason University, Virginia, USA, and **Thomas Dietz**, George Mason University, Virginia, USA.

This book series is devoted to investigations of human ecology, technology and management and their interrelations. It will include theoretical and methodological contributions to the analysis of social systems and their transformation, technology, risk, environmental problems, energy and natural resources, population growth, public health, and global economic and societal developments.

Women, Sexuality and the Changing Social Order

The Impact of Government Policies on Reproductive Behavior in Kenya

Beth Maina Ahlberg

Uppsala University
Sweden
and
Karolinska Institute
Stockholm, Sweden

Gordon and Breach
Philadelphia•Reading•Paris•Montreux•Tokyo•Melbourne

Gordon and Breach Science Publishers

5301 Tacony Street, Drawer 330	58, rue Lhomond	3-14-9, Okubo
Philadelphia, Pennsylvania 19137	75005 Paris	Shinjuku-ku, Tokyo 169
United States of America	France	Japan
Post Office Box 90	Post Office Box 161	Private Bag 8
Reading, Berkshire RG1 8JL	1820 Montreux 2	Camberwell, Victoria 3124
United Kingdom	Switzerland	Australia

Printed revised edition of doctoral thesis at Uppsala University 1988.

Abstract

Beth Maina Ahlberg, 1988, Women, Sexuality and the Changing Social Order: The Impact of Government Policies on Reproductive Behavior in Kenya. Gordon and Breach Science Publishers S.A., 274 + xiv pp., Montreux. ISBN: 2-88124-499-8

This study examines the process of mobilization of women, and analyzes their organizational dynamics, their survival strategies and concerns from a sociocultural and historical perspective. Furthermore, women's groups were conceptualized as agents who act from a subordinated position to try to transform or improve their situation.

The study has attempted to consider some of the forces involved in social transformation in general. But, it also considers two specific forms of social transformation where conflict and tension are the main forces of change. Firstly, women's groups represent actors struggling from a subordinated position. Secondly, women have been put into groups in the context of a specific social transformation process where colonial expansion to the periphery imposed new social structures, actors and processes. The groups are conceptualized in the context of the dynamic relationship and interaction between these actors and the system or structures created.

Perhaps the major conclusion arising from the present analysis is that people's orientations and perspectives need to be understood and accommodated in the design and implementation of human development. Only then can that development be meaningful and acceptable to them.

The study has also indicated that there is urgent need to use research methodologies which help strengthen people's capacities to deal with their problems.

Library of Congress Cataloging-in-Publication Data

Ahlberg, Beth Maina.
    Women, sexuality, and the changing social order: the impact of government policies on reproductive behavior in Kenya/ Beth Maina Ahlberg.
        p.   cm. -- (International studies in global change ; v. 1)
    Includes bibliographical references and index.
    ISBN 2-88124-499-8
    1. Women, Kikuyu (African people)--Kenya--Murang'a District--Societies, etc. 2. Women, Kikuyu (African people)--Kenya--Murang'a District--Social conditions. 3. Birth control--Kenya--Murang'a District.
    4. Murang'a District (Kenya)--Social conditions.
    I. Title. II.Series.

DT433.545.K55A35 1991
305.48' 896395406762--dc20

91-12553
CIP
r91

Contents

Introduction to the Series

This series brings together under one banner works by scholars of many disciplines. All of these researchers have distinguished themselves in their specialties. But here they have ventured beyond the frontiers of traditional disciplines and have developed new, innovative approaches to the study of social systems and social change.

Why? What has prompted this foray into uncharted territory? What is the reason for broadening theoretical perspectives and developing new methodologies? The impetus comes from the world we seek to understand. Scholars have traditionally made "boundary" assumptions that limited their scope of inquiry to the concerns of a discipline. Such limitations facilitate concentration, though they have always been artificial. The interpenetration of social, economic and environmental phenomena, and the precipitous pace of change in the late twentieth century make it clear that such convenient intellectual boundaries are not only unrealistic, they are untenable.

How complex waves of change sweep through the contemporary world, altering the natural environment, technology, the economy and social systems; the interaction of these forces, their impact on nations, communities, families and individuals; and the response to them by individuals and collectivities — this is the focus of the research to be presented in this series. The scholars writing in the series are themselves engaged in social change — the restructuring of our way of thinking about the world.

We are proud to have Dr. Ahlberg's study as the first volume in the series. It is symbolic of the scope of the series that its initial volume is written by an African woman working at a European institution. Her examination of the interplay between traditional culture, human reproduction, colonial politics, a modern disease and the women's movement exemplifies the complexity of modern problems, the intricate interplay of forces shaping social change, and the intellectual scope needed to understand the contemporary world.

                                                            Tom R. Burns
                                                            Thomas Dietz

Preface

This book is about how the forces that shape the social order relate to the regulation of human sexuality and reproduction. It focuses on women's movements in a major region of Kenya and analyzes from a sociocultural and historical perspective their changing roles in the regulation of sexuality and reproduction and more generally in societal developments. Through analyzing the mobilization and development of women's groups over time, the book aims to provide insight into the role these and other social agents play in historical transformations.

The material on which this book is based was collected in Murang'a, an administrative district in the central part of Kenya, and an area inhabited predominantly by the Kikuyu people. Murang'a, according to legend, is the point where the Kikuyu people originated.

Among the Kikuyu people it was customary for women to join groups after marriage and after the initiation of their first child. There were two main groups. The first consisted of newly married women; the second group, of higher status than the first, involved all women after the initiation of their first born. These groups were primarily concerned with mutual support during agricultural activities and during times of great stress, such as initiation ceremonies, childbirth and sickness. They also played a central role in the control and regulation of sex and reproduction. However, while collective support in agricultural activities and crisis situations continues today in forms similar to the past, their role in the control and regulation of sex and reproduction has declined. The regulation of sex and matters related to reproduction are increasingly left to the purely private (nuclear family) and professional spheres. This work is an attempt to analyze the concrete pattern and historical evolution of women's collective activities through colonial and post-colonial periods in order to understand how women's groups have maintained collective support in household or productive roles and crises, but have lost their role in the regulation and control of sex and reproduction.

Most countries in sub-Saharan Africa share a history of colonial domination and a post-colonial period where foreign domination and influence are still strong. Many of the changes examined in this book have generally been taking place in the entire region. In particular, most countries in the region have similar experiences in:

1) the breakdown of traditional social regulation and control systems in the wake of social and political upheaval;
2) agency lack of concrete knowledge about sex and reproduction in changing contexts; and
3) national and international governmental and nongovernmental agencies that are involved with local communities and networks in ways designed to impact on women and issues of sexuality, fertility and reproductive control.

Because of this, the concepts, questions and arguments raised in this book can be extended to sub-Saharan Africa. This extension enables one to systematically examine sexuality in its changing context and to discuss its impact on fertility and the current AIDS epidemic. Part 4 of the book addresses the difficulties of dealing with fertility and AIDS problems in the context of sub-Saharan Africa. The models and analyses of the theoretical and historical studies in Parts 1, 2 and 3 are drawn upon to identify serious problems in the family planning and AIDS programmes that will explain why so much funding and effort have often had little or no beneficial effect.

The production of this book has been a collective undertaking. From the moment I conceived the idea of studying women's collective participation, many organizations and individuals have contributed enormously, both professionally and materially.

Special thanks go to the Swedish Agency for Research Cooperation with Developing Countries (SAREC) for a financial grant which enabled me to carry out my fieldwork.

As a medical professional and advocate of multidisciplinary research, and the head of the Department of International Health Care Research (IHCAR), Professor Göran Sterky has encouraged my research and provided the necessary link with the medical profession. The group of social scientists and medical professionals involved in reproductive health at IHCAR (of which I am a part) has sharpened my views on sexuality and reproduction in their social, political and medical contexts. In our current research on reproductive health problems, and in particular the threat of AIDS, a broad perspective is essential. Gratitude goes to the Swedish International Development Authority (SIDA) whose financial support to IHCAR has not only trickled down to me, but is taken as an indication of support for this approach.

I am grateful to the staff of the Department of Community Health at the University of Nairobi, where I was affiliated during my fieldwork. In particular I would like to mention Dr. Miriam Were for her professional assistance at the inception of the study. As the head of the Department of Community Health, she assisted me with practical and administrative procedures during my stay with the department. I was immensely inspired by discussions with my friend and colleague Mrs. Violet Kimani, who has wide experience and knowledge of indigenous medicine and past Kikuyu practices.

I would like to thank all those who assisted in the field research. Great thanks go to the Women's Bureau in Nairobi for helping me to link up with the field staff. I cannot fail to mention the district administration, particularly the District Community Development Office. The office put at my disposal the locational officers, and coordinated other relevant authorities. To the six locational ACDOs in the Kiharu division, who not only assisted in data collection, but were at times subjects of research, a king-size appreciation for your assistance!

Many other Kenyan people contributed in many ways. I met with women from various professions and discussed their own individual capacities as representatives of organizations. I would like to thank Professor Micere Mugo for critically reading an earlier draft and discussing the cultural context of various Kikuyu practices and concepts. My appreciation would not be complete without mentioning Carina Odenyo and the 'Akina Mama' women's dance group. Our small talks on local gossip and laughter offered me strength and sisterly support that helped me through the long ordeal. The contributions of many other people too numerous to mention are also greatly appreciated.

The University of Uppsala and the Department of Sociology provided financial and academic support. In particular I would like to mention the Wallenberg Foundation which made available a planning grant during the early stages of fieldwork. I am most indebted to my supervisor, Professor Tom R. Burns, whose personal interest in this study and professional support and criticism have been a source of inspiration and encouragement throughout the entire process. I cannot forget Dr. Anders Olsson for helping me to untangle the mysteries of the computer. Professor Rita Liljeström of Gothenburg University, as my external examiner, provided valuable suggestions and ideas which have helped me in the re-organization of this book.

The entire process was facilitated by three men who constitute my family. Many days they had to cope by themselves when the wife, mother, cook, home manager and student was away gathering field data. They also put up with odd working hours. Towards the end, my two sons had joined in my concerns.

They woke up one early morning and found me working. They asked, "Mama, are you still writing about those troubled women?"

And above all, the toiling masses of rural women who are the subjects of this research. Their openness and readiness to have their overloaded daily routine punctuated with questioning and other forms of interference (and even more, their positive and enthusiastic posture) inspired me. It also provided an alternate vision of life. This study is dedicated to those women.

Part One :   **The Setting of the Study and Problem Formulation**

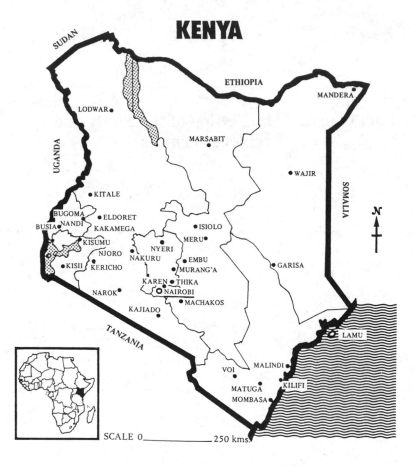

KENYA

SUDAN

ETHIOPIA

MANDERA

LODWAR

MARSABIT

UGANDA

WAJIR

KITALE

BUGOMA
NANDI
BUSIA
ELDORET
KAKAMEGA
KISUMU
ISIOLO
MERU
SOMALIA
NYERI
NJORO
NAKURU
EMBU
MURANG'A
GARISA
KISII
KERICHO
KAREN
THIKA
NAROK
NAIROBI
MACHAKOS
KAJIADO

TANZANIA

LAMU

VOI
MALINDI
MATUGA
KILIFI
MOMBASA

SCALE 0_____250 kms.

CHAPTER 1

INTRODUCTION

1. The Main Focus

This book is about social order as it relates to the regulation and locus of human sexuality and reproduction. It focuses on the small rural women's groups common all over Kenya. These groups are largely made up of women living closely together. The geographical location implies that group members are familiar with each other. Women's groups are thus localized networks which should not be confused with the larger national women's organizations.[1] This does not however imply that these groups have no links with the wider organizations and movements. Members of women's groups are also members of other organizations and groups. This forms part of their survival strategies.

My interest in a study of social movements and women's groups in particular arose largely from my own experience and that of women close to me. Growing up during the Mau Mau turmoil, I was part of those women left in the countryside while men fought from the forests, or were detained and imprisoned, or became migrant workers. As part of the emergency rules of the period, the Kikuyu people were huddled into colonial villages where women collectively built new homes, one at a time until all families had a roof over their heads.

During the 1960s, the Kikuyu people were for a second time in ten years, moved from colonial villages to settle on their newly privatized landholdings. Women then transformed the countryside by collectively constructing corrugated iron roofed and permanent houses. The mass movement of impoverished people within a short time period may have facilitated collective support in house construction. But thatching of roofs was in the past a women's job as well. Furthermore it was collectively undertaken. After house construction, women's

3

groups did not dissolve. They instead continued offering mutual support to enable members to improve family welfare and ease tensions around times of crises. Thus contemporary women's groups in the central part of Kenya seem to have retained forms and features of pre-colonial women's group activities. They have their roots in past social formations. But, at the same time, while mutual support around women's household and productive roles continue in forms similar to those in the past, women's collective role in regulation and control of sex and reproduction has diminished. The purpose of the study on which this book is based was therefore to understand the concrete conditions and processes under which women's collective partici- pation is reproduced and transformed as well as the forms it has assumed. Largely because of this, but also because women constitute a subordinated social category, I have analysed women's groups from two main perspectives.

Firstly, I have analyzed women's collective participation in the context of the recent theoretical approaches which recognize the role of social actors, including even those subject to domination, in the process of social transformation and change (Omvedt 1986, Burns and Flam 1987). Secondly, as the process of social structuration implies movement, it became necessary to understand the specific nature or patterns of historical evolution of women's groups and their activities. In this context, therefore, we can understand how women's groups have maintained collective support in household and productive roles, but lost their role in regulation and control of sex and reproduction.

These approaches would furthermore indicate the power, organi- zational potential and the benefits women gain from collective parti- cipation. Contrary to the once popularly accepted notion that sub- ordination of women is biologically determined, recent studies suggest that such subordination is a product of structural and historical processes (Boserup 1970, Aaword 1982, Kessler 1976, Rogers 1980). And given the paradoxical position women occupy everywhere, a socio-cultural and historical approach would illuminate not only the situation of women in Africa, but also the wider question of women's movements and struggles.

This form of analysis will, in particular shed light on the contro- versy surrounding the question of subordination of women in Africa. There are, for example, those who claim that modernization has

brought social and economic progress to many groups including
women in Africa. This view dominated early anthropological and
missionary writing, probably in part, to justify colonial domination.
Others see modernization processes during the colonial and post-
colonial periods as having led to the impoverization of the rural
masses and specifically to the subordination of women. They
nevertheless maintain that colonialism and the ensuing modernization
process only continued the subordination which existed in the pre-
colonial societies (Dumor, 1983). A third group constitutes those who
see colonialism as having led to a degeneration of the control and
measure of autonomy women had under pre-colonial systems (Clark,
1980).

In line with this third position, I argue that as a result of colonial
domination and the ensuing "modernization" process, new qualitatively different dimensions of marginalization and subordination of
women arose. This is particularly so in the area of sex and reproduction. Contrary to popular belief, Kikuyu women actively played a
central role in the regulation and control of sex and reproduction.
Through this, women could collectively moderate male domination. In
this sense I conceptualize women's collective actions among other
things, as a power base and strategy against subordinating forces. It is
therefore in this context that we need to understand how women's
groups operate, their dynamics, their areas of concern, their interaction with development agents and the specific ways they have
influenced or been influenced by these agents. This implies that the
question of improving conditions for women should be perceived in
the context of the specific socio-cultural, economic, political and
historical configuration of forces in a given area.

2.   Women's Groups, Sex and Reproduction

The issue of sex and reproduction is important from a number of
perspectives. Firstly, the pre-colonial Kikuyu society in general and
women's groups in particular were organized around social and biological reproduction. Women, for example, joined groups after marriage and initiation of their first child. In addition, women's groups,

played a central role in the regulation and control of sex and reproduction. Any study which conceptualizes women's groups as rooted in past social formation, cannot avoid the issue of sex and reproduction.

Secondly, contemporary groups have continued with mutual support activities around women's productive roles in forms similar to the past. Today however, research shows they play a minimal role in the regulation of sex and reproduction. There is thus a need to analyse and understand how this situation has evolved. Thirdly, these processes and developments have practical implications for Kenya and other countries in similar situations. What do they imply for programmes such as fertility and HIV/AIDS control which deal with human sexuality ?

My concern is therefore to understand the processes of transformation from a social arrangement where women collectively played a central role in the control of sex and reproduction to one where they have become collectively passive in this sphere of social life. Research suggests that in spite of increasing reproductive health problems, women's groups resist efforts of governments and other agencies to deal with problems of sexuality.

My concern with women's collective participation in the regulation and control of sex and reproduction is therefore in part based on the wider concern of the deteriorating state of health in general and women's reproductive health in particular. By and large, the poor state of health prevailing in Africa is a function of material conditions. But material conditions exist in contexts of socio-economic and political organization. Poverty is therefore a social and political condition which has consequences for the health of the people. Health care systems based on western medicine rarely address these social and political aspects of health.

Western medicine developed in response to disease as a natural phenomenon. The major concern of western medicine has therefore been the development of medical technology to cure disease (Doyal 1979, Illich 1975). Through colonialism, western medicine was introduced to Kenya and other colonial countries. In Kenya, western medical facilities were established at the pockets of white settlement and administrative posts mainly to provide services to settlers and colonial administrators.[2] This historically-produced structure and orientation has by and large been maintained during the post-colonial period.

The discussion of structure and orientation of health care is important here, because even sex and reproduction have been transformed into medical issues. They are handled within the prevailing health care services. In this context, it is imperative we consider the nature of health care in Kenya.

3.   Health Care in Kenya

The poverty which characterizes African countries is often expressed through health indicators such as life expectancy, mortality levels including infant mortality, disease and health conditions, availability of basic amenities like housing, water supplies and trained manpower.

Table 1: Kenya's state of health 1963-1982.

	1963	1982
Death rate / 1000	20	14
Infant mortality / 1000	120	86
Life expectancy in years	40	54
Hospitals	148	218
Qualified doctors	339	787

Source: Republic of Kenya: Development Plan 1984-1988.

Table 1 indicates the major trends in Kenya since independence, during which time there has been some improvement in health status. It is often claimed that this improvement is primarily a result of expansion of health services. But, the effectiveness of the health care system in improving the quality of life for the majority of the people in Kenya is hampered by its curative emphasis and maldistribution of services. In the 1970s, two thirds of the health budget went into cura-tive care in the form of construction, running and maintenance of large medical facilities. During the same period, rural health services received only 8.9%, while preventive health (communicable diseases, nutrition, public health and health education) received only 6.7% of the total health budget.[3] It is however interesting to note that while emphasis has been on curative care, major causes of mortality and morbidity are health and disease conditions which can be prevented through one or the other of community actions and improvement of other conditions outside medical facilities. In 1980, 70% of all deaths and 60% of the total reported morbidity were found to have resulted from such preventable disease conditions. During the same year, 33% of reported childhood deaths had malnutrition as a contributing factor (UNICEF/Kenya Central Bureau of Statistics, 1984).[4]

In addition, most of the existing medical facilities and staff are disproportionally allocated.[5] Urban areas take the largest share. In 1978, Nairobi alone had 12% of all hospitals in the country while serving less than 1% of the population (Economic Survey, 1978). Thus, in spite of the increase in the number of medical facilities and medical personnel, the effectiveness of the medical care in meeting health needs is limited by the nature of its orientation and structure.

The curative, unevenly distributed medical care has resulted in three specific patterns of medical care utilization. Large proportions of the population in general and more specifically in the rural areas are, due to the shortage of facilities and services, forced to continue using indigenous medical care. Studies focusing on utilization of medical care however indicate that medical facilities may be avoided for various other reasons. Women may avoid using the facilities (hospital or indigenous) nearest them for reproductive health problems, such as birth control, infertility, and treatment of sexually transmitted diseases. These sexually related health problems carry considerable social stigma. Women therefore use distant facilities to avoid being identified. Medical facilities may also be by-passed in search of those perceived as offering better care. Through kin and extended family support networks, rural people move to urban areas when they are sick or perceive they need medical care, even when their health problems can well be handled in rural facilities. This results in overcrowding in some facilities including referral hospitals such as the Kenyatta National Hospital in Nairobi. At the same time, medical facilities in the rural areas often go under-utilized.

Medical care, sex and reproduction

Reproduction including fertility regulation and control has increasingly come to be regarded as a medical problem. It is therefore handled within the health care structure described above. The type of problems which women face when they seek medical care for reproductive health problems are illustrated by the following observations in two rural hospitals.

In the course of my fieldwork, it became necessary to identify women with specific health problems of reproduction. The aim was to find how such women were dealing with the problems and the extent to which women's groups were involved in these actions. I approached the District Hospital within the study area for identification of such women. However, during the entire period of the study, the clinic remained closed due to lack of supplies and staff. The only gynaecologist in the hospital handled emergency cases such as induced abortions and related complications, miscarriages and deliveries, none of which came from the study groups.

The second case involved two childless women from the study area. They visited the Provincial Hospital Nyeri in order to consult a gynaecologist. But, the long queue and waiting reduced their prospect for medical check-up and treatment.

The third case shows that apart from shortage of supplies and manpower, the quality of those available is poor. This case was observed at the MCH/Family planning clinic at the District Hospital. There was a long queue of pregnant women waiting for their regular antenatal checkup. The midwife in charge was busy with her friends while a patient lay on the bed unattended. After ten minutes of waiting, the midwife made a one minute check-up, scribbled something on the patient's card, and handed the card to the patient without any verbal communication.

The effectiveness of the prevailing health care system in meeting health needs is limited by its orientation and structure. The response to problems of sexuality such as control of fertility and sexually transmitted diseases including HIV/AIDS, imply that there are many factors in the area of sex and reproduction which are poorly understood.[6]

I observed that women in Murang'a by-pass medical facilities nearest them when seeking contraceptives in order to conceal their identity. More important perhaps was the discrepancy between what women's groups claimed they were doing and what they actually did. Women's groups were eager to appear active in the government's family planning programme. But, some of their actions may even discourage contraceptive use. Reproductive matters were rarely collectively discussed within the context of the groups. However, exaggerated and frightening side effects arising from contraceptive use were openly and spontaneously discussed within the groups. Furthermore, after nearly thirty years of perhaps the most expensively supported family planning programme anywhere, Kenya still records less than 20% contraceptive acceptance rate. Ironically poor response to the government fertility control programme, and the decline in collective responsibility in matters of sex and reproduction occurs within a situation where women's health steadily deteriorates. In light of this, it makes little sense for women to avoid programmes such as family planning whose stated objective is to improve women's health. It seems however that current responses reflect the nature of transformation and in particular the use of models derived from contexts other than the ones where such models are implemented. Part of the task of this book is to discuss these processes and indicate their implication to the women's groups and their activities as well as development programmes aimed at regulation and control of sexuality and reproduction.

4.   The Organization of the Book

The book is divided into four parts. The first, comprising chapters one, two and three, sets the problem in its conceptual and methodological perspective. Part two focuses on the process of transformation of the Kikuyu society from the pre-colonial (chapter 4), through colonial (chapter 5) to post-colonial (chapter 6) periods and discusses its impact on women, and women's group productive and reproductive activities. Part three is a discussion of the patterns and dynamics of contemporary women's groups. That section in particular focuses on the patterns and impact of interaction between women's groups and other agencies including the government (chapter 7). Chapter 8 examines the internal structure and characteristics of women's groups and their pattern of change, while chapter 9 discusses the two major areas of women's group activities followed by a summary and concluding remarks in chapter 10.

Part four deals with specific programmes through which governments and various other agencies attempt to regulate and control sex and reproduction. Chapter 11 reviews and discusses the case of family planning programmes in Sub-Sahara Africa. The chapter indicates that family planning programmes failed largely because of lack of consideration of local contexts and realities. Chapter 12 focuses on the AIDS crisis in Sub-Sahara Africa suggesting the inability of development agencies, to draw from previous experiences and mistakes. Consequently, although HIV/AIDS has features which makes its control more problematic, agencies are repeating many of the mistakes of the family planning programmes, in dealing with human sexuality and reproduction.

CHAPTER 2

THE STUDY AREA AND METHODS OF THE STUDY

1. The Area

Kenya lies on the East Coast of Africa, with the equator cutting across roughly in the middle. The combined equatorial location and high altitude makes parts of the country agriculturally potential. But the amount of arable land is limited. Of the total land area of 569,000 square kilometres, only about 7% has adequate rainfall and good soils (UNICEF/Central Bureau of Statistics, 1984).

Table 2: Population growth in Kenya

Year	Number of people	Calculated Annual growth rate %
1948	5 408 000	-
1962	8 636 000	3.3%
1969	10 943 000	3.4%
1979	*15 327 000	3.8%

*Adjusted total 16 136 000, Population Census 1979, Analytical Report.
Source: UNICEF/Central Bureau of Statistics, 1984.

Kenya's population is usually shown to have undergone a rapid increase during the past few decades. There are geographical variations in population concentration. Higher density levels are found in the fertile arable highlands east and west of the Great Rift Valley which runs from the Middle East to Southern Africa. The 1979 population census showed an average population density of 27 persons per square kilometres for the whole country. However, average densities of 280, 261 and 202 were reported for Kiambu, Murang'a and

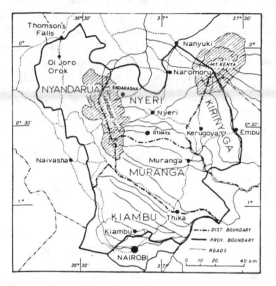

Kenya: Central Province (Source: Muriuki 1978)

Kirinyaga Districts respectively. Some sublocations of Murang'a, the study district, had densities of 700 persons per square kilometre. Population increase in relationship to land availability has been used since the 1940s (Mitchell 1952, Ward, 1953, Huxley 1937)[1] to justify a population control programme which the Kenya government and many governmental and non-governmental donor agencies consider central for development (USAID/Kenya 1985, Shepherd 1984, World Bank 1983).

But, while agriculturally potential land may be scarce, the distribution patterns of what is available are themselves a major limiting factor to the welfare of the people. From a historical perspective, land for colonial white settlement was taken from the fertile highlands which came to be known as the "White Highlands".[2]   After independence, families have been resettled on small holdings through a number of settlement schemes. The best known of these was the "Million Acre Settlement Scheme" which was introduced in 1961 and completed in 1971. But by 1965, the economics of small scale settlement was already being questioned. This led to postponement of such schemes and encouragement of willing-buyer/willing-seller transactions of former large settler farms (Okoth-Ogendo, 1981). This approach naturally excluded the largest proportion of the population from having access to land.

Kiharu Division

This study was carried out in Kiharu, an administrative division of Murang'a District of Central Province. Kiharu is divided into six locations Weithaga, Mugoiri, Murarandia,bordering the Aberdare Range

Table 3: Population of Murang'a District by sex and division

Division	Males	Females	Total	Sqkm	Density
Kandara	86,928	94,793	181,721	421	430
Kigumo	64,640	70,476	135,116	438	308
Kangema	61,938	70,974	132,912	341	388
Kiharu	65,934	72,248	138,182	407	339
Makuyu	31,192	29,210	60,402	643	93
Total	310,632	337,701	648,333	2,476	261

Source: Population Census, 1979.

to the west and Mbiri, Gaturi and Gikindu to the east bordering
Sagana township in Kirinyaga District and Nyeri District on the
northern side. Makuyu Division to the south-east has sisal, coffee and
pineapple plantation farms largely dependent on male migrant
labour. In early 1980s, Murang'a township, the District headquarter,
was raised to municipality status. It thus acquired a separate
administration.

Geographically and agriculturally, Kiharu Division is part of the
fertile and well watered highlands east of the Rift Valley. Both cash
crops (coffee and tea) and subsistence crops (maize, beans, potatoes,
bananas, cabbages, onions etc.) are grown on small holdings. In terms
of population, Kiharu is densily populated.

Table 4: Population of Kiharu Division

Location	Male	Female	Total	Sqkm	Density
Mugoiri*	24,422	27,085	51,507	119	431
Mbiri	3,825	4,241	8,066	27	298
Gikindu	4,277	4,746	9,023	81	111
Gaturi	12,358	13,800	26,158	103	253
Weithaga	13,331	14,807	28,138	50	561
Municipality	7,721	7,569	15,290	26	576
Total	65,934	72,248	138,182	407	339

* Murarandia Location was during the 1979 Population
  Census part of Mugoiri Location and that is why it does
  not appear separately here. Estimated Area: 33 sq. km,
  Population density: 403.

Source: Population Census 1979.

Except for the Municipality where male exceeds female population,
all the locations have a higher female population. Male exceeds

female population in Makuyu Division, to the south-east of Kiharu as well.[3] This is mainly because of the large sisal, coffee and pineapple plantations where labour is largely male.

2. The Choice of the Study Area

The complexity and sensitivity of issues of sex and reproduction and lack of written records on the mobilization of women for collective action were important considerations in the choice of my study area. As a member of the Kikuyu people, I was an insider who grew up in the study area (Huitzer and Mannheim, 1979). Without underestimating problems which I encountered, being an insider was a tremendous resource. In particular there were those practical considerations of inside knowledge of the language, experience, knowledge and familiarity with many unrecorded but relevant issues; the area and the people; their conditions of life, their moral postulates including acceptable and unacceptable behavior. In the absence of recorded information concerning living conditions at the closing years of the colonial rule, and women's group activities in early post-colonial period, such personal experience and familiarity became an important resource. All these were useful factors in the conduct of my research.

Moreover, for a research project of this nature, which extracted the bulk of information from group interviews in the form of discussion and observation, knowledge of the language proved essential for a number of reasons. Kikuyu people particularly the elderly make extensive use of proverbs and other special forms of communication. Such forms of communication become even more complex when the problem is sensitive and when the focus is on groups. It was thus possible to gain access to and decipher messages passed through special forms of communication.

Of special importance was the access to messages spoken or unspoken indicating that without negative undertones, people are indeed negative to many issues and programmes introduced from outside. This was clear from two observations. Firstly, group members used gestures and facial expressions in ways which indicated they were cautious about certain issues of reproduction. Secondly, there was spontaneous discussion of exaggerated and frightening side effects related to contraceptive use. At the same time groups were eager to be seen as being actively involved in the government's fertility control programme. These are insights inaccessible to foreign researchers including anthropologists who use immersing methods. Even when anthropologists gain such insight, because of the time lag, as Chambers (1983) also indicates, their results may be of little practical value. I made use of these common and special forms of communication to obtain more information, to ascertain its validity and to establish the extent of its usage.

Mobilization of women for collective action itself was an important factor in the process of selecting the study area. Murang'a District within which the study division is situated, is one of the areas where mobilization of women into groups in their current form and purpose started. Analysis of data collected by the Women's Bureau for five selected districts show that with 92% Murang'a had the highest percentage of women's groups forming before 1973. The other four districts including Kiambu, Machakos, Kisii and Baringo had 43%, 26%, 27% and 50% respectively (Monsted, 1978). The process of colonial domination was perhaps felt more intensively in this area because of its location in relationship to European settlement and the Mau Mau war. The effects on the people of Mau Mau confrontation- the toll of life, burning of homes, and life in colonial villages, displacement through imprisonment, detention and deportation, land consolidation and organization of women into clubs to counteract their active involvement in the Mau Mau- were more concentrated in this area (Gikonyo 1972, Hughes 1955, Wilson 1956).[4]

Given these and other factors, such as financial and time constraints, it was also necessary to select an area both rural and accessible. Kiharu Division situated about one hundred kilometres north of the capital city Nairobi, is accessible through a tarmac road which cuts its southern tip to connect Nairobi and the northern part of Kenya. Another tarmac road cuts across the area from east to west. Numerous smaller all-weather roads have been built through access road programmes. This made accessibility into the interior of the study division possible during the season of heavy rains which in turn provided an opportunity to observe groups and their activities during periods of intensive farm activities.

Besides accessibility, Murang'a District as a whole is well endowed with other forms of infrastructure. Some of the most successful agricultural co-operatives (coffee, tea and dairy) are found here. The study division has a number of medical facilities. The district hospital is situated in Murang'a Township within the study division. Maragua Rural Training Health Centre, one of the six such rural health centres which were established in the mid-1970s to cater for refresher courses for paramedical staff, is accessible to large proportions of Mbiri, Gikindu and Mugoiri locations even though it is situated outside Kiharu Division. Apart from these fairly large government medical institutions, each location has a government health centre or dispensary.

The Catholic Church runs a large and probably one of the oldest medical institutions (Muriranjas at Mugoiri Location) in the study area. The same church runs two homes for old men and women in the area.

From its agricultural potential and the pattern and availability of various infrastructures, the study area and in general the entire Central Province is often considered to be more advanced than other areas of Kenya. It can therefore be argued that the study area is not representative of the country as a whole. But while such regional variations exist and are a historical fact, it is also true that the process of colonial domination had a more profound impact in this area. Moreover, the study entails or aims to tap those unique features and forces shaping the process of group mobilization, their dynamics and strategies making the question of representativeness irrelevant.

3.   Methods of the Study

Survey of women's groups

I carried out a survey of women's groups to elicit information concerning group structure (numbers, size and composition), the nature of their activities and their interaction with other social agents within the wider system. The Assistant Community Development Officers (ACDO) were used for the administration of the questionnaire. The ACDOs are Government Extension Officers responsible for a location. They are at the bottom of the line of authority within the ministries of Culture and Social Services (MoCSS) and Local Government (MoLG), the latter of which is the employer. They are normally recruited from the same areas they serve or from neighbouring locations. They are thus well known to women's groups not only from interaction in the course of their duties, but because they are part of the communities they serve. In the course of fieldwork, all studied groups were found to know the ACDO (commonly referred to as CDA) in their area. It was also observed that apart from the chief, the ACDO was the best known among government extension officers.

The use of government officers for data collection posed a number of problems. The close contact between ACDOs and women's groups was an important consideration in deciding to use the officers for data collection. But in spite of this, as government officers, certain biases were apparent. The officers and the government in general, for example, considered as enterprising only those groups involved in commercial projects. This came out clearly during the initial stages of fieldwork. I approached the district officer in charge of the women's programme for the purpose of identifying women's groups. I had stressed that both registered and informal women's groups including those not engaged in income-generation were of interest. However, only registered groups and those involved in income-generation were identified. This was not just because the government was only dealing with registered groups. The feeling that women's groups were often engaged in small useless projects was apparent, particularly within the local administration. According to one chief, this was an indication of the failure of the ACDOs. According to the chief, ACDOs let women's groups make choices, instead of directing them to engage in large economic projects.

The use of the ACDOs also provided an opportunity to observe the social distance that normally hinders communication between simple rural people and government officers, including the subtle ways such differences manifest themselves. Whenever the ACDO visited the groups, he or she was offered special treatment. A table and a few chairs were organized for the officer, any other visitors and the group leaders. Members of the groups sat on whatever else they could lay hands on. In a number of occasions, I tried to discourage the use of chairs and tables by sitting among women. This was resisted mainly by the ACDOs who argued that such behavior would annoy women. While the officers felt that way, women appreciated my attempts to identify with them. The experience gained also indicates that a study of mutual aid groups outside of government rules and regulations would require a different research design.

In spite of these shortcomings, involvement of government officers in the research provided an opportunity to understand the nature and the dynamics of interaction between the groups and other agents. This was one of the objectives of the study. These considerations weighed more heavily than the biases which could arise. Besides, such biases were minimized through designing a simple questionnaire which avoided opinion-related questions. The ACDOs were trained for data collection, and were closely supervised by the investigator.

The questionnaires were administered mainly to the chairperson or in her absence the secretary or the treasurer of the 177 women's groups registered with the Ministry of Culture and Social Services.

The group interview method

A major part of the information on women's group activities and their involvement in the regulation and control of sex and reproduction was drawn from the case studies of groups, using group interview discussion method. The initial plan was to identify and study in depth, four types of women's groups, selected on the basis of the following criteria.

(i) Extent to which women's groups still use past forms of organization as indicated by their names and involvement in cultural dancing and singing.

(ii) Extent to which they have adapted new forms.

However, piloting and the early phase of the study, when groups were being identified and categorized according to the above criteria, indi-

cated that the field reality was more complex. The following observations led to the need to abandon the initial design in favour of
assessment of many diverse groups.

(1) The use of cultural names denoting reproductive performance of
women and the involvement of groups in cultural dancing and
singing had declined. Secondly, most groups had a mixed
membership in terms of religion. Many group members were at
the same time affiliated to larger women's church organizations.
These were some of the variables expected to indicate orientation
of groups.

(2) The existence of unregistered or independent groups was illegal.
The concept of a women's group thus referred to government
registered groups. This made it difficult to identify groups which
had nothing to do with the government.

(3) Interaction between the groups themselves and with the outside
world had intensified, particularly with the establishment of
women's group committees at various government administrative
levels. Members of groups belong to several women's groups,
church organizations such as Mothers' Union, Catholic Women
Association, church choirs and committees, school committees
and other mixed self-help groups.

(4) But probably the main indication of the need to abandon the
simple comparative design was the response to the question of
group's involvement in the regulation of sex and reproduction.
There were two main responses.

Groups indicated they had little involvement in sexual and reproductive problems including those that threaten members with childlessness. I used the concept of childlessness to present a concrete
health problem of reproduction around which other issues could be
discussed. The main reason given for lack of involvement was that
reproduction seemed to be regarded as a matter of concern largely or
only for individual couples. This response, however, contradicted what
followed: that groups were instead helping their members regulate
and control fertility.

Table 5: Tabular sketch of the original design.

	High Outside contact	Low outside contact
Cultural oriented	Dance groups at national level for resource mobilization	Dance groups at local level for recreation
Less cultural	Enterprising groups Oriented to church	Less enter-prising Oriented to church

These early findings led to the need to assess a larger number of women's groups, and to study more systematically the nature of women's group involvement in the question of fertility control.

The new selection criteria

The need to assess a larger variety of groups became apparent. It also became necessary to assess groups other than women's groups as defined here. Of the 12 groups assessed, two were outside the definition. They included a church organization (Gathukiini Mother's Union) and a self-help group (Kihara) mixed on the basis of sex. The rest were women's groups as defined here. They were selected on the basis of their life-span (formed prior or after 1980) and area (low potential eastern or high potential western part of the study area). Because of the influence of different Christian denominations on matters of reproduction, care was taken to select groups from predominantly Protestant and Catholic areas. However, except for two groups, Ithiki and Weithaga Mission, whose members were only

Catholic and Protestant respectively, groups had mixed membership even when they were situated in predominantly Catholic or Protestant areas.

Table 6: List of groups selected for assessment

Name	Year	Area	Predominant Religion
Gitumbi	1965	low	mixed
Weithaga	1968	high	Protestant
Gitungano	1969	low	mixed
Kiangochi	1970	low	mixed
Mwihoko	1983	high	Protestant
Ithiki	1984	low	Catholic
Nyakio	1971	high	Catholic
Utheri Munyu	1969	low	mixed
Thechi	1970	low	Catholic
Muiguithania	1975	low	mixed
Kihara	1983	low	mixed
Gathukiini	1962	low	Protestant

The interview setting

These groups were visited more than twice. The first visit was always organized to coincide with the group's regular meeting. Subsequent visits were organized collectively. Care was taken to organize these visits when most members could attend. My first visit to Thechi Women's Group coincided with two important activities. It was the last day for school children and parents had to be physically in school to sign their children off. It was also cattle dipping day. As a result, attendance was low. During these visits, group discussions were held. There were a number of problems with group discussion as an interview method. Although I had explained that this was a research project where groups were my teachers, I was still regarded as the teacher and therefore a resource.[5] This was perhaps because of the role I played in facilitating participation of group members in the discussions. Furthermore, elderly members felt that any discussion related to sexuality and reproduction should be directed to the younger women. It became apparent that to enlist participation of the entire group, discussions had to reflect the interests of the various age categories. Discussions were thus divided into two parts. Elderly women were encouraged to start by discussing sexual and repro- ductive matters in general and methods of fertility control in the past. It was probably here that group discussion as a method of gathering information was most suited. The elderly women discussed the past enthusiastically contrasting it with the contemporary situation. More importantly perhaps, they reproached the younger women for failing to control their sexuality. Naturally, the younger women defended themselves, bringing out vividly their paradoxical and vulnerable situation as they experience it.

Group interview method: a two-way learning process

Apart from the wealth of information obtained from group interviews, the possibility was provided to learn popular forms of communication used around sensitive issues. These popular forms of communication facilitated gathering information. I used the popular forms of commu- nication for encouraging discussion among women of varying ages.[6] Three expressions turned out to be particularly useful in this respect. These popular expressions reflect conflicts facing women in the area of sex and reproduction. The first was a jocular expression commonly used by elderly women that since they had packed up their tools, reproduction was not relevant to them. Whenever this expression was used, I re-addressed the question to focus on how they handled repro- duction when they had the tools. This turned out to be useful for discussing both past and present practices of reproduction.

A similar expression, " My child! Do not let them cheat you," was used by younger women to show that mothers-in-law opposed contra- ceptive use.

The third expression was a Kikuyu proverb used in relation to issues which are considered obscene, but educative otherwise. The

Kikuyu version, "Kirira ni waga thoni," means that an educator need not be embarrassed to use obscene language. This particular expression proved useful for discussing reproduction in groups which had male participants. In such groups male participants used the expression to remove any inhibitions, after which they discussed matters of sex and reproduction freely. In a number of cases, groups used this expression to get me to be more explicit. Groups in this case expected to be taught, as they probably are accustomed in such forums.

Dealing with groups as a unit provided the opportunity to gather information through overhearing and observing them in their inter-personal interactions. Three of many incidents of interaction observed indicate the nature of information obtained. During one of several public meetings I attended, the District Officer (DO) explained the objectives of government fertility control programme. He emphasized that people should reproduce the number of children they can support. The address however, ended on a warning note that, the government may be forced to deny maternity leave to women after their third child. A group of women in the crowd warned each other cynically, "Nimukuonio," implying that the government would be harsh on those who refuse to comply.

The second was overheard in public transport. A group of men and women discussed the soaring cost of living and concluded that child-spacing need to be taken seriously. The discussion centred on a family which could not raise enough money for school fees because four of its children were in high school at the same time. According to the small group of travellers, the concerned family could have avoided this stressful situation through proper child-spacing.

The third case was overheard during a women's group meeting. An elderly woman member of the group had recently suffered from bloody diarrhoea. She suspected sukuma wiki (collards) which is widely used as a relish to have caused the problem. She therefore decided not to eat collards any more.

In another group it was possible to make a quick cross-check to a question whose reply was clearly evasive. The question intended to find out the extent to which traditional healers were used in the study area. The first reaction was to deny any use. According to this group, people in the area had stopped using traditional medicine because they had been informed that traditional medicine is harmful. The same question was reversed to enquire whether they were not aware that most medicines were made from plants and herbs growing around them. This question was answered positively. A lively discussion concerning the variety of herbs, extensively used in the area followed. I took the opportunity to discuss the role of the various traditional healers. It was from this group that the existence of Traditional Birth Attendants (TBAs) commonly known as "Placenta Pullers" (Agucia Njogu) was discovered. This was further crosschecked with other groups.

Recording of information gathered through group interviews was problematic. The initial plan was to tape all the discussions. The use of a tape recorder was however opposed by the groups. One group was particularly unhappy with a previous researcher who had gathered extensive information concerning family size and economic status without being explicit about the use of the information being gathered. The group which had entertained the researcher extensively had expected receprocation with resources. This anger was therefore directed to me, and the mention of using a tape recorder became even more suspected:

"Tell us whether you have already taped us without our knowledge."[7]

The idea of taping the discussions was therefore abandoned. The tape was instead used for recording songs of groups which were assessed in greater detail.

Information gathered during group discussions was recorded by writing the main points during the meetings. Research assistants (mostly the ACDO), who prior to discussions were briefed on the main issues to be discussed, were also requested to note the main points. Their personal knowledge of group members was particularly useful in explaining peculiar behaviours. At the same time these officers provided relevant background information. The ACDOs were thus both research assistants and key informants as well. Through this double role a clear picture of the relationship between the government, the politicians and the groups unfolded. Furthermore, group discussions where women were encouraged to participate and give their views seemed to have some impact on these officers. Many were impressed at the ease with which group members expressed themselves on sensitive issues. This is probably because these officers are mainly used to giving directives down to the people, an approach which offers little possibility for feedback. At the end of each group discussion session, we exchanged notes. I prepared the full report of each discussion session the same night and before any other session.

The key informants and observation

A wide range of key people provided information on a spectrum of issues directly relevant to the study or provided background information. The administrative heads of the locations (chiefs), various other government extension workers, church leaders and a variety of women leaders in one way or the other provided relevant information. Living in the study area made use of key informants possible. It was easy to visit people in their homes or other situations when they were not pressed with other activities, such as during church functions. Through this network of key informants, I obtained detailed information on 15 women who had used or were about to use contraceptives. It was further possible to get access to detailed information on four childless women, who themselves became major key informants on the social problems of being childless and the options open to them. In many occasions, both direct and participant observation were used for gathering inf ormation on a wide range of issues. Direct observation was used during group discussion sessions and other group gatherings where members commonly used communication other than speech to express opinions or draw attention.

Although the study was designed to focus on women's groups, due to the observation that problems of reproduction were regarded as concerns of individual couples, it became necessary to identify specific women with such problems. Traditional healers from the area were consulted. Like the hospital, this method did not yield positive results. According to the healers consulted, women with such problems were likely to consult healers from distant places in order to conceal identity. The consultation of Traditional Birth Attendants (TBAs) who constitute an important category of specialists in the area of reproduction was not possible. This is not because TBAs do not exist.

Contrary to the Ministry of Health which had been unable to identify TBAs and was therefore not implementing its training programme in this area, I found that there are TBAs specially known by their function of pulling a retained placenta. It was however observed that the surviving ones were too old to practice. They could therefore not be used for identifying women with specific reproductive health problems.

Review of records and official documents

Review of secondary materials and official documents, provided both background information, and basic data. In particular the method retrieved valuable information concerning the situation of women during the colonial period, their interaction with the colonial government and the impact of this interaction to their collective activities. Through Uppsala University data base, records and documents of the colonial administration as well as other materials dealing with women were retrieved from various sources in Europe and Kenya. During fieldwork, official records dealing with the women's programme in the period 1970-1985 were also used to elicit information on the interaction between the groups and the government. Specifically this source provided insight on the issue of government funding, government support to groups including its presentation, formation and election of women's group committees and the training programme of women's groups.

Strategies of Handling Major Problems

Many problems encountered were related to the nature of the prevailing social, economic and political environment. The problem of contradictory and clearly evasive responses was apparent. As is usually the case in communities such as the Kikuyu, which have been exposed to intensive and at times aggressive targetting respondents carefully select and tell only what they figure the researcher wants to know.

I observed many incidents where women told what they thought was the view of the government and other development agents.

Women's groups were eager to show that they encouraged their members to use contraceptives, even though it was clear that some of their actions had the opposite effect. Secondly, there was denial of use of traditional medicine. As discussed further below, indigenous healing practices were forbidden by the missionaries and the colonial government. Moreover, until recently, African governments have neither encouraged its use. It therefore seems that the safest thing for the people is to deny its use, as an indication of compliance to government rules. However, when I encouraged the discussion through indicating that medicines are made from common plants and herbs, the denial changed into acceptance.

A third incident of this nature was observed when a group of extension workers visited a locational group secretary. I was already in the compound together with the group secretary, her daughter who had completed high school the previous year and was looking for a job and an orphan boy who had grown up in a government welfare institution. We were discussing the problem of unemployment. The group secretary was critical of the government for not creating jobs enough to accommodate the youth. However, when the group of women extension workers arrived, the secretary praised the government for its great achievements. In this way, target subjects are able to resist without exposing themselves.

Other problems were related to the design of this study. Involving government ACDOs as research assistants was problematic. Government officer's conceptualization of women's groups was limited to registered groups. I was therefore forced to exclude the informal, unregistered groups.

Problems also arose because I was an insider. Of special importance here was the nature of community expectations and demands on me. I was, for example, regarded as an important resource. This was not unique to me. Weithaga Mission Women's Group had similar expectations from a researcher even though she was not an insider. Being an insider, however, the problem of resource demand presented itself in a more forceful way. This is probably because an insider understands the people and their situation in a more involved way.

There were two major issues for which groups and individuals sought assistance. The problem of unemployment is critical. Most group members and individuals from the area requested help to secure jobs for themselves or their children. Groups such as Kiangochi even organized a special meeting to discuss how its members could be assisted to secure jobs. This was a frustrating problem because the existing socio-economic structure allowed for few solutions.

The second problem area was contribution to self-help (harambee) projects. There were a number of such self-help activities demanding monetary contribution from the community and the women's groups. The most critical was perhaps a harambee organized by the Catholic Women's Association. The chairperson had proposed that I should be the guest of honour. The role of a guest of honour is to conduct the harambee-calling and announcing the amount of money or item each participant contributes. In addition the guest of honour is expected to make the largest contribution. Guests of honour are therefore powerful, wealthy and prominent people. The idea of a researcher becoming a guest of honour can create biases. I made efforts to avoid being the guest of honour. Knowledge of the social network of relationships within the organization was useful at this point. The organization was made up of small groups from different localities. I managed to convince one of the local groups that the idea of a young unknown and inexperienced woman as guest of honour may not help their organization raise a large sum of money. They in turn conveyed the message to the chairperson. The proposal was dropped without jeopardizing the relationship. In these kinds of situations, drawing the line between research and service becomes critical.

Dealing with groups as the unit of analysis and the use of group discussion method for data collection was also problematic. As pointed out, the concept of group discussion among rural people who are used to being given directives in such forums was not well understood. Furthermore, group discussions and the use of unstructured questions also implied that women could raise issues and questions of central concern to them. Such issues were often outside the framework of the discussion. Two issues were commonly raised. The first concerned child adoption. The second revolved around problems of menopause. For information concerning the process of child adoption, groups were referred to the ACDO for clarification. It became clear, however, that part of their concern was the long and tedious bureaucratic procedures encountered in the process of child adoption. The concern of women with the problem of menopause gave evidence as to how the issue is neglected both from social and medical view points. Personally, I realized how little I knew about the subject and that attempts to interest medical experts were fruitless.

From another perspective, groups drew my attention to the fact that I had not been explicit.[8] They expected to be taught, as is usually the case in such forums. The group approach also meant dealing with women of varying generations between whom communication barriers in matters of sex and reproduction exist. These barriers have been reinforced by the government programmes which are only focused on fertility control of married women.

Group discussion with an insider was probably most suited under these circumstances. Familiarity with the language and the people facilitated understanding and use of popular expressions. These expressions could reflect, in what I would call a light-hearted manner, the nature of conflicts facing women in general and in the area of sex and reproduction. As a result, the expressions facilitated participation of women in group discussions, and at the same time they were used to draw more information.

Presentation of Data

Several types of data were gathered. Quantitative data on major features and characteristics of women's groups is presented mainly through tabulation. This is complemented by the qualitative data in the form of case studies of groups. The quantitative and qualitative sections are however fitted into the socio-cultural and historical analytical framework.

CHAPTER 3

THE CONCEPTUAL FRAMEWORK OF THE STUDY

1. The Actor-Systems-Dynamics Analytical Framework

The women's groups of this study are perceived as actors who formulate strategies aimed at influencing or shaping the social system in which they are a part. From this perspective my analysis fits in the recent theoretical development which recognizes the dynamics of social actors whether individuals or collectives in social structuration and transformation. But social actions take place within a social structure which offers opportunities and meaning while at the same time restraining the actors. In general, the actor-systems dynamics theoretical framework advanced by, among others, Burns is considered relevant in this particular study. According to this framework, social actors interact within the constraints and opportunities of existing structures at the same time as they act upon and restructure the system (Burns and Flam 1987). Social actors are thus the makers of their own history, a process which is not only continuous, but one where past experiences, knowledge and cultural traits are carried along. This framework further recognizes that even dominated groups are dynamic forces in the shaping of the social system and its change.[1]

The relevance of actor-systems framework

The actor-systems analytical framework is relevant to the analysis of women's groups because of the possibility it offers for interpreting complex social interaction settings. As the interaction scene is comprised of numerous actors, the framework provides the possibility of

32

seeing each set of actors, the nature of its actions and the specific forms of interaction in relationship to other actors and the system. But perhaps, more important is the recognition of the active role played by dominated or exploited groups in the process of social change. In this way, conflict, the main characteristic feature of interaction between dominated and dominating social groups is recognized as an important and moving force.

This is a move away from two lines of thought which have been influential in sociological thinking. Social institutions, according to the structural-functionalist school of thought play the role of maintaining social order, conformity and harmony. Conflict according to the proponents of this line is deviant behavior (Parsons 1951, Levy 1952). The second line of thought includes those who perceive the social system as all powerful. Accordingly social actors particularly dominated groups have little chance of influencing the system.[2] These lines of thinking are limited for elucidating major events of contemporary societies such as liberation struggles of colonized people and women's movements. These struggles and movements by dominated groups have led to major changes. It is possible to conceptualize and analyse these social issues and movements within a sociological framework.

The actor-system framework offers possibility to see not only conflict as a dynamic force but also the specific forms it assumes. Struggle and resistance takes various forms, given the characteristic features of the social system and/or its history which is itself a product of human activity. The struggle or resistance may be violent. It can take various forms of passive resistance (a phenomenon which has normally been identified with peasants). It may also involve taking actions, contrary to general expectations or patterns.

The issue of resistance is a major concern to students of social change including those involved in targetted social transformation. The latter often entails transfer of what has been developed within one social system to another be it technology or ideas. In this context, many development experts have been baffled by the apparent failure of poor peasants to accept that which change agents figure is beneficial to the peasants. Advocates of family planning face big problems in this respect. Given the enormous social, economic and medical problems women suffer from as a result of high fertility, family planning agencies fail to see why at the same time, contraceptives are unacceptable to these same women. In general, social organization, cultural values and beliefs of concerned peasants are blamed for being unreceptive to change (Forster 1962, Hyden 1983, Caldwell and caldwell 1988).[3] This subject is broad, and cannot justly be treated under the auspices of this analysis. It is however important to point out that the major problem is that development programmes are decontextualized. This is to say that as actors, development agents view things from their own perspective, which itself is shaped by the realities within which they live. According to Hutton and Cohen (1975), resistance to change only exists as far as the agents advocating it are concerned.[4]

In the context of women's groups, these issues are relevant. Women's collective activities are taken to constitute part of the women's struggle everywhere. At the same time, women's groups are part of the peasants to whom various development programmes are targetted. Because such programmes are decontextualized, women's groups may and indeed act or respond in forms which seem conservative even counter-productive. I am suggesting that the collective activities of women in Kenya can be conceptualized in terms of women's resistance or struggle. But this needs to be understood in the context of the specific conditions and social interaction settings within which women act to influence or restructure their conditions.

Women's struggle.

The use of the actor-systems theoretical framework provides the possibility to perceive women's groups in the wider context of women's struggle. Women mobilize themselves, reorganize to assert themselves constantly redefining the situation in the light of their past and present experiences and conditions. In other words, women's groups are analysed as actors in the context of the general framework of sexual stratification of societies everywhere, but more specifically, in relationship to colonial and neo-colonial conditions.

Sexual stratification is here defined not in biological form, although the physical differences between women and men seem to form some natural basis for this. Rather sexual stratification is used in its dynamic social and historical form, along which power, property, prestige and social recognition are organized, regulated, distributed and generally given meaning. In this context, women and women's groups mobilize, act and interact among themselves (as organizations) and within the constraints and opportunities of the wider system, where sexual differentiation and segregation is a basic principle in the organization and regulation of the division of labour and distribution of rewards. While this is the framework within which women interact with other social agents in the system, their actions are seen to constitute part of the struggle against subordination of women inherent in the sexual division of labour. The concept of sexual stratification is thus used to reflect on the hierarchical, unequal and exploitative relationships between men and women which feminist scholars of different ideological persuasion show to be a function of social arrangement and history (Boserup 1970, AAWORD 1982, Rogers 1980, Mies 1986, Sokoloff 1980, Huitzer and Mannheim 1979). An understanding of women's groups, their actions, interaction and forms of struggle or resistance, will therefore enhance the general understanding of the dynamics of women's struggle and the major forces involved. But because of the specific cultural, social, economic, political and historical conditions within which women's groups in Kenya are situated and act, specific knowledge pertaining to the struggle of women in similar circumstances will be gained. More specifically, this will yield invaluable knowledge on the plight and struggles of African women and those in the Third World generally.

What is being referred to as the women's struggle is mainly the struggle against women's subordination inherent in the sexual division of labour. Various theories have been advanced in support of universal female subordination. This implies that the subordination of women is a natural phenomenon. Collins (1971) argues from a Freudian perspective that women's subordination is fundamentally a result of men's sexual lust. Men, according to Collins have used their size and strength to coerce women. Tiger on the other hand asserts that male dominance arises from their social bonding. The following observations however suggest there exist forces other than motherhood, male sexual lust and strength in the sexual division of labour and subordination of women. Although sexual division of labour and subordination of women may seem a natural and universal phenomenon, it is known to vary from one system to another (Schlegel 1971, Caulfield 1981, Whyte 1978, Leacock 1981, Safilios-Rothschild 1979). This variation has also been observed through historical periods of given social systems (Engels 1891, Mies 1986).[5] During times of crises when human resources are scarce and in great demand, women have (as during the world wars and liberation movements) been recruited into roles they would have no access to in normal circumstances. After the crises, women are forced back to female domestic and other less prestigious roles and invisibility. Sokoloff (1980) observes that in the United States, although men and women may work in jobs requiring the same amount of education and training, they work in separate occupational groups and industries where women are paid less than men. In Scandinavian countries, where the struggle for sexual equality has made a major break-through, participation of women is still restricted to those less prestigious occupations (Haavic-Mannila 1985). The sexual division of labour and subordination of women is largely a social construction. Because of this, the analysis of the division of labour within the capitalist system is imperative. This illuminates not only the nature of subordination of women within the capitalist system, but also the forms it assumed as capitalism spread to encompass different cultural systems. We argue that the spread of capitalism had far reaching impact on the division of labour and the situation of women in the new regions.

2.   Subordination of Women Under the Capitalist System

Women's movements and the rise of feminist consciousness increasingly suggest that subordination of women is a social and historical phenomenon. Furthermore, evidence has mounted to indicate that capitalism violently forced women into the position they now occupy. There is a growing body of knowledge linking the development of private property ownership and capital accumulation for exchange with social inequality including gender inequality. This section thus discusses the division of labour in general and the process through which subordination of women has unfolded within the capitalist system.

Separation of production from consumption.

Perhaps the process started when production and consumption were separated. Pinchbeck (1930) has described the impact of this separation on the situation of women in England during the industrial revolution:

> In mid-eighteenth century the population of England was mainly rural, and women were largely engaged in productive work in their homes and in some form of domestic industry....women's opportunities for productive work at home were gradually lessened as the agrarian revolution proceeded, while at the same time industrial changes deprived them of employment in the older domestic industries....Now that the home was no longer a workshop, many women were able, for the first time in the history of the industrial classes to devote their energies to the business of home making and the care of their children.... pp 306-307.

The family became the centre of consumption while production moved to the factory (Sen, 1980). This separation however remained sensitive to the contradictory rhythms of the capitalist system. As the history of subordination of women unfolds, the contradictions and the specific form this process took at the dawn of industrial revolution is becoming clear. According to Mies (1986), the propertied classes, forced women out of productive domestic industry, to become the custodians of the home:

> The bourgeoisie, declared the family a private territory in contrast to the public sphere of economic and political activity. The bourgeoisie first withdrew their women from this public sphere....Even the French Revolution, though fought by thousands of women, ended by excluding women from politics.... pp 104

At the same time, large numbers of women were pushed into destitution to form, together with children, a large reserve of cheap labour force which was exploited for factory work. According to Phillips (1987), out of an adult population of six million women in Britain in

1851, more than half worked in overwhelmingly working class occupations. Moreover, two out of three of these working women were not living in proper families and were consequently supporting themselves and their children. Marx (1967) and Engels (1973) observed that conditions of factory work for women and children tended to be the worst. The appalling working conditions and overwork adversely affected women's health, resulting in high mortality rates. At the same time, women's domestic work suffered. The general poor conditions of early factory work, the high mortality levels among women and children, led to the fight for protective laws and family wage.

For capitalists, childbearing and rearing may have been of no immediate interest. The individual capitalist regarded the frequent interruptions due to pregnancy and childbirth as an expensive nuisance. But as Sen and Mies argue, the system as a whole depended on the reproduction of a healthy workforce. The need therefore arose to institute an upper class type of family among working classes.

For the male factory workers, the health of women and children was a major concern. The exploitation of cheap female labour had also meant loss of employment for men, a reversal of duties where husbands were forced, much to their dislike to undertake domestic duties of their working wives (Engels, 1973). Male working class movements thus fought both for freedom of workers to form families and a family wage (Mies, 1986).[6]

This can be said to be one stage in the development of the capitalist system, when various forces and actors with conflicting interests forced women into the domestic sphere and the realms of the family institution. This implied not just assumption by all women of economically dependent relationships. Unlike the propertied classes, working class women were as Mies states, "housewifized," without assuming total dependence. They too had to work to supplement their husbands' low salaries for the survival of the family, at the same time as they performed domestic chores. Once in place, this process was shaped by other forces such as state legislation and trade union pressure, as well as rationalizing processes and ideologies.

Romantic love and subordination of women under capitalism

Depending on their class position, the process of capitalist development shaped women to become either housewives or workers/house keepers. Concepts such as male strength (as the producers and providers), the weaker sex (consumers of male sweat), male sexual lust, maternal deprivation of children, love and romance became ideological justifications for rationalizing the emerging patterns of women's oppression. Mies points out that:

> The bourgeoisie, particularly the puritan English bourgeoisie, created the ideology of romantic love as a compensation for and sublimation of the sexual and economic independence women had had before the rise of this class. pp 104

Similarly, Sarsby (1983) argues that:

> ...the rise of the romantic novel in the eighteenth century can be seen in terms of diminishing economic power of women.

When romantic love and sex is taken in its social context, it is much more complex. As part of marriage and family institution, love and sex are placed in an arena of conflicts and tensions reflecting the contradictions of the system. Moreover, even where marriage is preceded by romantic courting, the process of getting a sexual and love mate involves choice based on socially defined criteria such as beauty, wealth, family name, etc. This is in itself a form of calculation which has tended to favour men.

Some of the criteria commonly used for evaluating and selecting love mates present for women other forms of oppression. Beauty and physical appearance is, for example, one of the more obvious and most widely used evaluation of a good woman. This includes size, shape, skin texture and colour. To improvise the accepted qualities, lucrative cosmetic, plastic surgery, fashion and advertising industries have grown. At the same time as these industries exploit women, they reinforce the need for beauty and sexual attraction, thus making women dependent on expensive products which are moreover hazardous to their health (Ahlberg 1982, Barrett et al 1985).[7]

In view of this, it is surprising that Weber, who seemed aware of the human suffering caused by the contradictory and institutional rationalization of the capitalist system, still regarded sexual or private life to be the only irrational institution which provide for the personal needs of the individual:

> Weber....points out that the sexual sphere has always been a nonrationalized force in the world. Erotic passion cannot be calculated,....We are weary of the rationalization of different life spheres, and the pressures to which they subject us. We need a respite from the impersonal realms of politics, economics, even from the contradictions of religion, the impersonality of science, and the irresolvable disputes of these different rationalized spheres against each other. Love is that respite. Precisely because it is irrational, it provides the personal element that the modern individual needs to give some meaning to a world of conflicting institutions that have become too rational (Collins, 1986).

Romantic love is itself rational. Its role as an ideological and rationalizing force is becoming more apparent as increasing numbers of women record their experiences and reality of living in the contradictory context of love and sexual violence. Weber's failure to see love and sex as an integral part of the contradictory process which is oppressive to women, seems a major oversight. As an upper class male however, Weber reflected upper class male experiences of romantic love and sex. The oppression of women is, as indicated above, complex and has many dimensions. Romantic love and sex inside and outside marriage are major subordinating forces. This suggests that efforts and struggles to liberate women is not just a question of equal job opportunities.

Capitalist expansion to the periphery

The emergence of gender division of labour and inherent subordination of women within the capitalist system is relevant to the analysis of the situation and struggles of women in Kenya. This is so because, as this division of roles was unfolding, the capitalist system was extending to other areas and cultures outside western countries.[8]

The spread of western capitalism through colonialism had far reaching consequences for the colonized people. It meant dismantling socio-economic systems which were rational in their own contexts. More specifically, realization of colonial goals resulted in the marginalization of the dominated areas and development of unequal dependent relationships (Rodney, 1972). Colonial intervention was not a peaceful process and the colonized people strongly resisted it. It was probably people's resistance to colonial domination which necessitated a ruthless colonial state machinery whose major preoccupation was maintenance of law and order. This was reinforced or rationalized by the missionaries as part of their "civilizing mission." The major contradiction was that, while purporting to civilize the indigenous people, by imposing the western system, the process forced a majority of the people into the periphery, by choking both the forces of indigenous culture as well as those necessary for the development of capitalism. Positive elements of capitalism that were suppressed include:

(i) private ownership of the means of production by entrepreneurs;

(ii) free labour force;

(iii) unrestricted markets;

(iv) calculable law in adjudication and public administration (Collins,1986).

Furthermore, the superior racial attitude inherent in the civilizing ideology, was a major factor shaping the kind of society that emerged from the mesh between western capitalism and other socio-economic and cultural systems. Besides dismantling the social organization of the dominated people, the psychological impact on the colonized people remains to be gauged (Ngugi Wa Thiong'o, 1987).

Impact of colonial expansion on women

Capitalist expansion to the periphery changed fundamentally the sexual division of labour and the position of women in these regions. The question of women's subordination within colonial and post-colonial structures, is of special interest here because of the widely persisting view, that women especially benefited by being alleviated from the bondage of traditions. It is commonly argued that literacy, a positive transforming tool, was introduced to these societies. Literacy is certainly useful (as the current author can testify), but it is positive only when it is used not as a dominating tool, and when it is equally accessible to all the people. As shown in the next chapter, education played two major roles which affected women negatively. For the colonizers, education became an important tool for dismantling customs and values which supported the Kikuyu social system. Secondly, during the early phase of colonial domination, women were denied education. When it was later allowed, as in the west it became a major tool for socializing women towards domestic Roles (Dobson, 1954).

There is a growing consensus that the process of colonial domination has deepened the subordination of African women. Apart from the plunder and exploitation of resources which marginalized and impoverished the colonized people, a western type of family which developed alongside deepening oppression of the western women was superimposed.

Women in the periphery were thus domesticated and socialized to assume dependent positions vis a' vis male wage earners. However, low wages, repressed union activities and high taxation which characterized the production setting in the periphery, meant in practical terms that male wage earners depended for their subsistence on female agricultural producers. The argument has been advanced that women's participation in agricultural subsistence has served to maintain cheap labour for capitalist expansion and accumulation (Deere, 1979). At the same time, the education system discouraged unemployed males from undertaking their former subsistence agricultural production roles (see chapter four).

For women, this implied doubling their workload as they assumed former male tasks in addition to their own. Secondly, surplus food production has for the majority of peasant women become a thing of the past. Thirdly, the psychological stress and reactions of men who, on the one hand have been socialized to play the role of producer/provider, but because of the structural formation, are either unemployed or receive salaries below the survival level, is apparent though not sufficiently researched. The conclusion to which we are driven is that in spite of superimposition of western social and economic structures, the emerging structural formation, and more so

its impact on the colonized people in general and women in particular, is fundamentally different from what took place in the western
societies. Thus, for those interested in problems facing women in the
periphery and Africa in particular, a deeper analysis of the structural
formation and its impact is necessary. There is no evidence what-
soever for the commonly cited claim that African men are usually
cruel to their wives, or that African women are more conservative,
and are for that reason less likely to question male domination. In the
same way, African women may achieve little, when men develop
defensive mechanisms which tend to view women's struggle as merely
a western issue.

Impact on sex and reproduction

The issue of sex and reproduction is important for any discussion of
women's struggles. It is the postulate from which and against which
such struggles take place. But for women in the periphery, capitalist
expansion and domination also implied the introduction of the
western family structure, romantic love and sex, within which even
western women were oppressed. This thus meant introducing dimensions of oppression related to those structures. The process moreover
dismantled a social system where women played a central role in the
control and regulation of sex and reproduction. As a result, new
patterns of sexuality separated from fertility and unrelated to the
economic structure have emerged. Most importantly as far as women
are concerned, these patterns of sexuality have reinforced the oppression of women in the following ways.

Firstly, child-spacing practices were dismantled. And as discussed
later, because of being decontextualized, the fertility control
programmes are not acceptable to the people. This has meant that the
majority of women spend their life-time in a continuous cycle of
pregnancy, child birth, child dependency and care. This, combined
with women's heavy workload and food shortages, has had far
reaching consequences to the health of women.

Secondly, adolescent sexuality changed as well. Among the
Kikuyu, pre-marital sex was prohibited. Although not clear,
Koponen's (1988) review of aspects of reproduction in Tanzania indi-

cates the existence of controls of adolescent sexuality among other people in East Africa. With the breakdown of such controls, adolescents in contemporary African societies become sexually active at an early age and outside marriage (Oppong, 1987). This explains why teenage pregnancies, abortions, school drop-out and baby dumping occur in large proportions (Sanghvi 1986, Akuffo 1987, Musoke 1988).

Lastly, because of economic problems particularly facing women, sexuality has been transformed into a commodity for exchange. The historical process of the commercialization of sex is discussed below.

Women's survival options and strategies under periphery capitalism

The vast majority of women live in the rural areas where they are engaged in agricultural production. Of women living in the rural areas in Kenya, 96% are smallholder agricultural producers. But, because of structural conditions which have lowered food production and dismantled social support systems, women in the capitalist periphery often cannot sustain themselves by subsistence agricultural production. They are therefore forced to seek other survival alternatives. At the same time, with no educational or skill training, women's employment opportunities are limited. Women have thus increasingly found themselves in petty trades such as hawking and beer brewing while large numbers are employed as domestic, un-skilled and semi-skilled workers in rural and urban areas (UNICEF/Central Bureau of Statistics, 1984). For many others, formal and informal prostitution is the only option for survival.

In urban and other production centres, prostitution and beer brewing thrived because of two major factors. Colonial laws prohibited African men from bringing their wives to their place of work. From a Weberian point, African male producers were by colonial state legislation denied sex and love, the only irrational area of life within the capitalist system. As a result, prostitution and related beer brewing and alcohol consumption became the only means of fulfilling those vital human needs. But, prostitution and alcohol consumption served the colonial capitalist economy in other ways. To the colonial capitalist employer, both prostitution and beer brewing and consumption were important tools for maintaining a stable cheap labour force. The combined forces of colonial exploitation had lowered the nutritional and health status of male workers. At the same time, when colonial employers recognized the high nutritional value of locally brewed alcohol, they encouraged its consumption. Similarly, prostitution was encouraged not just to fulfil the sexual needs of male workers, but also because women prostitutes prepared food for the male workers (see Doyal, 1979). This enabled the colonial capitalist system to exploit African workers and women at levels and dimensions qualitatively different from those of capitalism at the centre.

For women at the periphery, the process was contradictory at several levels. Ironically, prostitution and alcohol consumption were encouraged on grounds of maintaining good health for African workers. Over time however, the well known adverse effects of alcohol and prostitution on health set in. Hand in hand with this process of using prostitution and alcohol consumption to exploit African labour, European colonizers regarded African sexual morality and alcohol consumption to be abhoring. That is to say that the emerging patterns were regarded by the colonialists as cultural African practices. This view is widely held to the present day.

Women are moreover blamed for breaking strong cultural norms. They are considered as exploiters of men simply because they happen to have a commodity they alone can control. And although it is a right for every man, because of its short supply at least at the beginning, women could use it for exchange. At another level, the stage was set where men became accustomed to using their earnings for casual drinking and extra-marital sex. This, and the continued survival needs of large numbers of women within an environment where they have few opportunities, has reinforced prostitution.[9] Moreover, children and wives are exposed to suffering as the small family income is used on drinking and other women. This is the contradictory situation within which women inside and outside marriage live. Needless to say, this process has lowered the image of women, increased sexual and domestic violence and influenced reproductive health adversely. These are the historical, political and economic contexts within which

Table 7: Sexual division of labour and its impact on women in capitalist periphery

Women's Roles	Impact on Women
	Participation in productive sector limited, as women have had less opportunities to educational and skill training.
1 Subsistence production agricultural and petty trades.	Fatigue and poor health from overwork, continuous pregnancy childbirth and child dependency
2 Labour in commercial agriculture	Participation in petty trades such as prostitution leading to negative image, increased public and private sexual violence, numerous unwanted pregnancies, abortions and death
3 Domestic consumption management and childcare	
	General psychological stress and lack of confidence due to negative image, invisible roles and lack of control as they are regarded as dependents of their husbands.

the contemporary patterns and processes of sexuality and reproductive health have emerged and are being reinforced. Similarly, they need to be understood and analysed in that context.

Women's collective participation

It is within this same context that women have continued to mobilize themselves for collective participation. They mobilize to offset the impoverishment and marginalization of people in general. More specifically they mobilize themselves to meet the demands of a division of labour where their officially invisible but substantial contribution and workload has adverse impact on their health and image.

Women's collective activities have been shaped by many other factors. Commercialization of the economy or production for market, has necessitated transaction in monetary terms, banking, accounting and formal organization. Resource scarcity, emergence of a state bureaucracy based on colonial and neo-colonial structures as the major social transforming force and a political system, designed as though women do not exist or can be used at the whims of male patrons are factors which affect group structure, dynamics and mobilization (chapter 8). The nature of women's group activities and their major concerns perhaps not only reflect conflicts between needs and priorities of women and those of the larger system, but also the patterns and processes of change described above. Widespread persistence of activities hardly recognized by the wider system, indicates the nature of women's priorities (chapter 9). Similarly, the lack of involvement of women's groups in the control of sex and reproduction which was a central function of groups in the past reflects the changing patterns (chapter 4 and 9).

The foregoing section has discussed global conditions and structures within which women's struggles including collective participation take place. Thus far I have stressed that the sexual division of labour and the inherent subordination of women is part of the history of capitalist development both in the centre and the periphery. I now present a general model focusing on the social and political institutions within which women's group activities take place. One can see the collective activities of women's groups as a process which has both inputs and outputs.

3.   An Input-Process-Output Model of Collective Action

Women's collective participation is here perceived as a process with inputs and outputs. The inputs comprise the situational reality within which women live and act. This also constrains and influences their actions strategies, dynamics and organizational structure. The process entails a movement, where women mobilize and form groups to perform certain tasks which would help alter the problem situation. On the output end are specific activities undertaken. These activities articulate the group's needs, goals and strategies through which they aim to control or influence the realities, as well as hold the group together. As they mobilize to act collectively, members bring along their individual interests, perspectives and background from which they define and redefine their situation. The process involves inter-action with other actors who have different orientations, perspectives and interests. In the process of acting and interacting with these other social action agents, women's groups gain experience and knowledge which is then fed back to the various aspects of the process, producing both intended and unintended results. The feedback process is both short and long term. The input-process-output model of collective action is presented in figure 1.

The basic resource conditions

These are conditions women experience in their daily lives. Women aim to influence, control and change these conditions through their collective actions.

At the same time that these conditions constitute a driving force for collective action, they reduce the group's capacity for action and affect their strategies and dynamics. They also affect the way groups relate to other agents, as well as the outcomes of interactions with these other agents.

Resource scarcity or poverty

Living in poverty, as most women in the rural areas do, may actually facilitate collective participation. As discussed further below, food production and therefore the feeding of families is the responsibility of women. But when the resources at their disposal are limited, so that they cannot carry out such basic family survival

Figure 1: Actor-system dynamic model of collective participation.

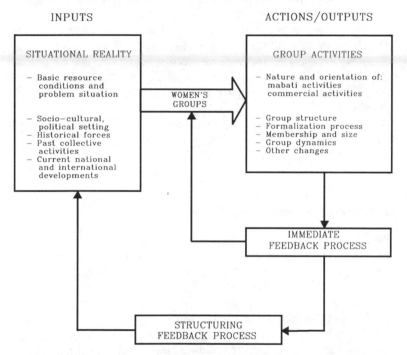

responsibilities, women are likely to exploit alternative strategies such as collective action. Women perceive the need to pool funds together, to perform an activity or offer a service which is otherwise beyond the capabilities of an individual woman. But the nature and extent of impoverishment, may prohibit long-term monetary contribution for most group members. Women who cannot make such contribution may not:

(a) join the groups or

(b) continue with all the activities of the group even though they may have joined the groups.

In addition, to enable a group to raise the required resources to accomplish a task which is far beyond its means may affect group structure and composition in a number of ways. Large groups may be formed while others may strictly recruit only women who can afford such long-term contributions.

Groups may compete with each other for the limited resources. This is particularly likely to occur when groups have knowledge of other groups, the kinds of resources available and distribution processes. This competition may be acute where specific agents such as government and donor agencies are known to have or are in control of resources.

But, poverty as a motivating factor for mobilization and its impact on groups cannot be discussed without considering other structural, institutional, historical and cultural factors which affect the position of women.

The social-cultural and historical forces

Past and prevailing forces which have shaped women's collective participation, can be categorized as internal and external. The Kikuyu cultural co-operative systems in agricultural activities (ngwatio) and mutual assistance in times of stressful demands (matega) constitute an internal force.

The external forces include structures and conditions arising from contact with outside agents starting with colonial domination. Within the new social formation, new dimensions of subordinating women have emerged. Women have assumed an increased workload against little remuneration in terms of actual returns or control over returns. This has led to more control of Kikuyu women by husbands who have more access to cash. Moreover, women's enormous contribution remain unrecognized. It is against this background that the mobilization of women for collective participation must be analysed.

The sexual division of labour

Sexual division of labour is considered important particularly because of the subordinating impact it has had and continues to have on women. In this sense, it is a situational reality which motivates women to mobilize for collective struggle. But it also influences the structure of the groups, their areas of concern, and what groups can accomplish. Women participate collectively in part to offset their heavy workload. But large numbers of women may be prohibited from participating due to time resource constraints, or poor health.

Furthermore, lack of education and skills influences women's group activities in a number of ways. The commercialization process has implied increasing involvement of women's groups in income-generation. In this way, women's group activities have also become commercialized. Moreover income-generating activities tend to require certain professional skills. But because women lack such skills, groups are forced to depend on other agents including the government which control other forms of resources. However, rhythms of operation and orientation of such agents are often antagonistic and insensitive to the needs and priorities of women. Groups may for example be encouraged to invest their time and material resources in activities which have few prospects for gainful returns. This is not just a question of lack of skills on the part of women. It is a wider structural problem and part of the effect of periphery capitalism or neo-colonialism on women's groups.

For the groups, this leads to instability and weakens the vigour with which women mobilize themselves for collective action. Furthermore, the time and material resource requirements of such activities prohibit participation of all women. This influences the recruitment process and group composition as well. The pattern and tendency seem to be emerging where women with few resources are forced out of groups even though they may need group support more than other categories of women. Secondly, the tendency has also emerged where women who already have access to resources form a group. Such groups have more possibility of gaining more resources from the system. While women largely mobilize themselves and struggle collectively to offset problems created by the system, their socio-economic position determine whether or not women can join groups.

The negative image of women who are forced into survival options such as prostitution limits chances for such women to participate and benefit from groups. Women's groups may only recruit those women who are considered socially and morally acceptable. This form of recruitment would therefore tend to leave out unmarried mothers, who may be in greater need of group support.

But, while subordination of women influences women's group activities, organizational dynamics and structure in the way discussed above, the general nature of group activities still reflect women's concerns and priorities. Groups have been encouraged to undertake commercial activities. Nevertheless, mabati or home improvement activities mainly concerned with household roles of women still constitute the core of group activities. These activities are based on past forms of collective assistance among Kikuyu women (see chapter 9).

The same can be said of women's group involvement in the control of sex and reproduction. Unlike past women's groups which played a central role in the control of sex and reproduction, contemporary groups play a minimal role in the same area. Groups tend to avoid undertaking activities which may lessen suffering arising from the new sexuality and fertility patterns.

The institutional forces

Besides being motivated and shaped by factors such as past forms of co-operation, prevailing conditions of resource scarcity and sexual division of labour, women's collective activities are part of the existing institutional framework.

The most important institution, with respect to the shaping of women's collective participation is the government. A national government is, however, part of a complex of national and international actors (figure 2). The specific historical relationships of depen-

dence between national and international governments and agencies
define the process of development and its orientation. In turn this
shapes women's collective activities. At the local level are two related
features. There is the government bureaucracy which has regular and
formalized interaction with women's groups. There are also political
forces which influence women's groups in ways discussed below.

Figure 2: Social and Political Organization of Actors,
Transactions and Institutions at the Periphery.

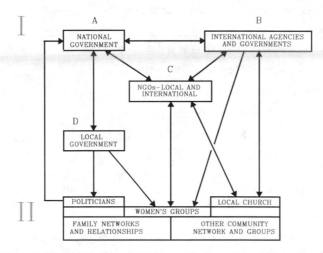

Note 1: Development policies and plans are designed at A
and targetted down to level II.

Note 2: The local scene II has varied actors who have formal
and informal links with D, A, C and B. Decision making,
survival and resistance strategies are defined and
designed at this level.

The major factor here is perhaps the use of women's groups as targets
for implementing government policies and programmes. But as
pointed out earlier, most agency programmes are antagonistic to
women's group interests and concrete needs.

Besides being antagonistic, agency targeting has placed new demands and organizational pressures on women's groups. The requirement for groups to engage in income-generating projects as a prerequisite for government support, within the prevailing conditions of severe resource constraints and the real need for women to obtain funds from sources other than their personal contribution, may have led to the increased involvement of groups in commercial activities. Many other rules and regulations have been instituted. Groups are, for example, required to:

(1) be registered with the government;

(2) have a regularly elected committee with specified composition, for example a literate secretary;

(3) have a written constitution;

(4) run a bank account;

(5) have a specified membership;

(6) recruit members from a base beyond the kinship group;

These rules and regulations have influenced groups in a number of ways. In a more general way, groups have increasingly become formalized in their structure and in their relationship with other agents. This has, for instance, put pressure on groups to have literate leadership.

To operationalize most of these rules and regulations, women's group committees have been instituted at various administrative levels (see chapter 7). Through regular and formalized interaction between women's group committees and the government, groups are exposed to both government operations and orientation. Given this, one can say that women's groups have in many ways become extensions of the government.

This is not to say that women's groups act on all rules, information and directives emanating from the government. In many cases, women's group actions or non-action are at variance with government expectations. They avoid, however, acting openly or in ways which may lead to open confrontation with the government. Groups generally accept being involved in government programmes such as the fertility control while at the same time opposing or avoiding regulations in a variety of ways. This may be called positive resistance. It arises because government interests, orientations and procedures conflict with those of women.

Similarly, in spite of pressures towards formalization, groups have a strong ability to adapt where necessary to past forms of organization. This seems to be the case with leadership composition and structure. To facilitate interaction of groups with other agents as the rules require, groups select a literate secretary and treasurer while the chairperson is usually an elderly woman who according to past criteria commands respect.

In another way, instituting women's group committees along administrative divisions, may lead to competition and complementality. Groups in one location may operate as a block in support of its locality and in competition with blocks of groups in other localities. At this level, women's groups may act in competition with each other, while at the same time complementing each other for the good of their area. It is at this level that women's groups may struggle to demonstrate abilities and potentials of women as a measure of gaining recognition.

The political system has also facilitated some of the observed processes and responses of the groups. In the context of resource scarcity, where women hold a majority of the political votes, tying government assistance to specific group activities may be exploited by politicians. Patron/client type of relationships arise. These relationships are however complex, and women's groups also exploit the situation. During political campaigns, when politicians particularly need women's votes, women's groups may form in order to exploit candidates whom they may have no intention of voting for. Whether it is the women or the politicians who initiate this, numerous groups form around political campaign periods.

Tying resources to group activities, within a political system which can be exploited by either the groups or the politicians, has led to various forms of competition. Groups form to secure resources from the government directly or through the politicians and other patrons. After formation, groups may aim at performing better than other groups or engage in those activities which the government is known to recognize and support. The resulting competition not only facilitates group formation, but also influences internal dynamics, activities and action strategies.

This chapter has looked at women's groups as actors within a social system where women are subordinated. The use of the concept of subordination necessitated a look at the prevailing views pertaining to the subordination of women. The sexual division of labour within the capitalist system is a major factor in the contemporary process of women's subordination. Colonial expansion to the periphery turned areas where women had control into forces of subordination. From the perspective of the actor-systems dynamics framework, subordination of women in its various dimensions is considered to constitute the situational reality within which women's groups operate. The following chapters will discuss the actual process through which Kikuyu society was transformed, the impact of this on women, group structure and their activities.

Part Two: **The Restructuring of Kikuyu Social Organization**

CHAPTER 4

PRE-COLONIAL KIKUYU SOCIAL ORGANIZATION

1. The Kikuyu Social System

The Kikuyu people had an elaborate system of social organization based on kinship and age-group systems. Both kinship and age-grade systems emphasized group life. Furthermore, the Kikuyu belief system exerted pressure for collective living.

The Belief System

The life of the Kikuyu people was influenced by the belief in ancestral powers. Ancestral spirits could punish the living for misconduct. To avoid their wrath and punishment, proper conduct by individuals, kinship and age-groups was of utmost importance in the daily lives of the people. Because of the belief in the unity of social relationships between the dead and the living, taboos, prohibitions and sanctions were observed in the daily conduct of the individuals and groups. The presence of disease and other misfortunes insinuated breach of conduct. Similarly, problems of reproduction including infertility, bareness, miscarriage, maternal and infant loss were believed to be signs of disharmony arising from breach of rules of conduct.

Related to this was the belief that the breach of conduct could be by a person other than the one suffering. This strong belief in joint responsibility for the well-being of the community and the individuals therein was probably the main basis for the strong spirit and actual collective living within kinship and age-groups.

The Kinship System

The most basic of the kinship group was the family unit (Mbari or Nyumba) comprising of members closely related by blood (Kenyatta 1938, Muriuki 1976). The family was the centre of economic and social life. Land ownership, food production and major social events such as ritual and religious ceremonies which were necessary for the well-being of the family and the Kikuyu people, took place within the family. All members of a particular family participated as a group.

The second level of the kinship unit was the clan (Muhiriga) which joined into one group, several family units. The clan assumed one name and the various family units were believed to have a common ancestor in the distant past. Members of a clan frequently interacted during events such as weddings, initiation, religious and ritual ceremonies.

The Age-group System

The other important feature of the Kikuyu social organization was the age-group. The beginning of an age-group (Riika) was marked by the rite of circumcision. Groups of men and women were circumcised together. The age-group system and the rite of passage has probably received most attention within the social sciences, but what Kinoti (1983) says seems appropriate for the purpose of this study:

> At the rite of circumcision, which was a group de passage, all those who were thus initiated into adulthood were given a particular age name....being initiated together meant that all members of the60 age-set or age-group (Riika) thus formed belonged to each other as age-mates. They were bound together by virtue of initiation, were responsible for each other's good and collectively responsible for the good name of their age-group. Age mates met most of the social needs of an individual as they were constantly in each other's company, both at work and leisure. Men and girls formed separate groups but there were social occasions, such as dances which brought them together. One of the age-group's main concerns was to maintain its honour and good reputation. Members were required to conduct themselves with integrity for

the sake of their own personal reputation, that of their family, and equally important that of their riika. Age-mates applied corrective measures to any of their members whose conduct they disapproved.

The family (Mbari and Nyumba) and the clan (Muhiriga) were independent social and economic units. But, the age-group system cut across clans and ridges (Ng'ongo) creating one political unit within the wider geographical area (Kenyatta 1938, Muriuki 1976).

Initiation into an age-group was perhaps the most important stage in the life of Kikuyu men and women. Because initiation took place at the start of puberty it had many functions. It marked the entry into adulthood. But, contrary to what is commonly believed, initiation was more than just physical operation. The physical operation was, as Worthman and Whiting (1987) state, only part of the educational process entailing a sequence of instructions, socialization and imparting of social values and subsequent adult behavior.[1] It constituted a period when Kikuyu men and women approaching adulthood were prepared to assume their roles. Ensuing initiation ritual songs and dances (Gitiiro) by married women, particularly focused on sexuality and reproduction.

Initiation and the period following it was thus important for the sexual life of the young men and women. Premarital Sexual intercourse was prohibited for both men and women. The newly initiated boys and girls were however allowed to sleep together and engage in incomplete sexual play known as Ngwiko. But the context or form within which ngwiko took place both reduced the chances of breaching the rules of conduct and promoted the spirit of collective living. Young men and women frequently danced, slept together and engaged in ngwiko. It was customary for the warrior class which formed after initiation to travel around the country. On such occasions the male warriors were entertained with food, dance and ngwiko. In this context, ngwiko not only provided sexual satisfaction, but it played an important role in mate selection (Worthman and Whiting, 1987). This helped to promote age-group solidarity and mutual identification on a wider geographical area. But, ngwiko was not casual. It took place in a context of strict codes of conduct. According to accounts of Kenyatta, men and women slept together with the woman's skirt tightly tied across her thighs to avoid possible penetration. Furthermore, the practice of a number of men and women having ngwiko together in one room (thingira), strengthened peer pressure and minimized chances of full sexual intercourse. Lastly, the concerned age-group guarded against this by punishing those suspected or found to have breached the rules.

Women in my study discussed the method of finding out which age-group member may have breached the rule. If during dances and other occasions when young men and women were together, men showed a favourable attitude to any of the girls, such a girl was suspected of having had full sexual intercourse. Such a girl was ridiculed, fined and at times ostracized.[2]

Initiation moreover formed the basis for acquiring social status and authority. This was however organized along sex. Most anthropological sources describing the age-group system, have however focused most of their attention to the male functions (Lambert 1956, Middleton 1953, Kenyatta 1938). These sources have described in detail the political career which men assumed after initiation. Kikuyu men joined the warrior class for the defence of the community. After marriage, which according to Kershaw's (1976) estimates was at the age of 25 years, and payment of the various fees. Men then climbed up the political ladder through the four grades of council of elders which constituted the government (see Leakey 1977).

Women are shown to have joined corresponding age-sets and councils by the same sources. But the details of these age-sets and councils are omitted. Lambert (1956) mentions the existence of women councils. He further notes that men (he presumably had only male respondents) were not aware of their functions. He however acknowledges the potential of women to organize themselves for concerted action particularly when their interests were interfered with. Lambert himself, a colonial administrative officer, made these observations at a time when intense changes and disruption of Kikuyu social organization had already been set in motion. It is however the view here that even in the pre-colonial society, women exerted their pressure through such organization and concerted action.[3]

2. The Division of Labour

Within the subsistence economy, tasks were organized on the basis of sex. Table 8 below shows that Kikuyu men and women each had extensive responsibilities. Women were mainly responsible for farm and household activities which had to be performed as a matter of daily or seasonal routine. From the point of view of a heavy workload, women were, even in the pre-colonial society, already oppressed. But within the Kikuyu social organization, there were various measures that controlled and balanced this situation. Food was the basis on which wealth (land and animals), status and influence was acquired by male elders (Clark, 1980). Since women were responsible for food production and its disposal, men depended not only on the ability of women to produce such food, but also their generosity. This provided women with a negotiable position thus integrating them into the Kikuyu political economy over which they exerted some control.

Secondly, the role played by polygamous marriage in lowering the amount of food surplus each wife needed to contribute to her husband, has received little attention (Boserup, 1970). This role has probably been obscured by the strongly held view that polygamy was no more than a means for male sexual domination over women. But as is discussed further below, sexuality among the Kikuyu was secondary. This view has nevertheless limited analysis of strategies and alliances employed by wives in a polygamous marriage to maximize their benefits, or assert themselves to resist male domination. Recent work (Obbo 1976) has indicated that within the dominant male ideology, women have had various options. Women have been actors who through power game at micro-level of societal politics have maximized their benefits in the society. Hobley (1922) observed that old women even participated in food related sacrificial ceremonies because of their responsibilities in food production and the feeding of families. Kikuyu women did thus assert considerable influence. This was further enhanced by the organizational nature of the Kikuyu where collective or group life especially among women prevailed in the day-to-day living.

The nature of collective participation in pre-colonial Kikuyu

The three types of co-operatives that women used to ease workload and stress in their productive and reproductive roles included:

Ngwatio co-operatives

Demanding tasks such as clearing of land, cultivation, harvesting, thatching, etc. were performed in special collectives known as Ngwatio. This was a definite group usually limited to kins, friends and age mates. There are few sources where this form of work organization is documented. But due to the nature of their responsibilities, women participated more frequently than men in these mutual work groups (Fisher, 1954). Perhaps Middleton (1953) also implies there was more co-operation among women when he states:

> It was a recognised custom (Ngwatio) for women to cultivate the fields as a group, but each plot was demarcated by pigeon peas or sorghum, so that at harvest time each would gather from her individual plot.

Whenever these groups performed tasks for its members, the particular family provided food. These were similar to work parties described as having been used by clans and elders, during the expansion of the Kikuyu in the nineteenth century to acquire new land (Clark 1980, Muriuki 1976).

Matega mutual collective support

Apart from Ngwatio, women had numerous other opportunities for co-operation. Most of these were tied to the roles women played in the area of reproduction, including childbirth, wedding and initiation ceremonies. During weddings, initiation and childbirth, mutual assistance involving presentation of gifts (Matega), or performing household and farm activities in the case of a woman who was recuperating from childbirth, was always done by women. These could be women of the same clan as the concerned woman, or other distant clans with whom a network of relationship had been established through mar

Table 8: List of male and female roles

Male roles	Female roles
1 Tending cattle and trading in livestock.	1 Looking after children.
2 Clearing the field, breaking up surface for women, cutting drains and water furrows, building roads and bridges.	2 Planting maize, millet, beans and other crops,hoeing and weeding and harvesting crops.
3 Planting certain crops like bananas, cutting and bringing home sugar cane for beer and straining the juice and and making tobacco.	3 Storing and caring for food supply, cooking, fetching water and firewood, grinding grain and pounding sugar cane for beer, tending hives and making honey.
4 Uprooting the grain stalks after harvest and burning to fertilize the soil and kill pests.	4 Thatching and plastering in hut building.
5 Collecting honey.	5 Sewing skins, making pottery, collecting iron, making strings required for making baskets and for tying leaves used at initiation ceremony, making baskets and bead work.
6 Hunting and fighting.	
7 Cutting and erecting timber for house building, building fences and granaries.	
8 Making wooden utensils and repair.	6 Trading in grains.
9 Legal and ritual duties.	

Source: Middleton 1953.

riage transaction or/and through friendship arising from belonging to the same age-group.

Gitiiro (initiation) dance parties

Initiation ceremonies were important forums for imparting discipline in sexual matters, knowledge, community values, and expected rules of conduct. Young men and women undergoing initiation had long periods of seclusion during which time they received education about the social expectations of adult life.

Following the physical operation, women in addition participated in dance and songs (Gitiiro) which mostly focused on the sexual and reproductive roles of men and women. Krige (1987) describes similar ritual ceremonies, songs and dances among the Zulu people in South Africa. During these parties, men kept away because women used a language which in normal circumstances would be considered vulgar or obscene.

In general, women had thus numerous opportunities for collective participation. Furthermore, this took place within the two age-groups Kang'ei and Nyakinyua which women joined after marriage, birth and initiation of their first child.

3.   The Pre-colonial Kikuyu Fertility Model: Sexuality and Reproduction

Children were highly valued among the Kikuyu for security and social status of parents, agricultural labour and continuation of the generation line. To the present, these factors are considered important in maintaining high fertility in Kenya. While this may be true, it is also true that children were not just born in a continuous and closely spaced cycle as happens to most married and unmarried women today. There were specific social mechanisms including beliefs and practices, taboos, prohibitions, social sanctions, and collective pressure commonly used to regulate sexuality in order to avoid conception and childbirth under certain circumstances.

Contraception regulating practices

Practices commonly used in the past to ensure proper child-spacing included:

(1) long post-partum sexual abstinence;

(2) sexual abstinence during many other occasions such as mourning and ritual ceremonies;

(3) sleeping in separate houses;

(4) polygamy;

(5) controlled sexual play (Ngwiko) for initiated but unmarried boys and girls, and couples in monogamous marriage;

(6) abortion and infanticide;

(7) late marriage particularly among men who first joined the warrior class after initiation.

Taboos, Prohibitions, and Social sanctions

Sex and reproduction operated within a socially regulated code of rules. Because of the strong belief in the unity between conduct and community well-being, individuals were unlikely to breach the socially expected code of conduct. However, to strengthen this, taboos, prohibitions, and social sanctions were extensively used in the daily conduct of individuals and groups to regulate sex and reproduction thereby maintaining social balance. But even so, taboos, prohibitions, and social sanctions were, contrary to what is popularly believed not considered sufficient on their own. In addition, the society was organized in ways that minimized the chances of breaching the rules of conduct.

The newly initiated men and women were, for example, allowed to sleep together and to practice a form of controlled sex (Ngwiko) in order to achieve sexual satisfaction (Worthman and Whiting 1987). In this context the Kikuyu people had a fairly open sexual order. But premarital sexual intercourse was prohibited. Sleeping together without sexual intercourse of course required strong discipline on the part of individual young men and women. Such discipline did not develop naturally. It was instiled partly through the long process of education which culminated in initiation ceremonies described above and maintained through social action and social organization. Ngwiko was mostly organized collectively. Many boys and girls slept in one room which in turn discouraged full sexual intercourse among those who may have dared. Similarly, elders who performed ritual and religious ceremonies were for instance prohibited from having sexual intercourse. To minimize the possibility of this happening, only the most senior elders, who by virtue of their age were inactive sexually qualified for these functions.[4] Apart from the mechanisms discussed above, group and peer pressure was collective exerted to help individuals maintain accepted behavior.

The Nature of group and peer pressure

Various social groups exerted pressure on community members to observed rules of conduct. As discussed above, sexuality including adolescent sexuality was fairly open. The newly initiated boys and girls were allowed and frequently engaged in non-penetrative sexual play. But to ascertain that full sexual intercourse did not take place during these occassions, the concerned age-groups collectively put pressure on their members.

The Kang'ei/Nyakinyua women's groups

These groups and the social status they acquired was based on the biological maturity through age, marriage and reproduction. Their importance for the purpose of this study is however the role they played in controlling sex and reproduction. This was perhaps the group which played the greatest role in checking and controlling not only its members but also men in matters of sex and reproduction.

Sexual intercourse was prohibited after about the fifth month of pregnancy, and during lactation which lasted 2-3 years. During this time, the wife abstained from sexual intercourse, but the husband had alternative sexual partners. He usually had a second wife, whose marriage the first wife may have encouraged. Pregnancy and semen in a

lactating mother were believed to poison breast milk killing the suck-
ling child. But, this belief alone was not considered adequate. Pressure from the groups played a greater role than has been recognized
to reinforce such beliefs and ensure that members lived according to
the rules.

The organizational nature of the activities of these groups particularly facilitated the application of this role. When
Kang'ei/Nyakinyua age-groups were together during numerous social
occasions and activities, Kang'ei undertook the more demanding
tasks. The elderly and weaker Nyakinyua who also had higher status
and authority, were assigned less demanding tasks such as looking
after babies for the Kang'ei women. During such occasions,
Nyakinyua women inspected and examined the babies to determine
whether mothers had broken sexual,rules. There were two main ways
of checking. The babies under the care of Nyakinyua were swayed up
and down and were passed around so that the Nyakinyua women
could feel the weight. Low weight on the part of a baby indicated that
the mother had slept with the husband, thus denying the baby the
continuous night feeds. During the same gatherings, Nyakinyua
women examined the colour of mother's breast milk as it dripped
down. Dilute looking breast milk, indicated that the particular couple
had engaged in sex. This information was passed around that the
particular couple had "harvested their sorghum while it was still
green." Songs were composed to ridicule both the wife and the
husband. Some Kang'ei women were known to refuse to leave their
babies under the care of Nyakinyua particularly if such babies had low
weight.

The above discussion suggests that the fairly open sexual activity
including Ngwiko was not casual. It took place within strongly regulated codes of conduct. Rules of conduct were socially defined thus
giving social actors, individuals as well as groups definite boundaries
within which to act.

Health and reproduction among the Kikuyu

Social groups, beliefs, practices and taboos were in general used to
ensure harmony and balance among individuals, families and the

community. Life and moral order stressed collective preventive or maintenance of good health and social balance.

But in cases of disharmony and disease, there was a collective approach in treatment. This collective responsibility is reflected in the belief held that the presence of disease and other health problems, including those of reproduction, arise from social misconduct. The imbalance may arise from misconduct of any member of the family, clan and the community, dead or living. For this reason, the ancestors were continuously honoured through good conduct and special ritual ceremonies in order to avoid their anger and punishment through disease and death. Health care among the Kikuyu had the following features:

(1) The society had designed many observations (taboos and sanctions) to guard against what could lead to imbalances.

(2) Collective responsibility was taken to help members of the community to maintain the balance. This is to say that health maintenance or what in the modern conception may be called health promoting community action was perhaps the basic and integral part of the entire life of the Kikuyu.

(3) Collective responsibility was taken to restore the balance in case of disease and other problems.

(4) Treatment of a disease thus applied a holistic approach, where members of a family participated as a group, and handled the medical, social and psychological aspects of the problem (Ahlberg, 1984).

The process of reproduction which started with initiation into adulthood was part of this moral order. The Kikuyu people were mainly concerned with preventing problems of reproduction. The numerous taboos and prohibitions were reinforced by collective responsibilities, in all aspects of the reproductive process including sexuality, marriage and procreation. An important feature was the association between marriage transactions with the outcome of reproduction. The maternal uncle was an important person in the reproductive performance of his sister. If there was infertility or child loss, the first ceremonies were directed at appeasing the maternal uncle. In normal circumstances, the maternal uncle was kept happy through gifts particularly before important occasions, such as the initiation of children (Kenyatta, 1938).

In the pre-colonial Kikuyu society, sexual intercourse was strictly prohibited before marriage, during lactation, and during many other occasions such as mourning periods and during religious and ritual ceremonies. This makes it seem that sexuality among the Kikuyu was secondary. However, it does not in any way mean that the Kikuyu people did not recognize the social and sexual needs of the people including young people. Nor does it mean as is popularly thought that sex was only for reproduction. Newly initiated men and women were, as discussed above, allowed to sleep together for the purpose of achieving sexual satisfaction without penetration. In this context, the concept of 'safe sex' was well understood and practised. This suggests that sex and reproduction was a process, which makes sense only when viewed in the context of the wider social and economic organization and the division of labour based on the family.

Women were responsible for food production and feeding of the families. Children, especially girls assisted their mothers in these responsibilities. This implies that reproduction was an integral part of the economic production. In this context, children were valued as part of the family labour and security. But in the prevailing conditions, where high infant and child mortality was a reality, the main concern of the families, was to procreate the necessary labour in a context that ensured maximum maternal and infant survival. The great concern with proper child-spacing should therefore be seen in the context of the whole concern with health maintenance discussed above and the level and organization of the economic system.

CHAPTER 5

THE SITUATION DURING THE COLONIAL PERIOD

1. The Process of Colonial Domination

This chapter discusses the process and pattern of colonial domination, its impact on the Kikuyu in general, but more specifically on the situation of women and their collective activities.

Kenya was opened for European settlement by 1902 when the Uganda railway was completed. This was part of the European imperial capitalist expansion of that period (Zeitlin, 1973).[1] As far as Kenya was concerned, European settlement was encouraged for economic considerations and the need to repay and maintain the cost of the railway. Secondly, the climate of what came to be known as the "White Highlands" was suitable for such settlement.

The subsequent period saw Europeans from Britain and her colonies including South Africa, Canada, Australia and New Zealand being encouraged to settle (Eliot, 1966). Settlers then just selected land holdings from what seemed like waste or unoccupied land. Later after a number of Crown Declarations, they bought land at nominal prices. The actual process of settlement is well documented (Rosberg and Nottingham 1966, Sorrenson 1968, Middleton 1965, Furedi 1974). There are two major but related colonial policies through which colonial domination was established. These include establishing of a colonial economy and dismantling of cultural values and customs which supported the Kikuyu social system.

2. Establishing a Colonial Economy

Colonial capitalist economic interests were achieved through:

(1) land alienation;

(2) taxation;

(3) low wages and poor working and living conditions;

(4) neglect of African reserves and prohibition of Africans from producing cash crops.

The process of establishing a colonial economy entailed mass migration of African males from the reserves (rural areas set aside for African settlement) to urban areas and European plantations in search of wage employment. Already in the 1920s, the Native Affairs Department estimated that some 69-77% of able-bodied Kikuyu males from Kiambu and 35-45% from Fort Hall and Nyeri were employed in any one given month (Stichter, 1982). As the process of colonial domination progressed, so were correspondingly larger numbers of males drawn from the reserves in search of wage labour or other survival alternatives. Between 1938-1952, the African labour force had doubled reaching 438,702 out of an estimated population of 5.5 million (Rosberg and Nottingham, 1966). By 1934, 110,000 or 20.5% of the estimated Kikuyu population was already living outside the Kikuyu reserves, while by 1948 the figure had risen to 294,146 or 28.65% of the total Kikuyu population (Sorrenson 1967, Ross 1927, Middleton 1965). These figures include resident wage labourers in the urban areas and European farms as well as squatters in European farms and other African reserves.

Characteristics of colonial African labour force

By and large the colonial economy was geared to serve capitalist interests at the centre. Because of this, it was not designed to or capable of transforming entire populations at the periphery into workers dependent on wages. Secondly, even the small proportion of the wage earning population was, through low wages, poor living and working conditions and suppressed union activities, not transformed into a working class, completely dependent on wages. Because they could not satisfy their basic needs, or support their families, African male wage earners were forced to maintain economic, social and political links with the rural reserves (Rosberg and Nottingham 1966, Furedi 1973 and 1974).

Another characteristic of the labour force was the exclusion of women either as dependents on their working husbands or as wage earners.[2] By 1948, Sorrenson (1967), for example, shows there were 23,354 men and only 5,535 women in Nairobi. Until the mid-1940s, even domestic jobs, which women came to dominate later, were not open for women. The early female migrants include the divorced, widowed and barren women. As a result of the breakdown of the Kikuyu social support system, these women were forced to escape into urban areas to become beer brewers and prostitutes (Furedi 1973, White 1983, Doyal 1979).[3]

But even with a low wage, inadequate amenities, poor living and working conditions, large numbers of Africans continued to migrate from the reserves, to swell what Stoneham (1953), a colonial settler, described as:

> A poor native community came into being, hideous locations of squalid huts sprang up on the outskirts of every town and became the bleeding ground for thieves and prostitutes.

The poor working conditions were compounded by various labour ordinances, the most famous being the 1920s Native Labour Ordinance (commonly known as the Kipande). According to this ordinance, all adult males were registered. They were then required to carry the registration card whenever they moved. This meant (as intended) that Africans could no longer desert their employment even where conditions of abuse prevailed without being traced and punished. Ross (1927) gives a vivid description of the inhuman treatment and abuse meted to African labourers by the settlers. These ranged from physical harm to denying them their wages. There were according to Ross a total of 40,000 men registered by 1922. At the same time the total number of offenders under the same ordinance was 8,377 with tens of thousands of detentions and interrogations. Government officials in the native areas had always been urged to induce able-bodied males to join the labour market. In areas where farms bordered native areas, women and children also had to be forced to join such labour (Ross 1927, Rosberg and Nottingham 1966). But, given the vagueness of the various labour circulars, and the fact that loyalty to the colonial administration by the African chiefs was measured and rewards given according to the ability to recruit such labour, abuse and force became a common feature. There was also constant pressure to keep wages low and to increase the taxes. This was not for revenue considerations but to force Africans into the labour market. In 1921 for example, the European Convention of Association organized and succeeded in having the African wages reduced by one third. At the same time the hut and poll taxes were raised from 12 to 16 shillings. This is well summarized by Ross (1927):

> For at least a generation there was a steady demand, often out-spoken but always operative, that the native should be impove-rished, under heavy taxation by the government, coupled with depressed wages.

In addition, large numbers of African men were recruited to fight or as carrier corps in the European wars. This resulted in considerable numbers of Africans dying.

3.   Confrontation with Kikuyu Customs and Introduction of New Values

Christian missionary activities

Missionary societies took an uncompromising stand against African customs and values. Efforts were directed to inculcate new ways of life and values through Christianity, western education and western medi-cine. Without proper understanding of the functional role of the various customs, in supporting and regulating African social systems, missionary societies prohibited most of the Kikuyu customs and prac-tices including:

(1) female circumcision and related ritual
    ceremonies;

(2) alcohol consumption and related ritual ceremonies (alcohol was
    mainly consumed during ritual ceremonies);

(3) polygamous marriage and marriage transactions;

(4) inheritance of widows;

(5) limited sex play;

(6) Kikuyu religion, ritual ceremonies and healing practices.

To the missionaries, abstinence from these customs by their African
adherents, became a symbol of genuine conversion. In general, the
missionaries passed laws prohibiting their adherents from indulging in
these customs and practices. Those who slipped back to customary
practices were suspended from the church, refused baptism and
confirmation, denied other privileges such as education and grazing
ground and those employed had their employment terminated. In
other cases, however, most notably the controversial and explosive
issue of female circumcision, the missionaries tried to secure government legislation against such customs and practices. The stand of the
various missionary societies with respect to African customs, the
African reactions and the precipitation of the crisis surrounding
missionary activities and approach is well documented (Murray 1974,
Strayer 1978, Middleton 1965, Welbourn 1961, Rosberg and
Nottingham 1966, Bunche 1941).

Missionary activities were part of the entire process of colonial
domination. Through the civilizing rationalization, the missionaries
probably played the greatest role in dismantling kikuyu customs and
values which defined male/female relationships and sex and reproduction. This directly undermined the position women held within the
society, and the base on which the Kang'ei/Nyakinyua women's
groups were organized. Four of the six customs and practices prohibited, including female circumcision, polygamous marriage, inheritance of a widow by a brother of the dead husband and the practice of
limited sexual intercourse, were in one way or the other concerned
with the process of reproduction, particularly the spacing of births and
the general security of women.

Missionary fight against female circumcision

Historical evidence (Murray 1974, Strayer 1978) suggests that by 1920s, Protestant missionaries had consolidated their stand against female circumcision. Missionary medical doctors were the greatest crusaders against female circumcision.[4] As early as 1906, Dr. Arthur, a missionary doctor at Kikuyu Mission Hospital, was already demonstrating that there was, contrary to Kikuyu belief, no relationship between circumcision of girls and childbirth. Missionary prohibition of African customs was nevertheless strongly opposed by the Kikuyu people. This African opposition of missionary activities however, coincided with the time when the effects of land alienation, taxation, forced labour, poor salaries and other forms of colonial repression were considerably felt by the Kikuyu. In this context, it is not surprising that the Nationalist Movement, the Kikuyu Central Association (KCA) took over the issue of female circumcision and used it to mobilize people for resistance. By 1929, Murray (1974) indicates that the missionaries were fighting both the issue of female circumcision and the Kikuyu Nationalist Movement. Because of the strong opposition, the missionaries managed to have the custom not totally outlawed, but regulated. They allowed a minor operation to continue. Dr. Philp of Tumutumu Mission in Nyeri had by 1915, compromised to let the custom be carried out under hospital supervision. He later found the procedure repulsive and medically dangerous and so requested the church to take more drastic measures. In 1931, the Kabare pastorate committee, supported by its white missionary, decided to allow the operation to be performed under the supervision of the church. Two Christian women were chosen to become operators (Murray 1974, Strayer 1978, Beck 1970, Philp 1925). Thus, even though the missionaries had condemned female circumcision as an unnecessary custom which posed medical problems during childbirth and deprived women sexually, the physical operation aspect of it was allowed to continue. Completely prohibited were what the missionaries considered to be the repulsive ceremonies, rituals and dance-songs (gitiiro) that accompanied the operation (Murray 1974, Strayer 1978).[5] To the Kikuyu, however, these rituals and ceremonies gave emotional meaning to the operation, and as pointed out, they were part of the educational process for passing knowledge, values and rules of behavior to the youth.

Strayer and Murray have come to the conclusion that, by readily accepting the minor operation, the Kikuyu seemed to demonstrate that the physical operation on women was itself as valued as that of males. While the Kikuyu probably had little choice in the circums-tances, the physical operation had the functional role of instilling and testing the capacity for both men and women to forbear pain. Besides, it marked the start of adult life and related responsibilities in general, and more specifically sex and reproduction. These functional roles, and the pattern of prohibition which allowed the physical operation to continue, may partly explain persistence of clitoridectomy.[6]

In addition, the possibility to perform the operation in secret, but to a great extent also the nature of colonial domination, where women were left to continue life in the reserves, may also have contributed to the continued existence of the operation. This is however not to say that the practice is as widespread as it used to be. Although there are no figures, with increased attainment of education and other forms of exposure, probably a larger proportion of the Kikuyu families have abandoned the practice. But for families which have abandoned or continue the practice, the functional role of the custom as basis for structuring the society or for controlling and regulating sex and repro-duction has been greatly undermined. This is important now when HIV/AIDS challenge has increased the need to address sexuality.

Introduction of western education

Native education was primarily used to facilitate colonial domination. The education provided was limited in quality.[7] Furthermore, the missionaries regarded excessive education to be harmful to the Africans. In 1906, the number of hours per day for the education of girls was reduced from 5 to 3. It was argued that this would encourage girls to do manual work and reduce the time they were away from home. The missionaries further attempted to limit the number of years a student could attend school (Strayer, 1978).

Education was often used as reward or punishment. The mission-aries often denied education to children of adherents who drifted back to one or another of the prohibited African customs. In addition, large numbers of children of the so called pagans were not allowed to join the schools. The situation was perhaps compounded by the colonial administrative approach where education was selectively directed to sons of colonial chiefs, a class the colonialists moulded, and then regarded as "progressive". Finally, with an education system tied to the benefit of the colonial economy, it was then geared to the social group, mainly the male who had been recruited to serve the colonial economy. This confirmed women as the true peasants and carriers of cultural life.

This inadequate and selective type of education led in the 1920s to widespread protests. But again as is clear from the timing, the tide of African protests, in this case striving for better and higher education, was precipitated by the entire framework of colonial domination both economic and cultural. By the end of 1920s and the beginning of 1930s, the Kikuyu took a major step by establishing Karing'a (pure) and the Kikuyu Independent School Association (KISA) schools. These schools provided the Africans with education on self-help basis within Christian environment, but outside European control.[8] Among other things, the independent churches allowed female circumcision to continue.

Karing'a and KISA schools and churches were run by committees. Church committees were made up of male elders only, while school committees were mixed. In a footnote, Welbourn (1961) comments that the involvement of women in school committees was probably due to the traditional importance of women councils which had considerable power within the Kikuyu society.[9] These protests and self-help initiatives reflected emerging needs, aspirations and readiness to oppose colonial domination by the Africans. By the 1940s, the colonial government was reconsidering improvement of African education.[10]

Introduction of western medical care

Western medical care was, like education and Christianity, geared to serve the interests of the Europeans. From the start, climatic and therefore health considerations played a major role in determining the nature of settlement in the colonies. The climatic and health conditions of the Kenya Highlands were advertised as suitable for European settlement (Eliot 1966).

The structure of medical care remained oriented to the European interests. In the early phases of the colony, English doctors were stationed in the main administrative centres to serve the colonial officials and their families, while Goan doctors and Indian sub-surgeons catered largely for the Indian labour force on the railway construction. With the development of the settler economy, a number of settler doctors were engaged (Carman 1976). Right from the start, therefore, a wholesale introduction of western medicine took place.[11]

By and large, medical needs of Africans were neglected. Even when there was realization of the need to expand medical care to the reserves, the plans were slow, not only for lack of resources as one might believe, but because of other factors as well. Beck (1970) for example shows how during 1919-1922 a dispute between the missionaries and the colonial administration over who should control health services in the reserves delayed its expansion. It was not until the mid-1920s when the plan was given impetus by the increasing demands and African protests, and was expanded at that time to include medical training as well. A medical training depot was infact began in 1929 to train African boys to become hospital, laboratory and pharmacy assistants (Carman, 1976).[12]

Kikuyu indigenous medicine, which for most Africans was the only care available, had been left fairly undisturbed except when missionaries prohibited it, not as a medical system, but as just another heathen practice. To the missionaries, the Kikuyu medical care system, comprising a variety of specialists including herbalists, diviners, birth attendants, etc, constituted witchcraft. But in the wake of African agitation in the 1920s, indigenous medicine posed a different problem to the colonial administration. In the face of deepening insecurity and frustrations, indigenous medicine increasingly played a significant role not just because it was the only available medical care for the majority of the Africans. As a system of belief, it was associated with the balance or lack of it in the social environment. It treated the whole person (physical and psychological ailments), and relied greatly on super-natural power, particularly the spirits of the ancestors. The Africans exploited it as a resource to resist colonial domination. The role of the indigenous medicine and diviners in the crisis which culminated with the Mau Mau uprising is well known (Rosberg and Nottingham 1966, Gikonyo 1972).[13] Even to the colonialists such as Majdalany (1962), for whom the use of Kikuyu diviners in the Mau Mau crisis denoted denial of civilization and a return to barbarism, there was recognition that Mau Mau was founded on the strength of those social groups whom the same civilizing process had offered nothing beyond misery and insecurity.[14]

Faced with an agitation which exploited indigenous medicine, the colonial administration passed the Kenya Colony Witchcraft Ordinance in 1925, imposing penalties ranging from exorbitant fines, long term imprisonment, deportation and death for those practicing it (Browne 1935, Roberts 1935). But despite this legislation, indigenous medicine continued underground, until today when tides are once again gathering in favour of reviving it.

The medicalization of reproduction

In addition, the process of institutionalizing reproductive matters around the hospital was intensified. This process of transforming reproduction into a medical issue and its institutionalization around the hospital was probably an issue which was unfolding within the western medicine (Mies 1986, Ehrenreich and English 1976, Doyal 1979).[15] But among the Kikuyu and presumably other colonized societies, there were specific interaction points which did not only medicalize health and reproduction, but also removed it from its social and cultural context.

Missionary activities were particularly important in this process. The problem of female circumcision has been discussed. The important point to mention again is that circumcision was part of the reproduction process, as a preparatory stage for adult sexuality, marriage and procreation. The greatest crusaders against it were the missionary medical doctors.[16] But even though these medical doctors led the crusade, the strong resistance by the Kikuyu forced them to allow the operation part of circumcision, against which they had so strongly campaigned, to continue within the mission medical facilities. Secondly, among the earliest trained African midwives, female circumcision (operation) was part of the training offered. Furthermore, women using the medical facilities for delivery and child care became major targets of missionary propaganda that, contrary to the belief held by the Kikuyu people, circumcision had no relationship to childbirth. Thus, female circumcision, which was central in the process of reproduction was expropriated from the people and suppressed through the hospital at the same time as it continued being performed within hospital precincts.

Medical research

The last issue to mention here is the lack of interest in medical research except for tropical diseases such as malaria and sleeping sickness which posed great threat to Europeans and their interests. Culwick (1944) shows, for example, that, in the 1930s, the colonial empire was faced with nutritional problems of great magnitude. Nevertheless, there was hardly empirical data to guide policies. He could easily count the number of nutritional studies in the entire eastern and southern Africa.[17]

African resistance and colonial counter-measures

Conditions arising from the process of colonial domination led to a deepening sense of insecurity, anxiety, frustration and alienation. The process was from the start, therefore, interrupted by various forms of resistance. By the 1920s, African protests (political, labour and religious) were organized, culminating in the Mau Mau confrontation in the 1950s (Middleton 1965, Welbourn 1961, Furedi 1973 and 1974, Kilson 1955, Kanongo 1977). Large numbers of able-bodied men and women ran to wage the war from the forests.

Besides fighting alongside men, women played an active role as individuals and in their traditional groups during the administration of the oath, in acquiring arms and ammunition, transporting or organizing the transportation of information and food between the reserves, urban areas and the forests. This active role is portrayed by the Mau Mau fighters themselves (Gikonyo, 1972). The colonial government recognized the potential of women in the Mau Mau. This point is underlined in the newsletter of the East African Women's

League (1953):

> The Kikuyu reserved lands come right up to Nairobi, and although the roads may be guarded and trains and lorries checked, goods can still be smuggled out of town in bags of vegetables and charcoal on the backs of the womenfolk: money and firearms can be circulated in the same manner. African women have recently been stopped carrying as much as £200 in bank notes !

The need thus arose for the colonial government to take a wide range of counter-measures to control the situation.

Counter-measures: Detention, deportation and repatriation.

In 1952 when Mau Mau broke out, a state of emergency was declared in order to restrict the movement of the people and isolate the Kikuyu in particular. Detention, deportation, imprisonment, death sentences and repatriation of the Kikuyu back to their already congested and agriculturally poor reserves were widely used in order to contain the situation. There were, by 1954, 17 000 convicts and 50,000 detainees (Rosberg and Nottingham 1966). Because of the large numbers of detainees and prisoners, and the harsh treatment including poor diet and hygiene, hard labour, physical and psychological injury inflicted during the interrogation and screening process, the health situation of detainees and prisoners was often critical (Likimani, 1985). Similarly, in order to weaken women's involvement, increasing numbers of women were imprisoned and detained. According to Shannon (1955) there were in October 1955, 6,800 Kikuyu women in prisons, detention and work camps.

The villagization scheme

The villagization scheme, by which all the people living in Central Province were forced into colonial enclosures, was part of the emergency measures. By the end of 1955, 1,077,500 Kikuyu and Embu people had according to Sorrenson (1967) been enclosed in 854 villages.[18] In many cases, because of the support of the Kikuyu population to the Mau Mau, many of their homes were burnt down prior to the villagization. This implied that, the majority of the people started life in the colonial villages in absolute poverty. In these villages, curfews were imposed, strong fences and deep trenches were erected round the villages to curtail movement of the people and consequently their support to the Mau Mau fighters. This also enabled the colonial government to use the population in forced labour more effectively.

Land consolidation and registration

The physical movement of the entire populations into the colonial enclosures provided the colonial administration with a chance to pursue the land consolidation and registration policy. This had been contemplated over a long period as a measure for agricultural improvement which would ease the problem of congestion and unemployment and avert violence. By the end of the 1950s, land consolidation and registration in Kiambu, Fort Hall and Nyeri was nearly completed. A report by Homan (1962), the secretary of Trust Land Board, shows that in the three districts, (total population according to the 1962 census was 1,161,500) a total of 666,525 acres were consolidated into 145,779 farms and registered under 126,713 titles (see also Pedraza 1956, Wilson 1956). As a punishment to those who had been active in Mau Mau, land was confiscated from a total of 3,533 Kikuyu (Sorrenson, 1967). Furthermore, the former Ahoi (tenants) who were accommodated within past Kikuyu land tenure were displaced and made landless. While the process of privatization of land created a landless class, production of cash crops rather than food was encouraged as the main strategy for improving the reserves. With the relaxation of emergency regulations, the population was again encouraged to move from the colonial villages, to settle in their private land. This implied building new homes. As shown further below, the mabati activities of women's groups started around this time of great need.

The use of indirect rule and targetting

(a) Using ngwatio groups in forced communal labour

Faced with all forms of resistance, even for programmes such as soil conservation, which the colonial government believed would help the Africans improve their living conditions in the reserves, the colonial government was by the 1940s increasingly using indigenous communal groups. Studies were carried out among the Meru and Kikuyu people to identify specific indigenous groups which could be incorporated in the colonial administration in general and in specific programmes such as soil conservation (Lambert 1947, Holding 1942, Rice 1947).

In Fort Hall (presently Murang'a) District, the concept of Ngwatio or agricultural mutual work group discussed above was being used to enhance soil conservation.[19] Within the pre-colonial division of labour among the Kikuyu, women were more frequently involved in Ngwatio work groups. This, and the removal of large numbers of men from the reserves during the colonial period implied that, for any communal labour enforced in the reserves, the majority of those participating were women. This point was underscored by the nationalist movement (KCA). As part of its resistance, KCA planned to stop women from participating in the soil conservation programme. Even though the motive of KCA was to defeat government's agricultural improvement programme, it was recognized that the work was being done by women.

But, the government forced communal labour differed from the pre-colonial Kikuyu work groups in a number of ways. Although as Rice (1947) seems to indicate, women were at times allowed to terrace their farms in turn as was the case with past Ngwatio work groups, colonial work groups were mainly used for public projects. Furthermore, a male overseer and a committee of male elders were instituted. This was the start of the formalization process of group life among the Kikuyu including agency targetting.

(b) The Maendeleo Ya Wanawake organization

Maendeleo Ya Wanawake Organization was established in 1952. The organization itself has been traced back to the 1940s and is believed to have had Canadian connection (Wipper, 1976). There is little doubt about its origin, considering that many white settlers came from Canada. As a British colony, Canada had a history of mobilization of women for mutual support and to resist colonial domination. Furthermore, the harsh conditions in the reserves had attracted the attention of many philanthropists and voluntary organizations such as the East African Women's League which was started in 1917 to fight for the rights of wives of European settlers. Many such organizations were carrying out social welfare activities prior to 1952. However, the Colonial Annual reports (1951-1962) indicate that by 1952, the government was more concerned with containing a situation which was not only threatening to explode, but where women had played an active role. This furthermore marked a turning point where the colonial government started dealing with women directly. Prior to this, instructions and information was given to the husbands who were then expected to pass it on to their wives. African women who had been given leadership training at Jeannes school for training community workers, were appointed by the government to help in the organization of Maendeleo Women's clubs both in European plantations and African reserves (Colonial Annual Reports, 1957-1962). Besides being used to counter women's active involvement in Mau Mau, establishment of Maendeleo perhaps also marked a major turn in the formalization of women's groups and their relationship with external agents.

Local women's clubs were organized with the help of volunteers mainly wives of settlers, colonial administrative staff and women government officials. The local administration comprising chiefs, headmen and elders was also required to mobilize women into these clubs (Wainwright, 1953). Because of the extensive use of volunteers, whose main role within the division of labour was the management of domestic consumption (Shannon 1954 and 1955, Wipper 1975, Mboya 1954), it is no wonder that Maendeleo Women's Clubs became preoccupied by "homecraft" (sewing, embroidery, handicraft, childcare, cooking and proper ways of entertaining visitors). This has been criticized on the grounds that African women were taught embroidery and preparing European foods such as cakes when they did not have homes and facilities to practice their new knowledge.

In this connection, one may sympathize with Wipper's uneasiness against these criticisms. Wipper (1975) contends that Maendeleo Ya Wanawake Organization has during the post-colonial period ceased being a pressure group fighting for the rights of women. This has been so because the national leadership has increasingly been co-opted by the government. Wipper seems to miss or avoid to accept that Maendeleo was from the start a government initiative.[20] It was initiated, funded and run by the Department of Community Affairs and Rehabilitation. The clubs were organized so that Local Native Councils could recover money used for buying sewing materials. Women club members were forced to make initial down payment for articles they produced to ensure as Wainwright (1953) indicates that they eventually purchased those articles, even though they may not have had use for them. In Central Province where the Mau Mau crisis was concentrated and the choice for women was between participating in harsh forced labour or Maendeleo Clubs, exploitation of the clubs as a source of revenue for the Local Native Council was probably widespread. According to information gathered during this study, even young unmarried girls joined the clubs, to escape colonial state harassment and suspicion of being Mau Mau supporters.

Conditions of women were bad enough to warrant concern, and did indeed raise some genuine concern.[21] But the paternalistic attitudes of those who were supposedly fighting for the rights of African women were overriding. Furthermore, problems of African women were misconceived by those who purported to be helping them. For example, while the East African Women's League recognized that African women were disadvantaged in the area of education, the same organization felt that Kikuyu girls could no longer be entrusted to Kikuyu male teachers. Instead, the feeling was that they should only be taught by European nuns (Shannon, 1954). The East African Women's League thus saw the problem not in the context of the colonial structures, plunder and exploitation of resources, but only in terms of the appropriatness of the Kikuyu male teachers.

Up until the late 1950s, one cannot therefore talk of Maendeleo as being a voluntary women's organization. The only voluntariness at the time was perhaps the role played by volunteer wives of European settlers to teach, supervise and organize African women Maendeleo instructors or organizers in close liaison with the Department of Community Affairs and the Local Native Councils. By late 1950s and early 1960s, colonial rule was coming to an end and emergency regulations were relaxed. The colonial government then started encouraging self-help activities. The salaries of Maendeleo organizers were stopped. The main tone and objective of the government had changed from force or directed groups, to formation of groups whose leaders and committees were chosen by the people themselves. After this, it was noted that, attitudes among the people were changing. Activities which had been resisted were now being performed with enthusiasm. Women are even described as having had a leading role in the formation of the new self-help groups (Colonial Annual Reports, 1957-1962).

By this time, African women who took over as leaders and organizers of Maendeleo Clubs were specifically shaped through training or supervision by European women volunteers and the government to take over those roles. These women emerged as a minority elite class, with values and conditions of life not only enormously different from the majority of rural women, but also conditioned to attain the positions and wealth of their trainers. The African women leaders were in addition going to play the role of wife and mother within a newly emerging structure which had been shaped as though women did not exist or could be used whenever it suited male leaders and the government.

The emerging social structure was not only male-dominated, but, women lagged behind in most of the new areas of defining status and social worth. The question of involving women in the political machinery therefore did not arise. Although the role of women in the Mau Mau conflict was well recognized, and was indeed the major factor in the formation and targetting through Maendeleo Ya Wanawake Organization, the Commissioners appointed to look into the methods for selecting African representatives to the Legislative Council, strongly felt that women were not yet ready for that role (Colonial Report, 1955).

Impact of colonial domination on women

The process of colonial domination described above, resulted in conditions which necessitated continued collective participation by women but also shaped the form it assumed. Perhaps the major impact of the process of colonial domination was marginalization and impoverishment of the Kikuyu people. This is not to say that social differentiation did not arise. The post-colonial social structure where political and economic power was taken over by a small elite class which had been selected and shaped through exposure to education and collaboration in the later part of the colonial rule is well documented (Leys, 1975). The simplest way to describe the situation is perhaps to say that at a macro level, relationships of dependence between capitalism at the centre and the periphery emerged (Rodney 1972, Ngugi 1987). Marginalization is therefore perceived at several levels and assumes many dimensions. A few of these will be discussed mainly from the perspective of their impact on women.

Food production

By the 1930s, food shortages and malnutrition had become a common feature. This situation arose from a number of processes. Migration of males for the service of a colonial economy whose main objective was exploitation of resources for external markets meant that, an important part of the subsistence agricultural labour was withdrawn from the reserves. In addition, agricultural improvement policies mainly extended commercial agriculture and cash crop production to smallholder African farmers instead of increasing food supply. These smallholder farmers then became dependent on external markets far beyond their control.[22] Moreover, land, which by then was registered in the man's name was increasingly used as security for acquiring bank or government credits and loans. Land thus acquired new properties which were in conflict with subsistence food production. As a result, women lost their former control over land use for food production and its distribution. The education provided had negative impact as well. Colonial education aimed at producing simple clerical or white colar workers. Education thus inculcated values negative to agricultural manual work. In this context education played a major role in lowering food production and the marginalization of women.

At the same time, colonial domination led to the depletion of other resources. One such resource was thatching grass, used by women in house construction. This was depleted not just through overgrazing and overcrowding of the reserves, but also the privatization of land which curtailed fetching thatching grass free from privately owned land. On the other hand, the demand for thatching grass and other building materials in Central Province was increased by the two movements of entire population, first to colonial villages and later to individual private landholdings.

It was during this time when Kikuyu Ngwatio groups involved in house thatching shifted from fetching grass to buying corrugated iron sheets. Monetary transaction and mobilization of funds became a central preoccupation of the groups. Up to the early 1970s, the need for permanent and improved homes for large numbers of people who could not afford constructing a new house on their own was extensive. The thatching groups were therefore larger. Work groups (selling group labour) for resource mobilization and traditional dancing and singing were also common features of the groups then. Around this time these groups were referred to as Nyakinyua. When the demand for housing eased towards the mid-1970s, the groups continued with other welfare activities. Even then, the concept "mabati" was still used to denote women's group activities and more precisely to refer to the amount of money each member contributes or in turn obtains from the group. But as will be seen later, groups assumed new features.

Sex and reproduction

From another perspective, the absence of men from home for short or long periods, implied also that observation of social rules of conduct, the control mechanisms and rituals which were effective when the society was intact no longer could apply with the same force. Taboos and social pressure groups such as the Kang'ei/Nyakinyua age-set were extensively used in the pre-colonial society to regulate sex and reproduction. But the joint responsibility taken by individual couples depended on knowledge about each other, particularly the menstrual cycle of the woman. This further depended on living together. The introduction of a hut tax had already by 1901 forced the Kikuyu to stop the practice of husband and wife living in separate houses to avoid paying extra tax. In addition, missionary opposition to Kikuyu sexual morality, where the community had joint responsibility as part of everyday living, disrupted most of the effective methods of controlling and regulating sex and reproduction. Because of this, combined with an education system which gave little alternative in these matters and an individualized medical care, a manner of viewing sex and reproduction in a narrow and mechanical sense emerged. The migrant husband therefore home only occasionally to an overworked wife with whom he shared a house and a bed. If it happened to be the period when sexual intercourse was socially prohibited, it would have taken a saint who had been forced into celibacy, or paid sex (prostitution) to avoid having sexual intercourse with his wife.

This sort of life had a number of implications. The wife was subjected to increased and closely spaced births with all the related health implications. For the Kikuyu men and women, the psychological impact of breaking sexual taboos and rules in a situation where necessary cleansing rituals could not be performed has been given little attention. The insecurity arising from the breakdown of controls, due to separation is evident. This was particularly clear towards the end of the emergency in the late 1950s. Large numbers of men were released from detention and prisons to find their wives and daughters with illegitimate children. During the emergency period, most women living in the reserves had been raped or forced to become wives of the notorious home guards. In spite of this, the presence of illegitimate children convinced husbands (who, besides being forced into years of celibacy had also been physically and mentally tortured) that women could not control their sexuality. And since husbands in many cases never stayed home after release, psychological insecurity arising from a sense of lack of control over one's wife continued. This psycho.social phenomenon, coupled with the overwhelming targetting of the current coital contraceptives to women, has made men even more insecure.

Fertility control programmes

The colonial government had by 1940s, realized that conditions in the reserves had to be improved if the growing protests were to be contained. Overcrowding of the Kikuyu reserves and related protests were blamed on rapid population increase among the Africans. The colonialists believed that, rapid population increase and overcrowding of the reserves arose not because of expropriation of African land and erosion of cultural norms which controlled and regulated sex and reproduction. These were, as indicated by the followin, believed to have arisen because Europeans brought under control menaces such as tribal warfare, famine, and infant mortality:

> Land hunger in Kenya is commonly supposed to have been caused by the rapid growth of the African population in the fifty years of British rule, through European control of inter-tribal warfare, famine, pestilences, infant mortality and so on.... But it is important to realize that while this is true, it is not because Africans (and in particular the Kikuyu) are confined to areas of land inadequate for this population that they suffer from land hunger. The Provincial Agricultural Officer, Central Province, has claimed in a letter to the East African Standard of 17th April this year,that, properly farmed, the Kikuyu reserves could easily carry that number. (East African Women's League newsletter, number 7, 1953).

The policies were at that time largely directed to agricultural improvement. But by the 1950s, the developed world in general was getting alarmed with what was then regarded as "population explosion" in the countries emerging from colonial rule. The subsequent years saw great attention and resources invested in population control programmes as an independent strategy for achieving social and economic development in the poor Third World countries. In the 1950s, the Family Planning Association of Kenya was for example distributing contraceptives in Nairobi and Mombasa. At independence, population increase was thus seen as the major problem hindering or threatening to hinder social and economic development. By 1966, a definite population policy "The Kenya National Family Planning Programme" was instituted. A team of experts from the US Population Council was invited by the Kenya Government to study the population problem and recommend a programme suitable and administratively feasible.[23]

But evidence seems to indicate that as a strategy for reducing fertility rate and achieving social and economic development in Third World countries, family planning has had limited impact. As Sindinga (1985) states:

> The programme's major objective was to reduce the rate of population growth from a national average of 3% per year at the time to 2% per year over a period of ten years. Now, nearly two decades later, one of the world's most expensive family planning campaign appear to have hardly made a dent on fertility. Instead the annual population growth rate has jumped to an estimated record 4%.

The entire process of colonial domination had far reaching implications to women's groups and their activities. The situation has arisen where women's groups have retained some of their past features and functions. Groups were for example observed to have adapted their former mutual aid activities into mabati activities to which they have added income-generating projects. But as indicated, groups have neither retained their past central role in the control of sex and reproduction, nor have they accepted the new fertility model targetted from outside.

CHAPTER 6

THE POST-COLONIAL WOMEN'S COLLECTIVE ACTIVITIES

1. The Commercialization of the Economy

Structural formations particularly the commercialization of the economy (agriculture) and the formalization of women's groups, not only in their organizational context, but also in their relationship with other social agents, have been intensified during the post-colonial period. The following section briefly discusses some of the major features of the emerging society.

Production of cash crops for external markets, backed with government extension services and credits, has during the post-colonial period been extensively extended to the smallholder peasants. Within the new land tenure, where rights of ownership are largely in the hands of individual men, commercial agriculture is increasingly under male control. Women continue to uphold the low status subsistence agriculture within a context where land is not only privately controlled but is increasingly used for cash crop production. Besides their traditional roles as food producers, women are also major providers of labour in the commercial agricultural sector. In this context women have assumed heavier workload at the same time as they have lost most of the control and autonomy over land use, food production and its distribution.

In addition, food itself has undergone the process of commercialization. The commercial milling, whose wide use can be traced to the colonial time when settlers increasingly grew maize on large scale, seems to have set this process in motion.[1] This has meant that even staple foods such as maize have been transformed. Instead of prepa-

ring whole maize where several ingredients including green vegetables, bananas and potatoes were boiled together in one pot, maize
flour has become the staple food. Furthermore, the preparation of
maize meal (Ugali) requires a separate relish usually vegetables
(cabbage, tomatoes, onions). A typical diet even in the rural areas
moreover includes sugar, tea, cooking fat or oil, salt, wheat products,
rice, etc. All these are cash purchased goods. The household has thus
increasingly become dependent on cash for its food requirements
(Hanger and Morris, 1973).

Given that it is men who have more access to regular cash, this
commercialization process has ironically reversed the situation of
Kikuyu women. While they shoulder greater responsibilities within
the rural economy, they have increasingly become dependent on their
husbands for cash. This seems to follow the pattern of capitalist
development discussed above. There are however two exceptions. In
the periphery, male wages remain too low. Moreover, a large number
of men are unemployed. For those who depend on cash crop returns,
such money is not received monthly. It is tied to the rythms of international marketing arrangements and state machineries whose decisions are often unfavourable to the producers (Weekly Review, April
7, 1989).[2] This has meant, for instance, that coffee returns are not only
small but payments are irregular. And even when payments may be
regular, they tend to be tied to needs of households such as school
fees. As a source of food, commercial agriculture is thus limited.

This seems to have set the stage where Kikuyu women, alone and
within groups struggle to assert themselves within the new society, in
ways which may seem strange or conservative to foreigners. It was for
example observed in the current study that while women struggle to
change this dependent situation, because of the same male dominant
position as cash earners/providers and the prevailing ideologies
supporting this position, women usually avoid direct confrontation
with men. They even avoid engaging in projects which may not be
approved by their husbands. Above all they avoid appearing to have
performed better than men, even when it is clear that this is the case
(see chapter 9). It is within this structural, historical formation of the
Kenyan society and its economy that the mobilization of women into
groups, both as actors on their own rights, and as targets of other
agents should be examined.

2. Mobilization of Women into Groups: Actors and Targets

In many ways, the emerging groups have elements of past Ngwatio and Matega mutual assistance discussed above. The home improvement or mabati activities discussed in chapter nine fall in this category. This is the dimension where women act from their perspectives and in their own rights. The second dimension in the mobilization process, is what will here be called targeting. The concept of targeting is used to refer to the situation where policies and programmes of other agents are implemented through women's groups. This in turn shapes or transforms women's groups in various ways.

The recent upsurge and concern to involve women in development has brought together international aid organizations, governments and voluntary women's organizations all targeting this or that through women's groups. This has therefore intensified the process of targeting which has been traced back to the period of colonial indirect rule. The targeted policies and programmes reflect orientation and ideals about social progress and development upheld by these local and international development agents even though such ideals more often than not conflict with needs and priorities of women and women's groups.[3] The following section focuses on the nature and impact of targeting during the post-colonial period. Three programmes which are considered relevant in the shaping and transformation of women's groups are discussed.

The Harambee Self-help Movement

Towards the end of the colonial period, when control of the population was no longer necessary, the colonial government encouraged self-help activities. Using the ideology of indigenous communal living (African Socialism) the post-colonial government promoted self-help activities as a major feature of development. The term Harambee (pulling efforts together) was then coined (Ng'ethe, 1983) to describe a movement in an arena of ideological and political activity. The 1960s and early 1970s saw widespread formation and registration of self-help groups composed of men and women. These groups were mainly oriented to public service projects such as construction of cattle dips, water supplies, schools, medical facilities, churches, bridges and roads (Godfrey and Mutiso 1974, Holmquist 1970, Ng'ethe 1983). Local communities make an average contribution in monetary, material and labour of up to 85% (Ng'ethe, 1983). Women were observed to have made greater monetary, material and labour contribution, while leadership was dominated by men (Mbithi and Rasmusson, 1977). Moreover, apart probably from water supplies, health facilities, churches and nursery schools, which women initiated much more than men, most harambee projects were a replica of the ideals of modernization, and not necessarily the priorities of women.

Even those projects which denoted priorities of women, the benefits accrued by women were limited by a number of factors as the rural water supply programme clearly demonstrates. One of the stated goals of the programme is alleviating the burden of fetching and carrying unprotected water for long distances. But until recently, when focus seems to be changing towards low cost water schemes with components of sanitation and community participation (Kwaho, Hesawa and Manicaland rural water supply programmes in Kenya, Tanzania and Zimbabwe respectively), huge and high technology water schemes which proved hard to maintain were constructed. Because of the belief that water projects had to be large to be of economic value, and because of the implementation of inappropriate technology, many schemes remained dry for most of the time. Furthermore, because of vested interests, local politicians and other patrons have facilitated construction of large water supplies in order to encompass large areas of their electoral or potential electoral constituencies.[4] Women have thus accrued few benefits from such water supply schemes (Ahlberg 1983). The Harambee self-help movement has been influenced by the political system in other ways. In a general way, the movement has been used as a platform where vying politicians compete to mobilize monetary and material resources thus having greater chance of becoming the representatives of the people. At the same time, as an arena of ideological activity, the local people are often reminded not to involve themselves in politics.

Harambee efforts were furthermore geared to provision of facilities, the running of which would be left to the government. It did not take long to realize that provision of physical facilities was not enough as many dispensaries and health centres for example remained unused after completion for lack of qualified staff and supplies.

The conclusion to draw from this experience is that there were strong forces which demobilized the harambee self-help movement. It is no wonder that by the late 1960s increasing numbers of women's groups were formed and registered with the government. Observations in my study seem to give a clue of the overriding factors. Many women's groups were found to have been part of larger mixed self-help groups from which they broke to form their own small groups. The question of use and control of group funds featured prominently as a reason why women broke away. This also became evident from mixed groups such as Kihara (discussed in chapter nine), where women felt more confident about participating with men as long as they (women) also held strong positions. According to women in this group, this is important for controlling male dominance in such groups.

The Special Rural Development Programme

In 1970, the government intervened more directly in the women's group movement through the Special Rural Development Programme (SRDP). This programme was strongly backed by foreign capital and expertise. It was introduced in selected districts all over the country to experiment the with an integrated team approach to rural development. Women's groups were within this programme, and were provided with material and technical assistance mainly to start income-generating activities. Furthermore, in line with the objectives of SRDP, attempts were made to integrate the services of the various extension workers.

But, in spite of the strong backing of the programme and the special attention given to women's groups in the programme areas, there was little success: by the end of the programme period, there was still little integrated co-ordination. Moreover, commercial activities for which groups had been given material and skill assistance had not faired well either. Pala (1975), for example, observed that handicraft production groups produced elaborate knitted and embroidered articles which had no markets.

Establishment of the Women's Bureau

In spite of these experiences, government intervention intensified along the same lines. By the mid-1970s, partly because of the increasing international pressure for national governments to "Integrate Women in Development", the Women's Bureau was established as a unit in the Ministry of Culture and Social Services. By this time, women's groups had demonstrated their capacity for development. The mabati activities were by the 1970s visible through shining iron roofed houses. Browne (1975) observed that chiefs in Nyeri District of Central Province were proud of the shining iron roofs which denoted development of their area. The Women's Bureau thus used existing women's groups to implement its policies and programmes. Mostly, the Women's Bureau supported income-generating activities (see chapter 9).

The intensified targeting of projects by the Women's Bureau also meant intensification of the the formalization process as well. Women's group committees at various administrative levels have been created. New formal rules and regulations which govern interaction between the groups and other agents have been introduced. The groups are, for example, required to register with the government, maintain a bank account, have a formal committee with specified number of members, a specified time period and recruit members outside the kinship boundary. This entire process of targeting, has resulted in increased interaction between the groups themselves, between groups and the government, and a formalization process which typically leaves women's groups more dependent on the government and other donor agencies. This exposes the groups to patronage and other abuses (see note four). The same process further affects group composition, internal dynamics and the mobilization process. Formal rules were found to undermine many of the informal rules and organization of the groups. I observed, for example, that informal groups (mainly smaller unregistered groups) which are still known to be widespread operate underground. Furthermore, the requirements for security by banks and the government has made obsolete the informal arrangements to have group projects in the compound of one of the group members. And probably as a result of increased and formalized interaction between groups and the government, salaried group leadership has been contemplated. The targetting process and the resulting formalization has had mobilizing and demobilizing effect on the groups and their activities.

Part Three: Patterns and Dynamics of
Contemporary Women's Groups

CHAPTER 7

THE INTERACTION PATTERNS OF
WOMEN'S GROUPS

1. Introduction

Interaction patterns and their impact on various aspects of women's groups are described in this chapter. Generally, two dimensions of interaction are conceptualized. The first dimension denotes the basic interaction as women join and participate in groups. The second dimension results from the targeting process. The two dimensions are loosely conceptualized, because in the process of interaction each may change and assume the properties of the other. Towards the end of the colonial and early post-colonial periods, the need for housing was, for example, a strong mobilizing force. In time, activities of women's groups became visible. The shining mabati roofed houses which denoted progress or modernization largely led to intensified government targeting including formation of committees at various administrative levels, training in skills and provision of material support for the groups. In turn the process of targeting shapes the groups in various ways. The more recently formed groups such as Ithiki and Mwihoko (discussed in chapter nine) state, for example, that they formed in order to benefit from the government resources. Analysis of interaction patterns helps to explain the nature of change within the groups themselves, their internal structure, their areas of concern and their relationship with other agents, particularly the government.

2.   The Basic Interaction Process

Rural women's groups are made up of individuals living close and familiar with each other. Leaders of groups of this study, for example, knew all the members of their groups. Of the 177 women's group leaders interviewed, 169 (95%) knew their group members very well. Members of these groups are homogeneous in many other ways. The groups are mostly comprised of married women. But, in spite of this, group members valued their groups for bringing together a variety of marital experiences, thus helping members to understand the general status of marital relationships. This in turn facilitates the definition of what constitutes marital problems. At this level of interaction, women bring along their concrete realities and experiences.[1] Through this basic interaction process, groups define and redefine their situation and design strategies accordingly. But as has been pointed out, the same women, either individually or in their groups are, members of many other organizations.

3.   Multi-Participation in Women's Groups

Members of women's groups were found to belong to other women's groups, larger harambee self-help groups and organizations. All studied groups were also found to be part of the government instituted committees. The most frequent combination of participation is shown in figure 3.

Participation in other groups and organizations was through choice of individual women, influence of prevailing conditions and the monetization and targeting processes. Women were members of more than one group simultaneously because of benefits which they accrue or more importantly expect to obtain from this type of participation. This raised the chances for a woman to receive extra support during times of crisis. There was also the calculation that, belonging to more than one group put women in an advantageous position because one of the groups may receive external support. Related to this was the need to reduce the risk, in cases when groups run into problems and disintegrate.

This form of participation has been facilitated by the monetization and targeting processes. During the 1960s and early 1970s, when groups were involved in actual roofing of houses, the physical presence of group members was essential, not only for the roofing activity itself, but for resource mobilization which then consisted of the sale of group labour. At that time, a deserting member risked removal of iron sheets from her house. The nature of activities and forms of sanctions and punishments restricted members from deserting or participating in many groups at the same time.

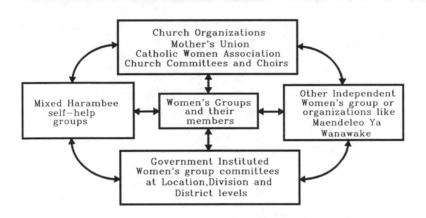

Figure 3: Groups and organizations to which women
and women's groups are members.

The nature of group activities, resource mobilization strategies and related rules and sanctions governing participation have increasingly changed. Members can now be absent from group meetings without penalty as long as they send their regular monetary contribution. This provides the possibility of sending contributions to more than one group. There are, however, sanctions for absentees and deserters who have no valid reasons. Late comers are still fined. But unlike the past, when groups themselves effected punishment to deserters, members who desert now are required to repay the money received before deserting. It was found, however, that groups experience problems. Members are either unable or unwilling to repay. When this happens, the case is reported to the CDA, who has no legal authority over offenders. If the CDA is unable to effect action, the matter is reported to the chief. Three such cases suggest that even for problems which can be described as internal, groups have increasingly come to rely on outside help.

(1) In Gaturi Location two Assistant Chiefs wrote letters ordering two group deserters to repay money they owed their groups. In one of the cases, the chief was threatening to send the offender to court because she had failed to respond to a previous letter.[2]

(2) Members of Kiangochi and Thechi women's groups in Mbiri Location belonged to a third group which had a problem of desertion. They appealed to the CDA whose intervention had little impact. This case was complicated because one of the deserters was the wife of the chief under whose authority the CDA is.

(3) In January 1976, the CDA from Mbiri Location wrote a letter requesting the chief to punish three members of Gituri and nine from Gaitega women's groups for deserting their groups for over eight months.[3]

4.   Other Forms of Interaction

The majority of the groups in the study area had exchanged visits with other groups. Of the 177 groups studied, 131(74%) had visited other groups at one time or the other. 106(60%) had had visits from other groups. A systematic study of the nature of these visits was not carried out. Nevertheless, a number of observations suggest the form this interaction takes.

Celebrating completion of an activity

It is common practice for groups to celebrate completion of an activity. In the past, groups celebrated completion of roofing of houses. With the changing nature of activities, groups celebrate completion of purchasing of household items (see chapter 9). This is probably the area where interaction is the initiative of women themselves and is limited to their mabati activities. In 1976, Mugoiri locational women's committee organized a tea party to celebrate completion of roofing houses.[4] Kimathe B1 and B11 organized similar parties after completing a round of sharing.[5] During such parties, other groups are invited to participate. In addition, a government officer, a politician or another dignitary is invited as a guest of honour. This occasion may be used for raising more funds.

Group participation in community work

Another form of interaction takes place when groups at various levels join to help an institution or poorer members of the community. Three such occasions were observed during the course of fieldwork. The first involved women's groups from Weithaga Location. A mother of ten small children had recently died at childbirth. This case was brought to the attention of the locational committee by groups from the village of the dead mother. Her family was described as extremely poor. The following three indicators were used to express the extent of poverty:

(i) Among the ten children, the last three, including the newborn, were incapacitated by severe malnutrition and consequently could not even walk.

(ii) The only blanket in the family was used for burying the mother.

(iii) The family was over-crowded in a two-roomed thatched house.

The locational women's committee therefore planned to make some contribution towards that family. The next group meeting was organized to take place at the compound of the poor family. Groups from the location and individual women were requested to bring along clothes, food or money. The press was invited to report on the occasion.

Similar contributions of foodstuff and money were made to the Koimbi Orphan and Gaturi home for old men. But unlike the previous case, the government was involved in the organization of these visits. Government officers announced the proposed visits during the preceding locational committee meetings. Furthermore, they urged women's groups to donate to the poor institutions generously.[6] The visit to the Gaturi old men's home was described as a success. There were nevertheless many complaints from both sides. Government officers complained that women's groups were not generous in their contribution. Groups on the other hand complained of the poorly organized government transport. Many women were stranded and only returned home late in the night.

One can say that even where groups are involved in community activities, two types of action prevail: where groups act on their own and as targets of other agents. The next section focuses on the nature of interaction between women's groups and other action agents. Government instituted women's committees and the training programmes of the government and other agents are discussed.

5.   Agency Related Interaction Patterns

Women's group committees

Women's committees have been created at various government administrative levels. Leaders of individual groups (the Chairperson, Secretary and Treasurer) from all the sublocations in a particular Location form a locational women's committee. The locational women's committee leaders represent the particular location in the division, forming the divisional women's committee and so on to the national level.

These committees have brought together groups from a wider geographical area. This has in turn facilitated the emergence of a women's movement with common organizational techniques regardless of the cultural variations.[7]   Furthermore, elaborate locational women's group projects have developed from these committees. The committees in Weithaga, Mugoiri and Murarandia Locations had such projects. Membership to the Weithaga locational project is open to members of groups other than group leaders. Care was taken to recruit women who can be trusted. Moreover, all the female extension workers in the Location were co-opted as members. There were two major considerations for this. Firstly, as government officers working closely with women, it was argued that they needed practical experience of women's group activities and related problems. Secondly, their access to government resources could be more ensured if they were themselves members of women's groups. The project in Weithaga Location was therefore more extensive than the committee.

Table 9: Participants in five divisional women's committee meetings.

Year	Women's Group Representatives	Government Officers	Total
1976 (Feb.)	9	8	17
1982 (Dec.)	4	10	14
1983 (Jan.)	19	10	29
1983 (Jan.)	13	6	19
1985 (Feb.)	4	5	9
Total	49	39	88

Source: Minutes of Divisional women's committees

In general however, it is probably at these committees where the most formalized interaction with the government occurs and therefore the most influence prevails. Government officers are part of the women's committees. CDAs commonly chair women's committee meetings. Table 9, indicates that a large number of government officers participate in committee meetings while according to Table 10, they also dominate women's group committee discussions. 14 (70%) of the 20 who participated in the discussion were government officers. In all the meetings, the Divisional CDA addressed the meeting first.[8]

Table 10: Participation in five women's group committee discussions.

Year	CDA	Other Officers	Women's Representatives
1976	2	1	1
1982	2	0	2
1983	1	0	1
1983	3	3	1
1985	2	0	1
Total	10	4	6

The nature of issues discussed

A look at the issues discussed suggest that, committees constitute a forum where women are mostly informed of government policies and plans. Government officers advise women's groups about the types of projects most likely to attract government support. Emphasis is put on economic projects. During these meetings, government officers report which areas and groups have received assistance. This is not the only forum where government assistance to groups is advertised. Government assistance to groups is itself presented in an elaborate ceremony presided over by a government officer (CDO, DO, DC, or PC). During such occasions, all government extension workers, local politicians, members of the public and other women's groups in the area are present.[9]

During a chief's Baraza (public meeting) which was attended by 300-400 people in Gaturi Location, the issue of women's groups was discussed by three of the four official speakers.[10] The local councillor, who spoke first, indicated that women's groups in the area did not demonstrate good progress. As a result, they could not expect to obtain government assistance. He exonerated a group from a neighbouring area as enterprising. Because of this, the County Council had donated iron sheets to enable this particular group to complete construction of a chicken house. The CDA discussed at length the issue of community organization and women's groups in particular. He too indicated that women's group activities in the area were declining. Similarly, the CDA blamed the women's groups themselves as the reason they and their area would not receive government assistance. The chief in his concluding remarks restated the issue of women's groups jeopardizing governmental funding due to lack of progress.

Women reacted to these remarks immediately. After the Baraza, two groups of women gathered around me and a woman agricultural officer. One of the group needed advice on the registration process of a group. The other group wanted to be assisted in marketing its baskets. What is important to note here is that the actual concerns of women were given little attention by the government officers. Government officers were concerned with other issues. It was often stressed that groups should assist institutions for the poor. Many of these institutions are administratively placed under the government.

Election of committee leaders was another area of concern for the government officers. The issue of election was discussed in four of the five committee meetings presented above. During one of the meetings government officers supervised the election. The officers stressed the need to elect leaders, who are educated and enterprising as well. Such leaders would be sure to be elected to committees at higher administrative levels.[11] Moreover, apart from encouraging women's groups to elect leaders according to ideals entailed in modernization, these officers also influenced the general composition of the committees. In November 1984, a letter was sent by the divisional CDA to locational CDAs advising them to encourage the newly elected committees to co-opt members of non-governmental organizations in the locations in order to strengthen their committees.

The training programmes of women's groups

Interaction within groups, and between groups and other agents, has intensified through such training programmes as educational visits and leadership training. These training programmes are organized by the government and many other agents.

Educational visits

Through educational visits, groups from one area visit other areas to be exposed to activities and organizational skills of other groups. Many women's groups from all over the country had visited the study area and Central Province in general to see the mabati activities.

Leadership training

The concept of leadership training is widely used to cover a wide range of seminars and courses aimed at improving skills of various people including members of community groups, civil servants and politicians. Many other agents, including voluntary and church organizations, offer leadership training as well. In the context of women's groups, leadership training is mainly organized for group leaders in the various administrative levels discussed above. The training programmes assemble women from a wider geographical area as well. Training sessions furthermore expose participants to specific skills related to income-generating activities, community programmes as well as family and home management. Leadership training courses which last for one week are routinely organized once-a-year for each district. The week long courses can entail as many as 30 subjects. Table 11 presents a list of 17 subjects.

These subjects indicate the nature of emphasis. Within the category of economic projects, overwhelming emphasis is directed to income-generating activities. The next bulk of effort focuses on women's domestic and consumption management roles. Apart from exposing women's groups to skills, training forums facilitate informal interaction among women themselves, particularly because participants are housed in a hotel or a training institution. This was the case with the leadership training programme for Murang'a District which had just taken place at the start of fieldwork.

Table 11: Subjects offered in the one week leadership training sessions.

Economic projects	Community projects	Domestic consumption management
Vegetable growing	Adult literacy	Sewing/mending
Poultry keeping	Water supplies	Nutrition
Calf rearing		Feeding infants
Pig rearing		Personal hygiene
Handicraft (weaving, dying, spinning, sewing)		Home Management
Marketing of goods		
Agriculture		
Animal health		
Budgeting		
Leadership skills		

Source : Kayongo-Male 1983

Training under Maendeleo Ya Wanawake organization

Maendeleo Ya Wanawake is a national umbrella organization where local women's groups are affiliated. Most of its training efforts are directed at home management and family life. With financial assistance from a number of international donor agencies, this organization has started a community-based contraceptive distribution pilot programme using women's groups. Leaders of selected groups are trained to handle non-clinical contraceptives which they then distribute to members of their community. Seminars and courses are organized to motivate women to accept family planning. At the start of my fieldwork, a three days seminar largely focusing on family planning had been organized for women's groups in Murang'a District.[12]

Training activities and influence of the church

The study area is under the influence of both the Catholic and Protestant (Anglican) churches. According to Bottignole (1984) the population of Central Province comprises of 32.7% Catholic, 34% Protestants and 33% traditionalist. Each of the two churches has a women's organization, the Catholic Women's Association (CWA) and Mother's Union, whose rules and objectives are closely tied to the entire church organization. The simplest unit is the local church. Members from various local churches interact at higher national and international levels through committees which transmit information and guidelines back to the village churches and the individual women members of these churches.

Most women's group members were either members of Mother's Union or the Catholic Women's Association, depending on what church was predominant in an area. Church women's organizations are largely concerned with marital relationships, child care and family welfare, both physical and moral. Participation in these church women's organizations directly exposes women to messages emanating from the church. But, although the church is concerned with the same kinds of development issues as the government and other agencies, differences of emphasis are apparent. In the area of population control, the Catholic church is, for example, opposed to contraceptive use. Its training programmes focus rather on natural fertility control methods.

During my fieldwork, the Catholic church organized a one day seminar to instruct couples on the practice of natural family planning. However, according to groups from the area and individual key informants, this seminar was poorly organized. The organizers had overlooked, for example, that a large number of Catholic women are single mothers. As the seminar was meant for couples, single mothers could therefore not participate. Secondly, even for married couples, the timing on the Sunday following Easter weekend was inappropriate. Most husbands who work outside the area had traveled home during Easter and could not afford an additional visit so soon. These organizational constraints prohibited participation of husbands who may have wished to participate.

6.   Interaction Patterns within Kiangochi Women's Group

Kiangochi Women's Group is discussed in more detail not only as a concrete example but more importantly in order to elucidate the complexity of interaction. Kiangochi Women's Group as a whole or some of its members participated in many other groups and organizations in one time or the other.

Affiliation to Catholic Women's Association

Majority of women in this group were also members of Catholic Women's Association. Probably the major impact of this participation was in the area of family planning. Kiangochi Women's Group and a number of other groups in this predominantly Catholic area were conscious of the church's stand against the use of contraceptives. Catholic women, including leaders of CWA, nevertheless used contraceptives, including the highly controversial tubal ligation. But groups in predominantly Catholic areas expressed a stronger need for the involvement of husbands in fertility control. This is probably because natural family planning methods require closer co-operation between husbands and wives.

Participation in mixed groups

Kiangochi Women's Group was divided into two. Each half was part of one of two other groups mixed on basis of sex and organized along clan lines. Membership to a clan is determined by husbands. Kiangochi Women's Group was thus divided into two because husbands were from two different clans. Muita mixed self-help group was formed first. It had purchased a plot at the adjoining Maragua Township. Construction of residential rental houses was nearly complete. At the same time the group was collectively producing maize and beans on a hired plot. These successes facilitated formation of the Kihara mixed self-help group which claimed the other half of Kiangochi Women's Group.[13]

Leadership, including the important position of group treasurer was equally shared between men and women. Women thus felt more secure because the chances of men embezzling group funds without the knowledge of women were reduced. Participation in these mixed groups was based on the principle and calculation of multiple returns and protection against risks and crises. Members of Kiangochi, for example, clearly perceived the need for their husbands to be involved in group activities. This form of participation provided husbands with a chance to benefit from government funding as well. These mixed, clan based groups however existed in spite of government regulations prohibiting formation of groups along kinship lines. This was so mainly because the local CDA accepted to treat the mixed groups as women's groups. Women leaders of Kiangochi represented these mixed groups in the women's group committees at various administrative levels. This was a case where alliance was formed between government officers and the community for the benefit of the community.

But from another perspective, these local initiatives and strategies to capture external support is a function of the the nature of agency targeting itself. The channeling of resources through women's groups, but more importantly the intensified political and bureaucratic rhetoric that government resources are limitless as long as women are organized may have encouraged these initiatives.[14]

Agency targeting in the forms discussed, and increased exposure of groups to government policies and plans has had another effect. Women have increasingly become aware of government assistance and aware of some of the basic constraints that could prevent this assistance from reaching them. According to this group, the women's programme had been allocated large amounts of funds. But instead of being invested in women's group activities, those funds were being used for the construction of a bridge which was of no use to women who have no cars. Furthermore, they were aware that women's programme was neglected because of poor representation in the development committees.[15] Members of Kiangochi Women's Group thus requested me to join and assist in their fight for improved representation of women in these committees.

Participation in other women's groups

Members of Kiangochi had participated in three other women's groups. However, this participation had been discontinued because of a number of problems, related partly to the pressures arising from the targeting process and the nature of the political system.

The elderly members of Kiangochi were, in the past, part of a Ndumo dance group. Ndumo is a Kikuyu dance for elderly women. The leader of this dance group had herself been an active member of the nationalist movement during the colonial period. She had been imprisoned for her active role in the movement. Other women had tried to mobilize resources to secure her release. She had, however, advised them against such a move because they would be forced to do that each time she was arrested. This woman was admired for her bravery during those hard times. After independence, she became the leader of the dance group. Because of her political stand, her dance group was invariably chosen to entertain during political celebrations. But soon, this leader became too dominant. Food donated to the group by politicians who needed services of the group was always prepared in her house. This gave her the opportunity to consume the remains alone. Most of the other favours went to her as well. She was the only member in the group for whom two politicians had each built a house. This had led to the break up of the dancing group and at the time of the study, these elderly members of Kiangochi requested me to assist them in reviving traditional dancing within Kiangochi Women's Group. These elderly women made two requests. They needed protection against those who may want to disrupt their new dance group. They also needed assistance to secure ornaments and a uniform.[16]

Members of Kiangochi had also been members of a group from another village. They withdrew their membership, however, because leaders favoured members of the other village when sharing group resources. Furthermore, after receiving their share, those members deserted the group. A wrangle thus developed. Members of Kiangochi constantly pressed the CDA to help them recover their money from that group. This created a dilemma because the CDA has no legal authority over the groups. Moreover, one of the deserters was the wife of the chief under whose authority the CDA is placed.

The last group had problems of leadership. According to the members of Kiangochi, the chairman of that group, a childless woman, favoured and worked closely with only a few committee members who were newly settled in the area. At the same time, this chairman accused her committee for not cooperating with her. The issue became a public case involving the chief and the CDA.

The rift was deep and the group could not be saved. The registration certificate was retrieved by the CDA. Later, members who had broken away formed a new group with a new committee which seems to have never been changed. Hostility between the two groups however continued. Members of Kiangochi Women's Group said the following about the childless chairperson:

> "Why is she (childless chairman) so hostile to us ? Are we the ones who closed her birth canal opening so she should not give birth. If she thinks so, why does she not come so we can open it for her ?"

CHAPTER 8

THE INTERNAL STRUCTURE AND CHARACTERISTICS OF CONTEMPORARY WOMEN'S GROUPS

1. Features of Contemporary Women's Groups

This chapter describes some characteristic features of contemporary Kenyan women's groups, including group distribution, size, naming system and marital composition, and discusses the nature or pattern of change over time.

Women's groups in their current form have been in existence since the mid-1960s. This is not to say that there were no groups prior to this period. In the context of this study women's groups are traced back to the pre-colonial Kikuyu society. But the changing social, economic and political processes have also affected group form and structure. The targeting and monetization processes which started in the colonial period have, in particular, had far reaching impact.

By the 1940s, the colonial government increasingly turned to the use of indirect rule through existing social structures in order to enhance acceptance of its programmes. By the 1950s, Maendeleo Women's Clubs were established. In a study of women's mutual aid groups in Central Province, Mwagiru (1985) observed that 3% of the 46 groups in her study had been formed between 1950-1955. These were years when the colonial government encouraged formation of Maendeleo Women's Clubs as a policy and strategy to minimize women's active role in the Mau Mau. The same Study observed that no groups were formed between 1956-1960. Mwagiru has concluded that groups may not have formed because these were the years of Mau Mau conflict. However, although earliest groups in my study were formed and registered from the 1960s, the reason given for non-existence of groups in the period between 1956-1960 is questionable. This was the period when the Mau Mau crisis had been brought under control and the colonial rule was coming to an end. The emergency restrictions were thus relaxed and women were then being encouraged to form self-help groups with voluntary unpaid leadership and male participation. It is probably because of this change of policy and the increasing male participation in self-help activities (which records indicate led to male leadership of the groups) may account for the failure to record formation of women's groups in the period. At independence in 1963, the new government embraced Harambee self-help as a major aspect of development.

Not all women join contemporary women's groups. Furthermore, group size itself has been fluctuating so that current groups are smaller than the earlier mabati roofing groups. The naming system seems also to have undergone a change in a pattern where groups now identify themselves with the development ideals held by the wider system. In terms of marital status, current groups expose some of the past cultural patterns and rules of inclusion and exemption. Marriage is still an important criteria for recruiting women into groups. But unlike the Kang'ei/Nyakinyua groups in the past, women do not automatically become members of groups after marriage. Unmarried women are in general still excluded from the groups. What is important however is that unmarried women are excluded for reasons other than those used in the past.

2.   Distribution of Women's Groups in the Study Area

There was a total of 177 groups. Table 12 shows their distribution. Weithaga and Mugoiri Locations which are situated in the highly populated and the more agriculturally potential western part of the study area (see table four) have the largest number of women's groups. Murarandia is exceptional. Apart from being the smallest of the three locations in the western part, it borders the Aberdare Ranges. Agriculturally, the location is a tea growing zone. Tea picking

is a daily activity which may interfere with group activities. Furthermore, Murarandia was recently cut from Mugoiri to make a separate
location. This may partly explain why it has a lower percentage of
groups than Weithaga and Mugoiri.

Table 12: Distribution of women's groups by location

Location	Number of Groups	Percent of Total
Weithaga	36	20
Murarandia	17	10
Mugoiri	32	18
Gaturi	27	15
Mbiri	14	8
Gikindu	20	11
Municipality	31	18
Total	177	100

In general, the drier eastern part of the study area (excluding the
municipality) has fewer groups. Mbiri Location also became a
separate location in 1979 when Murang'a Township was upgraded to
the status of a municipality. The municipal boundaries were extended
into rural Mbiri which then acquired its own separate administration.
Gikindu is perhaps the driest location. It has acted as a frontier,
receiving migrants from the congested parts of Murang'a District and
more specifically the neighbouring western part of the study area.

3.   Formation and Registration Pattern

Table 13 suggest that a large number of groups were formed and
registered between 1965-1975. The pattern of group formation and

registration seem to coincide with a number of government policies. The period between 1965-1975, when 61% of the current groups were formed and registered, was also the period of great demand in house

Table 13: Group formation and registration by year

Year	Number of Groups	Percent of Total
1965-1970	84	49
1971-1975	20	12
1976-1980	37	21
1980-1985	32	18
Total	*173	100

* Date of formation or registration of four groups was not recorded.

construction. Land had been consolidated. The government was encouraging people to move from the colonial villages and settle on their private land. It was also a period when the mixed Harambee self-help activities were becoming established. But, as indicated earlier, this movement was insensitive to the needs and priorities of women. The experiences of women within the Harambee self-help movement had probably then persuaded women to form separate groups. By the 1970s, the targeting process had intensified through the Special Rural Development Programme (SRDP). Although it was implemented in 1971, SRDP had been conceptualized and ground-work laid back in 1966 (Livingston, 1981).[1] The next major stage was the establishment of the Women's Bureau in 1976 and the related campaigns prior to this date. These and other factors, such as a political system which may exploit the large numbers of women in the rural areas, are both mobilizing and demobilizing forces.

4.   Group Size

It is difficult to discuss the size of women's groups prior to the 1970s, because there is little information on women's group activities during this period. However, most women, particularly the elderly women in the study, recalled having participated in larger house roofing and dance groups which no longer exist.

Table 14: Group size at the date of formation

Year Formed	Total Number	Size 0-49	%	50-99	%	100+	%
Up to 1970	80	32	40	31	39	17	21
1971-1975	20	4	20	10	50	6	30
1976-1980	37	19	51	13	35	5	14
1981-1985	32	20	63	11	34	1	3
Total	*169	75	44	65	39	29	17

* 8 groups were omitted because the year of formation or size had not been recorded.

Table 14 seems to confirm what the elderly women indicated: that there were larger groups in the past. Current group membership ranges between less than 50 to several hundred. A considerably large number, 44% of all the groups formed and registered between 1965-1985, started with less than 50 members. 39% had 50-99 members and 17% had 100 members and over. There is a progressive rise in the formation of smaller groups (category of less than 50 members). This trend is observed when average membership at the time of formation is compared to the current period. By 1985, there were a total of 8,758 women in the groups, giving an average of 50.6 members per group.

This was a decline from the average membership of 65.2 members per group when the groups were formed.

Overall, 88 (52%) of the 169 groups whose date of formation and size were recorded had membership decline. Of these 50 (57%) were started between 1965-1970, 14(16%) between 1971-1975, 13(15%) between 1976-1980, and 11(12%) between 1981-1985. It seems that the longer the life of the group the higher is the membership decline.

5.   The Naming System

In the context of women's groups, the naming system plays two major roles. Firstly, names are used for identification. Secondly, the particular name used may reflect the base from which group members are drawn. Names denoting kinship affiliation, for example clan (Mbari or Nyumba) and age-group (riika) Kang'ei and Nyakinyua have been used by groups for identification. Kinship groups such as the clans were in the Kikuyu society distinct and autonomous units.[2] Groups which identify themselves with such distinct clan names most likely recruit their members only from the clan or sub-clan concerned. The group naming system has however been changing.

It was not possible to compare all the locations, because of the poor state of available records. Records from Gaturi Location may, however, demonstrate the nature of change in the naming system. In 1976 there was a total of 46 women's groups in Gaturi Location. There were 28 and 27 groups in 1981 and 1985 respectively. Among the 46 groups recorded in 1976, 11 (24%) had names indicating clan based membership. In 1981, the figure had dropped to 11% and in 1985 only 4% of the groups were clan based. The groups whose names indicated clan based membership seem in general to have fewer members. All the 11 groups based on kinship membership in Gaturi Location in 1976 had 8-15 members per group.[3]

There is not enough information to show whether groups discontinue or just change their names. Most probably both occur. In Gaturi Location in 1976, three clan based groups applied for deregistration. The only reason they gave for this decision was that in their view they had not continued to develop.[4]. Examples of groups which had changed names were encountered while many case study groups reported having been members of larger groups which later dissolved for one reason or the other but emerged in new forms.

Groups have increasingly assumed names which denote love, trust, self-help, self-reliance, work, progress, plans etc. A total of 53 (30%) of groups had such names. Of these, majority 34 (64%) were started in 1975. The bulk of the other groups, 93 (53%), used names of places, mainly their own villages.

6.   Composition of Groups in Marital Status

Contemporary women's groups have roots in the pre-colonial Kikuyu social organization where marriage and reproductive performance were important factors in the mobilization of women for collective action. Women's groups then played a central role in the control of sex and reproduction. Composition of Women's groups in terms of marital status was therefore studied in order to indicate the extent to which women's groups are still concerned with matters of sex and reproduction. The various marital status categories in a given group were not studied. Rather, the aim was to find whether groups recruit members from the various marital status categories.

Unmarried women

Except for 11% of the groups which had recruited unmarried women, the rest were composed of only married women. Information on the characteristics of individual unmarried women members of groups was not systematically gathered. However, a general picture of this category of women emerged from a number of groups which were studied in depth, key informants and direct observation. The unmarried group members are women who have had children outside marriage. Furthermore, they are fairly advanced in age, thus reducing their chances of marriage.

Table 15: Women's group composition in marital status

Marital Status	Number of Group	Percent of Total
Married childless	64	36
Unmarried	19	11
Divorced	22	12
Widowed	148	84
Men	26	*15

N = 177 * choices are multiple

In general, young unmarried women are not encouraged to join groups. There were a number of reasons for this. Firstly, such women are likely to marry outside the area. This implies losing a group member. More seriously, groups were concerned about the possibility of such women exposing group secrets to new groups where they marry. Such was less likely to occur for women who had slim chances of marrying.

Secondly, young unmarried women have needs and priorities different from those of married mothers. But the main fear is the likelihood of such women becoming loose in morals. Groups pressured their members against loose behaviour such as alcohol consumption, drug use, indiscriminate sex including prostitution. Such behaviour would endanger the image of the groups and women in general. Rules against drunkness and drug addiction (Kureba) were clearly stipulated and members who were drunk at the wrong time risked termination of their participation.[5] Three groups had dismissed members for such behaviour.

One of the groups had started as a mixed group. Later women found out that male group members were secretly using group money for brewing liquor. Women responded by breaking away to form their own group.

The second group had six male participants who used the funds they received from the group on alcohol at the local bar. Apart from failing to spend such funds to improve their families' welfare, the women were concerned that such members could, under the influence of alcohol, easily reveal group secrets or behave indecently. Their membership was therefore terminated.

An incident of a drunkard group member was observed in Kiangochi Women's Group. The member concerned was an elderly woman. She had come to the group meeting late and drunk. This annoyed the entire group particularly also because the woman misbehaved. While the meeting was going on, the drunk woman kept talking. Worse still, she was sitting indecently exposing her private parts (guturama). It became hard for the other women, especially the elderly to concentrate. They kept drawing the attention of the chairperson, demanding her immediate dismissal.

At the end of the meeting, the elderly women having been most humiliated because traditionally the drunk woman belonged to their age-group, directly confronted the drunkard woman. Her participation was terminated.

The figure of unmarried mothers in the groups is small, however, considering the growing proportion of premarital pregnancies and motherhood. Recent studies suggest that increasing numbers of young women become pregnant outside marriage. To indicate the extent and nature of the problem, members of groups in Mbiri Location had coined the term "cia magendo" meaning black market children. This problem has aroused great concern among the people in general and women's groups in particular. Specific request for the institution of sex education for primary school girls, who often drop out of school, was frequently made by the groups.

Early pregnancy not only has numerous health complications but, it terminates schooling for girls. The role of education as a basis for social security and status partly explains the great concern about the problem. Families which can afford to put their daughters back to school do so. The majority of girls from poorer families usually find themselves in urban areas looking for jobs, only to swell the rate of unemployment and related social problems including prostitution. Moreover, parents of such girls assume the burden of raising their grand children alongside their own large families. Thus, apart from having social stigma, this problem has far reaching implications to the families concerned. But, even with all this concern, it seems that as long as the young mothers are still what is commonly referred to as "child mothers", the problem is internalized as a problem and demand on women. In many cases, the problem of adolescent pregnancy is seen as the failure on the part of the mothers.

Women's groups and other community members were clear that this problem reflected the breakdown of social control systems in the area of sex and reproduction. It was explained that a large number of boys and girls still under-go the rite of circumcision. As in the past, the initiated boys are provided with a separate house or room, detached from the parents. Accordingly, these boys assume adult sexual life. However, current initiation involves only the operation without related educational, social control mechanisms and sanctions which instiled discipline in matters of sexuality. Ironically, with all the concern and knowledge that the growing problem of adolescent pregnancies has mainly resulted from the breakdown of past cultural sexual moral order, parents oppose any suggestions of providing adolescents with family planning services and related information. This situation has arisen because fertility control programmes are narrowly targeted by government and other agents without taking account of people's perspectives, cultural contexts and realities within which they live.[6]

Married childless women

I had a number of related assumptions with regard to recruitment of childless women into women's groups. These were mainly derived from the prevailing views and available literature regarding why women in Kenya avoided using fertility control methods. A commission of experts from the US Population Council helped Kenya design a population policy. The commission considered cultural values and attitudes which favour high fertility as a major factor which hinder acceptance of family planning.[7] Because of this purported high cultural value of children, I assumed that women's groups would thus encourage their members to have large families. Moreover, they would discourage childless women from joining groups. Following from this, I expected groups would be active in prevention of reproductive health problems which would render members childless.

It is interesting to note that a substantial proportion (36%) of the groups had recruited childless women. This is a category of women who had suffered from one or more of the reproductive health problems. Yet, groups had little involvement in these kinds of problems. Reproduction and related problems were considered by the groups as largely the concerns of individual couples.[8] This is a major departure from the pre-colonial situation where sexual and repro-ductive issues were a matter of public concern.[9] The commission of experts and others responsible for designing population policies did not consider cultural values and attitudes in their concrete social con-text and/or the prevailing reality. The pre-colonial Kikuyu fertility model for instance suggests that, the high value of children occurred within an elaborate social order which offered regulating and control mechanisms. It is therefore not the existence of cultural values and attitudes favouring high fertility, but rather the breakdown of cultural systems which previously regulated and controlled these values. This, coupled with the ensuing modernization processes, but more speci-fically the medicalization of reproduction, explains moreover why women's groups may not concern themselves with reproductive matters any more.

Widowed women

84% of all the groups had widowed members.[10] The figure was high in all the locations, but the relatively poorer locations including Gaturi (81%), Mbiri (100%), Gikindu (100%) and the Municipality (90%), had slightly higher figures compared to the 75%, 76% and 72% in Weithaga, Murarandia and Mugoiri Locations respectively. This type of recruitment indicates that groups are also concerned with widowhood and related problems.

7.   Some Factors Explaining the Changing Features of Women's Groups

Changes in the various characteristic features of the groups observed in this chapter need to be understood in the context of changes taking

place in the wider social system. The emerging Kenyan society torn on
ethnic and regional basis has, for example, necessitated institution of
policies aimed at enhancing national feelings and achieving a political
balance. In 1979, the government instituted a total ban on the use of
names denoting ethnic background for welfare organizations. This
move was directed against giant welfare associations such as Gikuyu
Embu Meru Association (GEMA), whose enormously growing
economic and political power posed a threat to the new regime.

This ban also affected small rural women's groups. During the
registration process of a new group, one of the questions raised by the
government officer was whether the group had wide representation or
was limited to a single clan. The group had even decided to use the
name of the entire sublocation, thus indicating wide representation.

During the same registration process, the group had to comply
with many other bureaucratic demands. Registration cost the group
65 Kenya shilling. The group was further expected to complete
elaborate forms, elect a committee of 12, prepare a list of office
bearers, a list of members and by-laws all to be submitted to the
CDO's office in four copies. The medium of communication was
English, even though the majority of the group members were
illiterate or semi-literate.[11]

Despite government intervention encouraging the formation of
groups with wider membership base, the general tendency has been
towards formation of smaller groups. The requirement that groups be
engaged in economic projects as a prerequisite to receiving government support has largely put a monetary strain on many group
members who cannot make such long term monetary contributions.
Many groups lose members when they embark on income-generating
activities.[12] Economic and bureaucratic demands have had other
effects on the groups. Mwihoko Women's Group in Weithaga Location was for example formed in 1983 with the express aim of tapping
government assistance. In the process of formation and registration,
the group encountered bureaucratic rules and regulations, stipulating
the group size and membership recruitment base to be followed.
Apart from trust, the ability to pay a large amount of money over a
long period was the main recruiting criteria.

Women's changing workload may have affected women's groups
as well. Group membership decline was greater in the three locations

to the west. These locations are coffee and tea producing zones. Tea is a crop which is harvested every day of the week throughout the year. In terms of time resources, tea production may take all the women's time, particularly where no extra labour is available. A young mother from Murarandia Location, with a husband working in Mombasa, explained that tea harvesting took all her time, making it difficult for her to join groups. Although coffee picking is seasonal, this period is critical and most women probably have little time to participate in group activities.

Impact of the political system

The dynamics of the Kenyan political system have shaped some of the processes and changes in the groups. The process of electing political representatives in particular influence group structure and internal dynamics. Although Kenya is a one party state, each electoral consti- tuency attracts several candidates all vying for votes. And, because majority of the people living in the rural areas are women, they hold most of the votes as well. In general, politicians direct their efforts to win women's votes. At the same time, they rhetorically caution women against being involved in politics, thus insinuating that politics is a men's province. Women's votes are exploited by male politicians not just because they are the majority in the rural areas. Women are also disadvantaged in many other ways, making them susceptible to all forms of exploitation. Election campaign periods are especially cri- tical for exploitation of women's groups in Kenya. In response, many women's groups form, lose or gain membership around this time. The chief of Weithaga Location indicated that most groups forming during election campaign periods do not survive long after the campaigns, mainly because they are mobilized by the politicians. The following cases demonstrate the complex interaction situation, the nature of conflict of interests and its impact on women's groups.

In Mugoiri and Murarandia Locations, membership decline can for example be attributed to the nature of politics in the mid-1970s. This area was, since 1963, represented by a powerful politician. By the mid-1970s however, an equally powerful politician came on into the scene. In order to gain women's support, the new politician closely associated himself with land and house buying projects. Groups from the two locations mobilized resources to purchase a rental house in the city. The older politician, whose wife was at that time, the national chairperson of the Maendeleo Ya Wanawake Organization in which many women's groups were affiliated, encouraged his women supporters to withdraw their membership from the house buying groups. The new politician however won the election. But, because the housing project is a long term and costly investment, it has not been possible to recruit new members or groups into the project. This politically engineered conflict continues, and in the 1983 elections, the rift between the supporters of the two politicians had deepened.

A similar politically engineered conflict was observed in a group in the municipality. During the early phase of my fieldwork, the group in question invited the district CDO to help solve a long standing dispute which had split the group into two. The problem had started in 1979 when the election of a new committee took place. During the same year, parliamentary elections also took place. The two giants discussed above campaigned to win women's vote in this area as well. Similarly, they created a division within this group. To complicate the matter, the chief and the CDA who are the other main actors in the settlement of group disputes had girl-friends and a section of the group loyal to either of them. The election of the group committee should therefore be seen in the context of this complex background. When the new committee was elected, the old leaders refused to surrender the office or recognize the new committee. This affected the group's banking because funds could not be credited in or withdrawn. Consequently, group activities came to a halt.

The problems of this particular group were difficult to solve because of the many conflicting interests and divisions. Furthermore, the nature of the administrative structure creates more problems. The Department of Social Services has administrative responsibility over women's groups without legal authority. The Department could, of course, recommend the dissolution of the group. But, according to the CDO, this would be working against the very objective the government supports. Past attempts to solve the problem had left the group contemptuous of the department, mainly because solutions recommended aimed at reconciling the two divisions.

The dynamics of the political system and related conflicts emerged in other situations, such as the District Development Committee (DDF) meeting at Murang'a in 1985. This committee allocates government funds and materials to various development projects, including women's groups. It is composed of all local and national political representatives from given Districts, government officers and women's committees. Women's group committees at the Location recommend groups to receive government assistance. Although this may appear so on paper, these committees are, as indicated below, not free from official influence and other interests. Nevertheless, the list of recommended groups is forwarded to the District Development Committee.

During this particular District Development Committee Meeting, there developed sharp disagreement between the politicians and the civil servants on the criteria used for selecting groups. In order to please the politicians and secure their own positions, the civil servants had selected groups from areas where politicians had enough support. But the politicians had a different plan. Being half-way to the next elections, politicians were more interested in building support in areas of their electoral constituencies where they had little or none. The politicians therefore blamed the civil servants for selecting the wrong groups. Because of this disagreement, selected groups did not benefit from the allocated funds. Furthermore, new groups could not be selected because of time constraint. Consequently the funds were returned to the treasury. This conflict of interests, which is characteristic of the Kenyan political and administrative scene, have implications for women's group dynamics.

The combined administrative and political interests exploit some other elements of the groups. The groups are, for example, increasingly called upon to contribute food and funds for various occasions. Furthermore, they are used for entertaining important dignitaries through songs and dances during many ceremonies.[13]

CHAPTER 9

THE ACTIVITIES OF WOMEN'S GROUPS

1. Productive and Reproductive Activities

This chapter focuses on and discusses the productive and reproductive activities of contemporary women's group. The productive activities comprise mabati activities which acquired their name from the original roofing of houses and commercial or income-generating activities. Mabati activities still constitute a major component of women's group activities, but groups are increasingly involved in commercial activities as well. This reflects the nature of change and in particular agency involvement. In general, commercial activities rather than replace, are only added to the ongoing mabati or mutual support activities.

The last section examines the involvement of women's groups in sex and reproduction. Within the pre-colonial Kikuyu society, women's groups played a central role in reproductive roles. But, while women's productive activities have continued, contemporary women's groups play a minimal role in the control and regulation of sex and reproduction. This also reflects the nature of change, the role of the modernization and specifically agency involvement and the medicalization of sex and reproduction, which removed these issues from their social and cultural contexts. This chapter is based on information derived from case studies of groups.

2. The Mabati or Home Improvement Activities

Mabati activities were started in the 1960s from the rising demands of

134

roofing houses. The structure or form of the mabati activities reflects past cultural women's groups. The mabati activities have followed a definite chronological order. Groups started with actual roofing of houses. After roofing, groups provided their members with selected items and services essential to women's household chores. The next widespread undertaking was the provision of water tanks which enabled women to harvest rain water from their newly improved roofs. Thirdly, groups purchased cows or goats to improve household

Table 16: Major home improvement or mabati
activities of women's groups

Activity	Number of groups	Percent
Purchasing land, farm animals and improving farming	81	46
Purchasing household items	148	84
Purchasing water tanks and pipes	70	40
Paying school fees	118	67
Sickness and funeral expenses	41	*23

N = 177   * Choices are multiple

milk supply. Currently, groups purchase household items such as furniture and utensils. The term mabati is thus used to encompass this whole range of home improvement activities of women's groups. Table 16 indicates the major mabati and welfare activities, to which group resources are allocated. From this table, it is clear that home and family welfare are central concerns of women's groups.

Resource mobilization

During the actual roofing period, groups were larger because of the nature of their activities, the rules which governed participation and conditions of life. During this time, members could not simply withdraw their membership after their houses were roofed because this risked removal of the roofing material. Furthermore, apart from individual membership fee, groups mobilized resources through sale of group labour or workgroups. This required physical presence of all members for group activities. Table 17 suggest that prior to 1975, a large number of groups mobilized resources through workgroups. The widespread sale of group labour for resource mobilization, was

Table 17: Participation in workgroups by year

Year	Total	Workgroups	Percent
1965-1970	84	62	74
1971-1975	20	13	65
1976-1980	37	8	22
1981-1985	32	3	9
Total	173	86	50

largely due to the conditions of life at that time. The demand for new homes was pressing. All families were being moved by the government from colonial villages to settle on the newly privatized land as a measure of improving agricultural production.[1] But because of the conditions preceeding this period, most families were too poor to afford building a house on their own.

Sale of group labour for resource mobilization declined after the mid-1970s. This is a result of many factors. A wider problem is the inability of a rural economy to absorb all available workforce including women's groups. According to ILO (1972) and Ndegwa (1985), unemployment is a major problem in Kenya. Furthermore, as pointed out earlier, women have assumed a heavier workload. Besides their responsibilities in subsistence production and household care, women constitute the main labour force in the commercial agricultural sector. Moreover, women's groups themselves are increasingly involved in commercial activities, which for group members implies investing extra time and labour as a matter of routine. These factors limit the time for women to participate in workgroups as well.

However, in spite of the official emphasis and orientation in favour of commercial activities, mabati activities, particularly provision of simple household items continue to be a major component of women's group activities. I visualize mabati activities as an area where groups act within the context of their own perspectives. Through mabati activities, group members obtain immediate, concrete and tangible results. This was a source of great pride.

Allocation of group resources

Groups have rules which govern use of their resources. As a general rule, most groups meet once every month to discuss group matters and to pay their monthly contribution, a proportion of which is allocated to one or two members. This is rotated until all members have been allocated. This is what groups call "one round." Most groups allow their members to buy what they have expressed to be their priority. There is, however, great concern that members actually buy what they have indicated to be of priority or at least identify items acquired through their groups.

There are a number of ways to ensure that this is followed. During the roofing days, all members of a group not only contributed money, but participated in workgroups. The entire group purchased and carried iron sheets to a member's house. For women's groups then, this was an occasion for dancing and singing. This, and the shining mabati roofs, made groups and their activities visible and popular, particularly within the local administration.[2] Current mabati activities are less outwardly visible because they involve provision of simple household items which are only useful to women, in their invisible household chores. But groups still require their members to identify group purchased items. Members of groups proudly displayed items which had been acquired through group activities whenever, they served tea or food to visitors. This is group strategy to make their otherwise invisible activities and achievements visible. This is important in facilitating internal group solidarity and generating respect from other actors within the wider system.

The concern of the groups to make their achievements visible need to be seen in the context of the sexual division of labour and subordination of women. Although Kikuyu women in the pre-colonial society were overworked, they had some autonomy and control over production and reproduction. Colonial capitalist expansion introduced new dimensions of subordinating women. Besides the complex and heavy workload, women's overwhelming contribution passes unrecognized. Moreover, they live within contradictory realities where due to their disadvantaged position, some of their survival strategies damage their image.

These observations indicate that women's group activities are part of women's struggle against subordination. Members of groups indicated that they value groups for reducing women's dependence on their husbands even for small things such as salt. At the same time, the same women were also concerned with not appearing to be doing more or seeming to be competing with their husbands.

Two contradictory cases were observed. A member of one of the groups did not inform her husband what she received from her group. When this came to the attention of the group, she was given two choices: to leave the group or inform her husband. Another member bought a cow with proceeds from her group. She did not dare bring it home for fear that her husband would feel surpassed. She therefore kept it, as is customary with herds, in the compound of another woman (Kuhithia) until such time that the husband was tactfully informed about it. These kinds of behavior should not be construed to imply that women are conservative. Women's struggles will reflect the conditions and realities within which they are placed. It is probably within these silent struggles of women that mabati activities should be evaluated.

Some groups meet more than once a month. Gitumbi women's group regularly meets at least twice. The entire group meets usually at the end of each month, to deal with general group matters including its pig project. Furthermore, the entire group visits the member whose turn it is to receive group contribution around the middle of the month. According to the group, these home visits are also used for assessing the needs of individual group members.[3]

3.   The Income-Generating Activities

Income-generation constitute a second part of women's productive activities. Income-generating activities are thus not mutually exclusive from the mabati activities described above. Both types of activities aim to achieve one goal. There are however two major differences. Mabati activities are part of the spontaneous support systems which offer immediate benefits to women. They are concentrated in those areas which women recognize to be of priority to them. Income-generating activities are on the other hand long term investments which have increasingly received external local and international agency backing.

Increasingly large numbers of groups are involved in commercial activities. 126 (71%) of the groups had one or the other of the commercial projects. Those already not involved in commercial activities were planning to do so in the future.

The main income-generating activity areas

Women's group commercial activities are concentrated in four major areas including:

(1) Animal Production (pigs, poultry, goats, cattle bees, rabbits);

(2) Crop production;

(3) Small-scale business;

(4) Handicraft production and sale.

57% of all the groups were involved in animal husbandry, 19% in crop production, 10% in small-scale business, such as selling charcoal and firewood, and 40% in handicraft production and sale.

Groups are sometimes engaged in several income-generating projects simultaneously. 34% of the groups engaged in the production of handicraft and one of the other commercial projects. This is the most common combination probably because handicraft articles can be produced while performing other activities such as meetings, walking, or during leisure time.

Groups also shift from one project to another for a number of reasons. A project may be completed. A group which keeps a cow, may for instance sell the cow and invest the money in another project. More often than not however, new projects are started because the previous ones have failed. Many groups for example abandoned poultry and pig rearing because these projects were too expensive to run. Furthermore, they require special skills which are not readily available to women or women's groups. In many cases groups incur losses. But, in spite of these limitations, involvement of groups in commercial activities has increased. Income-generating projects are popular because they are perceived to constitute an alternative strategy for mobilizing resources. Secondly, the agency targeting process discussed earlier has also facilitated involvement of groups in income-generation.[4]

The Women's Bureau channels material and skill assistance through women's groups. But prior to receiving such assistance, groups are required to be already engaged in economic projects. Women's groups are exposed to information concerning government assistance, conditions and regulations regarding such assistance during the numerous committee meetings, training programmes and public meetings.[5] This information, but more so the form in which it is presented, leaves little choice for women's groups but to engage in programmes which are likely to attract government support. Groups therefore start new projects, besides what they may already be engaged in, or abandon their on-going projects in favour of those more appealing to external assistance.

Major problems with commercial activities

Groups are commonly encouraged to undertake projects which are inappropriate in many ways. Women lack skills and financial base necessary for running commercial projects. Apart from lack of skills and prohibitive running costs, women's groups face problems of marketing. This is because they may be unaware of the available markets, or face competition from other producers.

The experience with poultry and pig projects seem to illustrate this. Most poultry keeping groups lost their stock from diseases which women had no knowledge of. Moreover, government officers with professional knowledge are not accessible when women's groups need them. Weithaga Mission Women's Group was forced to abandon its poultry project because most of the government-donated chicks died from a cause unknown to the group members. Many pig projects were abandoned because of high running costs.

Most groups producing handicrafts had large quantities of unsold items. The same was experienced by groups involved in animal production. Gitumbi Women's Group, for example kept a large number of pigs which at the time of fieldwork should have been disposed off. The same group had suffered a loss of five pigs, during a preceding drought because of inaccessibility of the only pig processing factory.[6]

These factors are rarely taken into account by funding agencies particularly the government. Government records indicate a pattern in which groups are allocated each a sum of Ksh 10,000 regardless of their size and nature of activities. It seems that funds are allocated to women's groups mainly on political criteria. Furthermore, given the prevailing ideals, women's groups are encouraged to produce for markets and not for local consumption. In the case of handicrafts, women's groups produce for an already over-flooded tourist market. Consequently, income-generating activities perform rather poorly. But, in spite of this and frustrations arising from losses, groups commonly invest in new projects. A number of groups in Weithaga Location were, after the pig projects, directing their efforts to small scale businesses such as selling charcoal and firewood, which require little initial investment and running costs. It seems that practical experience with externally backed commercial projects is teaching groups to try new activities.

In addition, group membership is affected by income-generating activities. Gitumbi, for example, indicated that its membership dropped dramatically in 1983, when a pig project was started. According to the group, most of the members left the group because they felt the project was no longer a priority to them. This may have been so, but monetary contribution also doubled. This may have meant that most members could no longer afford such contribution.

4. The Case study Groups: Additional Features

Table 18 presents the groups which were assessed in depth. They are divided into old and recently formed groups.

The old groups

Groups commonly start with mabati activities. Three of the four groups forming in 1970 or earlier, including Gitumbi, Gitungano and Kiangochi, have evolved through the phases of:

(1) actual roofing with corrugated iron sheets;

(2) provision of water tanks;

(3) purchasing of a cow or goat to improve family milk supply;

(4) provision of household items-cups, plates, chairs, beds, etc.

These mabati activities, continue to form the major component of activities of these three groups which are situated in the poorer part of the study area. Furthermore, all the three groups had, in the past, sold group labour for resource mobilization.

Weithaga Mission Women's Group, on the other hand, has had experiences similar to an old group. At the initial stages, it was, like the other three, involved in mabati activities, although actual roofing was not mentioned. Like the other three, Weithaga also sold group labour for resource mobilization. Weithaga Mission, however, replaced its mabati with income-generating activities at an early stage. But, while the three older groups have had two or three income-generating activities running consecutively, Weithaga has invested in more than five different income-generating activities, consecutively. These include:

(1) poultry-keeping where most of the chicks died. The remaining ones were sold and returns invested in:

(2) handicraft production whose proceeds were invested in:

(3) a cow which was later sold to enable the group to start:

(4) a pig project. Because of the high running cost, the pigs were sold

by the beginning of 1985. The group then embarked on:

(5) charcoal selling business. This business was chosen because of its low initial investment capital and running cost. Unlike poultry or pig-keeping projects which involve investment of women's time and labour, feeding and medical care, buildings and other security measures, charcoal and firewood business is free from most of these problems.

6) The group plans to purchase a rental house. Ten of its members who otherwise are less active, have bought shares in this future project. This qualifies them to continue being considered as members of the group.

Recently formed groups

The more recent groups, Mwihoko and Ithiki, represent concrete examples where group formation is facilitated by the prevailing socio-economic conditions, agency targeting and the political system. Mwihoko, for example, formed to tap government resources through the newly elected member of parliament who came from the same area as members of this group. The new political representative furthermore, was appointed the Minister for Culture and Social Services. This is the government ministry responsible for women's programme. Being a government minister gives him both power and accessibility to resources.

Mwihoko is the only group among those assessed which had only income-generating project. Its main goal was to mobilize about Ksh 1.5 million for the purchase of a rental house, preferably in a large urban area such as Nairobi. The size of the planned project affected the recruitment criteria because only categories of women such as local teachers, traders, and wealthier farmers who can afford substantial, long term monetary contribution were recruited into the group. But, as the planned project was a long term investment, the locational CDA and the chief advised the group to start a smaller, income-generating activity. This, it was argued, would help foster group solidarity. Besides, there are rules and regulations stipulating that groups should be registered and engaged in an income-generating

Table 18: Summary of the case study groups

Name of Group	Year Formed	Membership Past Current		Major features and activities
Gitumbi	1965	150	65	-Mabati/commercial -Turnover high in Mabati -Mixed religion and age -Assisted
Weithaga Mission	1968	300	43	-Mabati/commercial -Turnover high in commercial -Mixed ages only protestants -Assisted
Gitungano	1969	65	180	-Mabati/commercial -Turn-over high in Mabati activities -Mixed age and religion. Assisted
Kiangochi	1970	60	65	-Mabati/commercial -Turn-over high in Mabati activities -Mixed age and religion -Assisted
Mwihoko	1983	50	50	-Commercial only -Mixed age and religion. Assisted
Ithiki	1984	45	45	-Mabati only -Mixed age -only Catholic -Not assisted

activity before they can get support from the government. This group therefore started a pig project. Although Mwihoko was one of the youngest groups in the area, it had already received a government grant of Ksh 10,000. This had raised some antagonism among other groups, especially the locational women's committee. As the committee chairperson explained, after recommending groups for assistance, the assistance went to a new group which was not even a member of the committee. She explained that when the locational women's committee recommendations came to the District Development Committee (DDC), they were not considered because a recently formed group situated in the home of the current member of parliament, had campaigned against the recommendations. The chairperson had thus refused to attend a second meeting which had been scheduled to discuss the same issue:

> "When they telephoned, I told them I would not attend a meeting which was going to discuss the same thing that had already been passed."

Similar remarks were recorded in a letter sent out in October 1985 by the divisional CDA to locational CDAs complaining that women's groups had formed a habit of communicating directly with the Minister for Culture and Social Services. The locational CDAs were thus requested to advise women's groups to stop this practice and use the established channels of communication to forward their grievances. Although this letter did not mention the groups concerned, it was not hard to tell that this referred to Mwihoko Women's Group, which had openly admitted that its formation was timed to exploit the presence of the Minister for Culture and Social Services.

In spite of this, the group was considered by government officers to be one of the most enterprising and development-oriented group in the area, not just because of its ambitious project, but also because it was composed of educated and therefore understanding women.

Ithiki, the other recently formed group, was engaged only in mabati activities, mainly the provision of household items. It also aims to start an income-generating project in the future, but compared to Mwihoko, the nature of the future project was unclear at the time of fieldwork. Formation of this group was, as in the case of Mwihoko, facilitated by the targeting process, particularly government assistance to women's groups. But unlike Mwihoko, which had formed to exploit the presence of the Minister for Culture and Social Services, Ithiki women's group reported having just heard through the radio that women's groups all over the country would obtain government assistance. Ithiki was therefore formed to attract government resources from a more modest level. Its process of formation and recruitment of members is therefore typical of most groups.

Organization of group activities

Groups engaged in activities such as animal rearing, which requires feeding and other care, share the duties in a rotation. Gitumbi, Gitungano, Kiangochi and Weithaga had this kind of organization. The four groups had their projects located in the compound of group chairperson. Because of time constraints, Mwihoko has employed one of its members to look after the pig project for a small salary.

In general, groups meet regularly once a month. But some groups, such as Gitumbi and Kiangochi, meet more than once mainly to off-set financial and organizational constraints. The case of Gitumbi and Kiangochi indicate the various strategies employed by women's groups to circumvent time and financial constraints.

Besides their own mabati and income-generating activities, members of Kiangochi Women's Group participated in two other mixed groups which had monthly meetings and monetary contribution as well. This added time, labour and financial constraint on members of Kiangochi. To avoid the problem of non-payment and probably also desertion, Kiangochi organized to have its monthly contribution paid in two instalments at the end and middle of the month.

Gitumbi Women's Group also meets regularly at least twice a month. The entire group meets at the end of the month to discuss general matters of the group including its pig project. In addition, the entire group visits the member whose turn it is to receive group contribution around the middle of the month. These mid-monthly visits are social occasions where members are invited to a cup of tea. According to the group, these home visits enable the group to assess the needs of individual group members. At the same time, members are pressured and encouraged to keep themselves and their homes clean and proper.

5.   Involvement of Women's Groups in Sex and Reproductive Health

There are several contradictory observations regarding involvement of women's groups in matters of sex, health in general and reproductive health in particular. Many activities of women's groups, particularly the mabati activities, have implications for sanitation, personal hygiene, nutritional status and the general welfare of families. But in spite of this, women's groups "considered" their involvement in health matters to be minimal. Only one group made a direct association between its activities and the improvement of nutritional status of children.

Similarly, groups "considered" their involvement in health problems of reproduction to be minimal. At the same time, they were eager to show that they encourage fertility control. This was, however, contrary to what I observed. Fertility control was not handled within the context of the groups. In fact, some of the actions of the groups may even discourage contraceptive use.

These contradictory responses are part of the historical process in which the Kikuyu society has been fundamentally transformed. Through this process, the Kikuyu fertility model, for example, ceased being part of the social and moral order within which the community and in particular the Kang'ei/nyakinyua women took collective responsibility. Reproduction was instead narrowed down to a medical and technical issue. Moreover, coital contraceptives directed towards married women of reproductive age became the main method of fertility control. In other words, technical solutions replaced social responsibility.

The nature of women's concerns

Women's collective activities reflect women's perception of their situation, needs and priorities, which are commonly different from those supported by agents such as the government. Women's groups may therefore seem concerned with issues which appear unimportant but nevertheless constitute the reality or context within which women exist. The simple mabati activities still constitute the major component of women's collective activities, even though they are unrecognized. Table 19 indicates that women value their groups from the perspective of the realities they face.

Concern with marital relationships

Concern with marital relationships and related problems was strikingly central. 47% of the group leaders interviewed considered groups to be beneficial because they expose members to marital experiences of other women. The main concern of group members is to maintain stable marital relationships. A frequent response was:

> "Through meeting other women in the groups, we get to understand that women everywhere have similar problems. We learn how to handle husbands by discussing with other women."

The concern with marital stability is a function of the vulnerable and paradoxical situation of women and the conditions of life in the rural areas. Survival for the majority of peasants in the rural areas is a struggle. Under such circumstances, the family becomes an important unit where inputs from husband and wife are necessary for the survival of those in that unit. Furthermore, because of their disadvantaged position, women are more dependent on their husbands for social and economic support. On the other hand, marital instability has increased. When there is such instability, divorce or separation, women are affected in two major ways. More often than not, women are blamed for such instability and the problems arising from it. When separation occurs, the woman is returned to her parents or simply thrown out of the home. In practical terms, marital instability and divorce not only takes away the husband's support, it also displaces the woman from land she may still have cultivation rights to. In these circumstances, the struggle for survival becomes more strained.

Table 19: Benefits accrued or perceived from participating in women's groups

Responses	Numbers	%
Facilitates collective problem solving.	105	59
Forum for exchanging ideas.	77	44
Helps women understand their common problems especially those related to marital relationships.	83	47
Exposes members to new methods of child care.	43	24
Helps to improve social welfare and status of women and their families.	64	36
Pressures women to keep themselves, their families and homes clean and proper.	44	25
Improves confidence and perception of women.	33	19
Gives women chance to rest and relax.	33	19
Attracts outside resources and assistance.	28	16
Helping the poor, aged and sick.	35	20

N = 177 and responses are multiple choices

Groups' concern with marital imbalance and related forms of insecurity was expressed in another way. A large number of groups (84%) had recruited widowed women. Widowhood raises a number of problems for women. There is the general psychological stress and depression which follows bereavement. Secondly and probably more important is the problem of loss of social and economic support for the family unit. Where the bereaved woman has a large young family, the strain is enormous. Although our data did not yield this evidence, it is likely that a bereaved family slumps down to a lower socio-economic status, while those already down may sink further down into desperation. In addition, there are other forms of insecurity, such as the loss of respect and recognition commonly tied to the presence of a husband as the head of a household. Viewing the man as the head of the household is not only strongly upheld, but is reinforced through certain official policies.

This attitude and the related official position was demonstrated in 1984. During a seminar in preparation for the end of the women's decade conference, women in Kenya called for employment of more women in decision making positions. The president of Kenya responded by reminding women that God had not made a mistake in making man the head of a household. Moreover, even if women were appointed to high positions, they were still expected to be subordinate to their husbands at home.

It is at the level of property ownership where this attitude has been most officially reinforced. Until recently, when laws have been changed so that women can also own land, land was, since the colonial period, registered in the man's name. It is therefore the man who receives bank loans, credits, extension services and returns from sale of crops such as coffee. The great concern of the groups with widows may be a product of their experiences under a structure where the husband is the most prominent figure. When a husband dies, it is common practice for male relatives to claim the land particularly if there are no male children. Even where the law may stipulate that the spouse has the right of inheritance, the process of legal settlement is long and tedious, especially for the large numbers of illiterate and less informed women. Besides, the same law demands marital proof from bereaved women. Where a marriage is consummated under customary law, there may be conflict because such cases are dealt with through civil law. The following cases observed in the field illustrate some of these conflicts.

A member and chairman of a group had lost her husband a year before this study took place. She had ten grown children who were also successful in education and jobs. The question of economic support for this particular woman did not arise. One of her daughters was getting married however. Marriage transactions, including the actual giving away of a daughter at a church ceremony, is one of those roles strictly played by a father. In the absence of a father, a close male relative takes his place. This role has never been played by women. In this case, however, the local priest advised the concerned woman to play that role, because according to the priest, the husband had entrusted everything to his wife prior to his death. The wife thus played this role and it was according to her the most trying time in all her life. Her group added that this had been possible because their church had at that time a young and therefore less conservative priest.

Another case involved a woman whose husband had died three years before. She had been absent from her group during the entire period I visited the group. This woman had been struggling to secure a piece of land which her husband was in the process of buying. The seller had tried to reclaim it. For this reason, she was allowed to be absent from her group without a fine.

Concern with the image of women

Women were also concerned about improving their image. This concern and the specific ways for improving their image was seen vividly in the Weithaga Locational Women's Committee. The following observations were made during my first visit to the group, a visit, that was not pre-arranged. I explained the purpose of my visit, but did not make attempts to interview the group. The group had a written agenda which included health. The health issue discussed was cleanliness and hygiene among women themselves. The chairperson explained how and why women should clean themselves:

> "You realize that women's bodies are dirty. We need to clean ourselves in order to avoid smelling when we are in public places. You should clean your body and underwear everyday, because otherwise you will smell."

To elaborate this, the chairman explained the experiences of women when they go for training at the agricultural training centre. As most of the women in this group were group leaders, they probably had at one time or another been involved in such training. Women are not only taught to be clean, they actually attend to their cleanliness. They wake up at six o'clock and bathe in cold water.

> "This is what the groups should teach women to do. We must embark on a cleanliness programme within the groups."

She gave examples of other programmes which had been adopted by many women in the area. The first was kitchen gardening using waste water. This is one of the techniques taught at the training centres. The second was family planning.

> "Even though adoption of family planning is not made public, I
> am sure that many women accept it. It is secretly done, but we can
> see the results. I am thus convinced that the cleanliness pro-
> gramme will succeed."

The important point to note is that no mention was made of how
women should clean themselves to reduce or avoid infections. Rather,
the main concern was that women should be clean to avoid odors,
particularly in public. Such odors nauseate men and lower their
respect for women. The cleanliness debate had been lively. Individual
members narrated their nasty experiences of malodorous women in
public transport. The discussion was even extended to include other
acts such as urinating in public, which is considered shameful.

A health action such as personal cleanliness and hygiene may thus
be valued, not as a health issue, but as a strategy for improving the
image and respect for women. It seems that daily encounters, experiences and realities within which women live are more important and
convincing than questions of infections, germs and bacteria, which
even the doctors cannot see with their eyes. Whether to avoid
smelling or to reduce infections, observation of personal hygiene
would lead to good health. The critical issue and major concern
should be promoting that which would ensure the promotion of
personal hygiene. Furthermore, this suggests there is a need to change
orientation in order to accommodate perspectives of women and
prevailing concrete realities in programmes of health. The following
section will discuss specific women's groups. The main focus is the
involvement of women's groups in reproductive matters. The main
question posed was whether groups were concerned with reproductive
problems which lead to childlessness. These cases suggest the complex
situation within which fertility regulation takes place and the limitations of the family planning programme.

6.   The Case Studies of Groups

These cases highlight a variety of issues and concerns of women in sex and reproduction. Current groups play minimal role in regulation and control of sex and reproduction and related health problems. Practices and control systems used in the past are elaborated in these case studies. Although I had used similar guiding questions, different groups put more emphasis on different problems. The various responses however give a general picture of what constitutes reproductive problems. Furthermore, the cases illustrate the context within which the fertility control programme is targeted but also indicate why acceptance of the programme is low. The fertility control programme is directed to women even though they have little control over their sexuality. Women emphasized that their husbands did not allow them to use contraceptives.[7] Case studies of contraceptive users present concrete conditions and contexts within which women opt to use contraceptives.

Kiangochi Women's Group

This group had no childless members in the child-bearing age. There were, however, several childless members among the category of women past child-bearing age. This category of members receive monetary contributions more frequently in order to compensate for their loneliness. Young women with problems of reproduction normally go to hospitals.

The elderly members of the group were nevertheless encouraged to explain how problems of reproduction such as infertility were handled in the past:

> "When a woman failed to conceive, after she was married, the entire extended families on both sides consulted a traditional healer. The maternal uncle was very important here. If he was not happy with the dowry he received, he could be angry and decide to tie (Kuoha) the womb of his sister. The traditional healer mostly conducted ceremonies to appease the maternal uncle."

The prescribed treatment included symbolic sexual intercourse by the parents of the girl. If the actual parents could not perform this for some reason, close relatives could be requested to do it. While the elderly members were explaining this, younger women shyly laughed.

"If the problem persisted, many traditional healers were consulted. But if all failed, the concerned man and wife could agree to marry a second wife, for the purpose of getting children. Such children were brought up jointly by the three people. In some cases, children loved their step-mother more than the biological mother. If a woman was however married into a bad family, and failed to have children, she was simply returned to her parents. It was never thought that men could have been the problem. Women these days go to hospital for treatment (Guthambio)."

This group indicated that health problems of reproduction are increasingly left to hospitals. But, at the same time, the group claimed it was concerned, and encouraged its members to accept family planning. However, various actions undertaken by this group seem to indicate that this may not have been the case. A special meeting comprised of members who had special problems was organized so that I could meet and help them. There were two categories of such women.

The first was a childless woman. Although not a member of the group, she had been advised to come to the special meeting. When, however, the time came to discuss her problem, members of the group left the room. She was not sure what her problem was. But she had been sick and hospitalized. Her husband, who was working in Nairobi, had been married before. The first wife was childless as well. The mother-in-law forced her to leave. She herself had once run away because people had told her that her husband was incapable of impregnating her.

In spite of having two childless wives, the husband had never had a medical check-up. A key informant and member of this group explained that the husband had at one time been suffering from a venereal disease. Although the key informant could not elaborate, she vaguely recalled a time when women ran away from the man.

The second category of women in this special meeting involved those who required family planning. There were three such women, all members of the group. Two of them were widowed. One of the widows was a young woman in her twenties and a daughter of a member of the group. Her mother-in-law was also a member of the same group. She had four children and, according to her mother and several other members, she looked pregnant. I was therefore requested to help her have a pregnancy test and then family planning devices. However, I later found out that both the group members who had organized this special meeting and the young woman were more interested in securing a job which would enable her to support her four children. And as in the case of the childless woman, all the other members left the room when the problem of this young woman was being discussed.

The second widow was the group secretary. She was the only one accompanied by two members of the group. In spite of having a large family of ten children and an additional two grand children born outside marriage, she too felt that her main problem was unemployment. She argued that she did not need to use contraceptives because she had no husband. At this point, her friends drew her attention to her fear of being raped while visiting them at night. I later learned from a key informant that this woman had had a number of children after the death of her husband. This was also the main reason why her friends were so concerned that she should use contraceptives and preferably the more permanent tubal ligation.

The third of this category was a young woman in her early thirties. She had seven children. She now wanted a tubal ligation. The District Hospital had a two year waiting list.[8] She was therefore forced to use the Family Planning Association of Kenya clinic at Nyeri, some 70 kilometres north of the village. The operation cost Ksh 200 in these clinics. Secondly, before an operation is carried out, a husband's consent is required. The main issue here was not only lack of money, but having to convince her migrant husband of the necessity of the operation. As with other younger women, this member was left alone when her case was being discussed.

Ithiki Women's Group

Similarly this group had no childless members. Furthermore, health problems of reproduction are generally not handled within the group framework. The group further explained that few births take place at home. If however a delivery occurred at home, any woman can help. This implied that no traditional birth attendants (TBAs) are consulted. This response raised the need to find out more about the existence and role of the TBAs. According to this group, there were no TBAs except those selected by the chief to register births and deaths in the villages. The group was then asked whether it had knowledge of the "Placenta Pullers." This is a specialist about whom another group had discussed. There were such specialists in the area. Moreover, elderly members of the group gave specific examples of such women. But, while this discussion taking place, young women who sat in one corner with babies strapped around their front in order to breast-feed them with ease were making mischievous comments:

> "You think we would wait to deliver at home? And you think we would allow anybody to touch us or help us? We board a matatu [this is the most common means of transport] and go to the hospital."

But in order to obtain more information on women's perceptions about hospital delivery, I posed a negative suggestion that many women did not like to be delivered by men as was the case in hospitals. Contrary to expectation, an elderly woman in the group immediately responded that the services of men are better. Another member of the group wondered where this particular woman had obtained her experience with male services since all her children were born at home. She had learned from those who had delivered in the hospital.

To strengthen the view that male services are better, other members of the group narrated the story of a woman who delivered just outside the hospital. The woman had hardly stepped from the matatu when the baby fell down. She had no time to prepare herself. The umbilical cord broke, the baby fell to the ground and the placenta reversed. A woman nurse who happened to be near was busy quarreling with the helpless woman while another male nurse rushed over, picked up the baby and started caring for it. Another elderly woman told about her own personal experience. The women nurses had quarreled and asked why she had allowed herself to become pregnant when she was so old. She had replied:

> "I had gone to get school fees."

She had become pregnant when she visited her husband in Nairobi to

get fees for her children. It was then agreed that the services of men
are better possibly because they have no experience with pregnancy
and delivery, they tend to be kinder to the suffering women.

In addition, the issue of past and current forms of fertility control
and regulation was discussed. Accounts similar to those of other
groups were given. There was agreement that fertility control and
regulation was by and large the concern of the entire community
where women's groups had a central responsibility. I then posed the
question why control and regulation of fertility had become a
shameful concern of the individual couples.

The elderly members suggested that the question should be
addressed to women of child bearing age. However, I raised three
issues to encourage participation of elderly women. Both old and
young women had formed groups to assist each other with some of the
burdens arising from large families. The elderly women could therefore not escape such basic issues. Secondly, the role of mother-in-law
which had been discussed in other groups was suggested to constitute
a major problem blocking acceptance of family planning. Thirdly,
elderly members have a duty to educate younger women about past
cultural practices. Attention was mostly directed to discussing the
meaning of family planning. What came out more from this particular
group was that the concept of family planning was only vaguely understood. The chairperson and one of the elderly members had asked:

"Are women supposed to start planning even before they have
had one, two or three children?"

A member in child bearing age gave the following answer:

"In my opinion, I think family planning does not mean stopping to
reproduce when one has up to three children. It means giving
birth to a child and then having another only after that one is
grown up and independent."

But to demonstrate just how private fertility control is, especially
when dealing with concrete cases, a young member of the group
pretended that she wanted a lift to town after one of the meetings.
She then moved nearer and whispered that she was not interested in a
lift. Instead, she wanted to know whether the CDA could help her to
secure tubal ligation. She had heard that the CDA was helping

women in the matter. The elderly chairperson kept peeping curiously, perhaps suspecting what the young woman wanted. The CDA suggested that the young woman should contact another member of the same group who had undergone the operation. But the young woman vehemently opposed this suggestion. The CDA then suggested that she would bring the necessary forms at the church service. This too was opposed. The woman would instead visit the CDA at her home, where nobody else would suspect what she was up to.

Nyakio Women's Group

This group had one childless woman whose husband had married a second wife. According to the group, the children of her co-wife loved the childless woman as much as their biological mother. They often come from their place of work to visit her. She was thus not considered lonely or requiring special help.

Past and contemporary child-spacing practices were discussed. As in other groups, elderly members of this group focused on past practices and concluded by accusing younger women for lack of control in matters of sex.

> "In the past, when a woman gave birth, the husband moved into a separate house. He never returned until the child was sent by the mother to take snuff to him. This was a sign that he could return to her bed. The husband was meanwhile allowed to have extra-marital relationships. He could have a lover who was known to the wife. The lover was herself a married woman and her husband knew about the affair. The two lovers used to exchange gifts, porridge on the part of the woman, and meat on the part of the man, and this way the affair became an open secret. This relationship did not however affect their family responsibilities. There were in addition many taboos which guarded sex and those who broke these taboos were punished."

This group discussed some specific methods of determining whether sexual rules and taboos had been broken. According to the elderly women, younger women no longer restrain themselves when it comes to sex. Furthermore, they refuse to take advice from elderly women.

At the same time, they prohibit their husbands from having extra-marital sexual relationships. The young women had the following to say in their defence:

"These days, a husband and a wife can only afford one house, one bed. They sleep together even when the wife has just delivered. It is not that we [the young women] stop our husbands from having lovers outside marriage. But when this happens, they neglect their family responsibilities. They use the family resources on their women lovers. The problems of today are numerous. Children, especially boys are no longer given advice because most of the time they are in schools. But above all the problem is the failure of contraceptives. We know four women from this area who have undergone tubal ligation. In spite of this operation, they have become pregnant. After undergoing this operation, a woman forgets the worries of having to think about those things. But then suddenly she is pregnant. No one can convince us that there is any safe contraceptive."

The problems for the young women are the changing and complex conditions of modern life and the failure of the family planning programme in general and contraceptives in particular. Even the controversial tubal ligation failed. Attempts to find the specific women who had become pregnant after tubal ligation failed. It seemed that as long as women discussed the experiences of other unknown women, these things could be discussed. Perhaps because of the combined opposition and support of contraceptives by the various agencies, including the church, the government and voluntary organizations such as the Family Planning Association of Kenya and the Maendeleo ya Wanawake Organization, women, it seemed, were also trying to find more information about contraceptives in general and tubal ligation in particular. This was a Catholic dominated group, and a stronghold of the Maendeleo Ya Wanawake Organization. Women were therefore exposed to strong opposition from the church and at the same time strong support for contraceptive use from Maendeleo.

Utheri Munyu Women's Group

There were childless members, but the group did little to control or prevent problems of reproduction. I was in particular requested to assist childless members and advise the group what can be done.

To facilitate discussion, a similar procedure as in other groups was used. This group gave accounts similar to those of other groups with regard to past child-spacing practices and the communal responsibility in the prevention and treatment of problems of reproduction. The maternal uncle was mentioned in this group as a major cause of such problems. The group furthermore indicated that infertility was never associated with men. There was therefore no treatment for men.

In addition, the group was encouraged to focus on current problems of fertility control. According to this group, control and regulation of reproduction, infertility and child-spacing was problematic because of the following factors:

(1) The husband is sometimes opposed to the wife using contraceptives or family planning methods because he loses control over her.[7] The role of the husband was however not as dominant as in Thechi Women's Group discussed further below.

(2) Side effects arising from contraceptive use was given as another reason. Among other things the pill is believed to sit somewhere in the stomach forming a large stone which later makes the woman sick. The IUD was also thought to have frightening effects. In some cases, it was believed the IUD moves through the blood stream to the brain of the user making her sick. It was also thought to stick in the infant's forehead during birth. In one such case, the belief was that the IUD had cut deeply into the baby's forehead making an operation necessary. More striking was that none of this was the concrete experience of any member of this group. Each one had heard it from other sources.

(3) Opposition by the mother-in-law was also mentioned. When young women go to clinics or are involved in some seminar or course, elderly women advise them not to accept being cheated. Family planning is focused on women of childbearing age. This opposition is probably due to the omission of elderly women, a group which otherwise played a significant role in the past.

(4) The naming system, where children are named after relatives starting with grand parents, was also mentioned as a factor encouraging large families.

Thechi Women's Group

Unlike in other groups, where past cultural practices were discussed enthusiastically, the major concern of this group seemed to be current problems of fertility regulation. It became apparent that women in this group were mainly interested in finding solutions to some of the major problems facing them. The majority of women in this group were in the sexually active age. This explains their concern with contemporary fertility control and child-spacing problems. I was again viewed as a resource and was expected to offer solutions.

According to women in this group, wives are expected to protect themselves from becoming pregnant, although they at the same time have little control over their sexuality. Moreover, the majority of husbands work outside the area, coming home only over weekends or at the end of the month. When husbands come home, it is hard to avoid sexual intercourse, even though wives may be unprotected. The women laughingly dramatized how they are ordered to stop cooking and put children to bed, when husbands arrive. It became clear that involving women alone in fertility control is self-defeating and as they put it:

> "We know these things. We are taught about family planning when we visit the clinics. But what is the use when we cannot use it at home !"

They also felt that the issue of fertility control was too sensitive to be handled within the framework of women's groups.

> "Men are happy about our participation in collective activities, as long as they can see tangible benefits such as improved houses, increased milk supply etc. We are not sure they would approve of the involvement of our groups in family planning."

These women were clearly concerned that male participation in family planning was overlooked. Based on their experiences and realities, they suggested, for instance, that seminars and courses intended to educate men and women should be organized to take place on the last weekend of the month when men are home. They were, however, aware of the difficulties of getting men to participate in such seminars and fertility control in general. For that reason, men would have to be tricked in some way to participate. These women discussed the limitations of a seminar organized by the Catholic church to educate couples on the practice of natural family planning methods. The organizers of this seminar overlooked the high prevalence of single motherhood, absence of husbands and their financial constraints which prohibit frequent visits home.

The other factor which arose here is the question of church influence. Other than natural family planning methods, the Catholic church forbids the use of contraceptives. This explains why the cooperation of the husband seemed critical in this group. This may also explain why the group was not keen to discuss contraceptives. An elderly woman raised the problem of side effects from contraceptive use. The problem which was extensively discussed in other groups was here discussed only briefly.

Muiguithania Women's Group

This group had no childless members. But the chairperson of the group had confided in a childless woman in the village about me and my interest in problems of reproduction, including infertility. The childless woman had therefore requested the chairperson to be positive if the question arose next time.

The same procedure where elderly members were encouraged to lead the discussion was followed. The division of views between old and young members was striking. To the older members, family planning and child-spacing in particular had failed because of:

(1) The failure of women to discipline themselves in matters of sex. They nevertheless believed this to be due to the increased consumption of hot foods. Most people of late depend on foods purchased from shops. Such foods are hot and their increased consumption naturally makes the blood hot.

(2) The young women do not allow husbands to have sex with other women.

The young women blamed the men and the worsening conditions of life. The complex and paradoxical situation or reality within which women of reproductive age find themselves was vividly expressed by the young women:

"It is not lack of discipline or control on our part. Rather it is men who are uncontrollable. If for example a woman decides to abstain, as in the past, the man does not agree. Secondly, people can only afford one house and they often share a bed. Even if they wanted to abstain, it is a little unpractical. When a woman decides to move and sleep on the floor, the man follows. If she refuses to have sex, the man hates her and moves out to other women. If we allow them, they not only move away, but also take all the money with them. This is why we do not bother. We have given up and have decided to give birth continuously. It is the only way we can keep men. It is their responsibility to provide for those children. And, unless men discipline themselves, this thing will never succeed."

The young women were quite clear about the vulnerable situation they find themselves in. Through sex, they aim to keep their husbands at home. This, however, leads to many births in close succession. According to these women, the responsibility of looking after a large family leaves little time for the woman to look after herself or to give attention to the man. A young woman with a small baby strapped round her back summarized by saying:

"Many times I have no time to clean myself because of children. It would therefore be easy for my husband if allowed, to go to the cleaner women, where he would also spend our money, leaving us with no food."

Kihara Self-Help Mixed Group

This is one of the two groups outside the framework of women's groups. The assessment of groups mixed on the basis of sex was considered important, not only to show the interaction between women and men together, but also to obtain views of men on issues of reproduction.

There were two main observations. Firstly, women behaved differently when they participated with men. Secondly, by using proverbial language, men had no inhibition in discussing matters of reproduction.

I had extensively interacted with these women in their own group. They were lively and capable of expressing themselves. It was therefore surprising to find them silent while among men. Except for officials who discussed group activities, and elderly women who elaborated the past practices, most of the discussion was dominated by the few men present. Furthermore, the sitting pattern indicated men's superior position. All the men sat on proper chairs while women sat on the ground wherever they could secure a space. While the discussion was going on, women were busy preparing tea and bread. But when it came to serving, priority was given to men, so that a shortage only affected women.

The discussion in this group centred on the role of men in reproductive matters in general and fertility regulation in particular. The chairman, a man of about 50, spontaneously explained that fertility regulation, particularly child spacing, was not new. This gave an opportunity for the older men and women in the group to discuss the specific traditional practices. Most of what the group discussed was similar to other groups.

Perhaps the most important observation here was the procedure of discussing sensitive issues. Each time a man talked, he used the following expression:

"To advise and educate is to be shameless."

This gave the concerned man ease to utter words and explain things which otherwise would be embarrassing or even obscene. Men, too, thought that the contemporary situation where children are born in close succession is a result of the changing conditions of life. The following factors were discussed in this group.

(1) Currently, couples are forced to share one house and one bed. Where a baby is born, it is provided with a separate bed. The

father and the mother continue to share one bed.

(2) The problem of the separation of couples was also mentioned. When migrant husbands come home, there may be little chance to avoid sexual intercourse. Many women conceive during this time. Later, one of the women confided how she used to escape sexual intercourse. If her husband came home during her unsafe period, she invented things which he had supposedly neglected. This was followed by heated arguments and quarrels. There would then be no climate for sex. Since migrant husbands come home on Saturdays, the following day he would return to his place of work. When the woman was safe, she would travel to him.

Later on, this particular woman got support from her husband to use contraceptives.

(3) Strangely enough, free education was mentioned as a factor which encouraged large families. Primary education is free in the sense that no fees are paid. However, parents provide books, buildings and uniforms. Fees in secondary schools are exorbitant and are considered emergency expenses for most groups.

(4) The last factor mentioned was the problem of the young people. Single girls give birth, when they are too young and poor. The responsibility of looking after their children falls on their own parents. This encourages them to have more children because they do not feel the pressure of bringing them up. These wider issues were discussed extensively. The question of contraceptive use was, however, not discussed.

Gathukiini Mother's Union

This is a protestant church organization made up of a cross-section of women from the local church, comprising several villages. Recruitment into the mother's union is based on the commitment of individual women, although old members normally recommend those who wish to join. The recruits undergo a three month course, during which time they are oriented about the rules, regulations and expectations of the organization. New recruits are accepted into the order by an elaborate ceremony presided over by the Bishop of the area. During this ceremony, the new recruits swear mainly to uphold and protect their marriage and bring up children as Christians.

In addition to its Sunday meetings, this particular mother's union meets regularly one day during the week. These meetings are mainly for worship and prayer, but sometimes the organization performs community activities like helping the sick, poor and the aged, within and outside the organization. This particular mother's union reported having been active in health issues of reproduction and child care. This, however, seemed to refer to courses and seminars organized through the church. The church is active in organizing seminars where outside experts are invited to educate members on a variety of issues, particularly family planning and child care. In this respect, the group is used as a target. As in other women's groups, I was regarded as a resource.

The same procedure where members of the groups were encouraged to discuss past and current practices around reproduction was applied here as well. Most of the discussion however centred on the issue of fertility control. The oldest member started by expressing disappointment at the prevailing irresponsibility of young women:

> "I have had 13 children during my life. My husband died in 1945 when I had 11 children. In the old days, we had large families. But, they were well spaced. After the birth of a child, the husband moved out of the house until the child was grown-up. Besides, when a woman delivered, she was fed with a lot of nutritious food, to regain strength fast. I am very disappointed to see the trend these days. Even when women well know that they have no food to eat to recover fast, they still deliver every year. As a result they become too weak and the children do not grow properly either. I wonder why women do not abstain from sex or use the family planning devices!"

To demonstrate how bad the current situation was, the old woman pointed to her daughter. She too had 14 children and her husband had died in 1970. Compared to her old mother, the daughter looked older and worn out.

In response to these sentiments, the chairperson decided to demonstrate the problems involved through her own experience.

According to the chairperson, who was a school teacher nearby, the mother's union had tried to encourage women to talk about their own experiences in matters of reproduction. She talked extensively about her own experience and attempts to control and regulate her fertility:

"Between 1956-1968, I had 8 children which means almost a child every year. I practised family planning only for the last two children. The first device I used in 1964 looked like a small cup. A special cream is smeared all round and then inserted inside the woman. The main problem was keeping the device clean and hidden from children. However, I don't know what happened, maybe it broke. I became pregnant while still using it. But this time I managed to stay a little longer without becoming pregnant.

Next we tried the condom. The main problem with this device is its practical application, because the man has to wait until he is erect. This method is not liked by men and I knew when I became pregnant because he removed the condom. When I went to the clinic during this pregnancy, I was told not to deliver at home, because I was anaemic. I used to eat soil even though I knew it was dirty. Something was missing in my body. So I went to deliver in the hospital. All the other children had been born at home.

After this delivery, I started using a coil. It was fitted in 1968. I had been asked to return three months after delivery. But I pleaded with the doctors because there was a high risk of becoming pregnant before that time. For all the previous pregnancies, I had not resumed my monthly period after delivery. Each time before the next monthly period, I was already pregnant. The doctors therefore agreed to fit it six weeks after delivery, and I still have the same one 17 years later."

The issue of side effects from contraceptive use was raised by a number of women. Similarly none of them said the experience was personal, in spite of the open account by the chairperson. A young member had, for example, sought to know which was the best family planning method. She had heard that people got sick from the pills and heavy bleeding and backache from the coil. She buried her head behind the church desk when others confronted her with the question of whether the experience was personal. The chairperson demonstrated through her own experience once again:

> "During the 17 years I have used the coil, I have never had extra bleeding or backache. This however is the work of God. And this is not to say that there are no side effects. I do not for example personally like to take pills, because I always wonder what else these medicines do to the body. I have avoided having tubal ligation because I do not want to have an operation when I am not sick."

This discussion of personal experiences by the chairperson was exceptional. As she narrated this, many women, particularly the younger ones, laughed shyly and were keen to hear more. A young woman added:

> "This is a good teaching session which has just been introduced. We should learn to discuss these things within the groups, because these groups are suitable for such issues."

The fears people have about pills is perhaps reflected in the kinds of questions raised by members of this group. The question whether unmarried girls become infertile from using pills was raised. This concern with young girls is perhaps related to the increasing problem of teenage pregnancies. The group was encouraged to discuss the possible causes. The chairperson once again led the discussion:

> "I had avoided this issue, but since it has been raised, I would like to say something about it. We had discussed this issue another Sunday if you can remember. During that time, the members upheld the stand of the church and the bible. We agreed not to allow unmarried girls to use contraceptives. If this is allowed, it would encourage girls to have sex indiscriminately thus breaking the tenth commandment. Use of contraceptives would also encourage them to have sex with many men again raising chances of contracting venereal diseases such as gonorrhoea [Gatego] and syphilis [Gicununu]."

At the end of the discussion, the members drew my attention to the fact that I had not explained these issues explicitly. According to an elderly member, one should avoid being shy when educating other people. This indicates that, as probably is usual with this type of discussion, this group expected to be taught.

Because of the complexity of the issues of reproduction and the contradictory statements about the involvement of women's groups, it became necessary to present cases of individual contraceptive users. This would provide concrete situations or reality within which such actions are taken. The following section thus presents a few of the cases.

7.   Case Studies of Contraceptive Users

Through use of key informants, information was gathered on a total of 15 contraceptive users. The majority (12) of contraceptive users had used the controversial tubal ligation. Half of those using tubal ligation had six children or more. Furthermore, contrary to expectations, more than half (8) of the contraceptive users were Catholic.

Case one: Bypassing local clinics

This case was narrated by the Health Field Educator at the District Hospital. The hospital runs a Maternal Child Health (MCH)/Family Planning clinic. A wide range of health problems of reproduction, including mothers and children, are handled under one roof, so as to reduce the social stigma related to contraceptive use. But according to the Health Field Educator, this arrangement does not reduce, stigma for all women. If a woman who is not pregnant or who has no small children visits the clinic, it is understood that the purpose of her visit is family planning. Because of this, many women who need contraceptives use distant facilities.

In one such case, the woman concerned traveled secretly to the National Hospital in Nairobi. She dressed as she always did when going to the farm. She took a clean dress, changed at the farm and boarded a bus for the city. She prayed she would not be involved in an accident because she had not informed her husband about the journey. After finishing her business, she went through the same ritual and pretended she had been working on the farm all day long.

Case two: husband's neglect of responsibilities

This case was observed at the Family Planning Association of Kenya clinic. The concerned woman had traveled from the study area to undergo tubal ligation. The idea of having a tubal ligation was her own. Her husband who worked in Nairobi had neglected her and her children. Because of this, she started a fruit business, which involved buying fruits in the rural areas and selling them in the city. While in the city she would visit the National Hospital to obtain contraceptives.

At first she used the pills, but as she rarely met her husband, she decided to have a tubal ligation which a husband must endorse. When he came home, she requested him to endorse the necessary forms. His first reaction was to strike her (she did not explain why). He later accepted and even offered to accompany her, as long as she met all the expenses.

Case three: Tubal ligation

This case was a woman teacher and a leader of a Catholic church women's organization. Although a Catholic, she had undergone tubal ligation. She explained in detail the circumstances leading to this decision.

She had seven children: five boys and two girls. The girls were born last in line. Both had however been born by breech birth. The first of the two breech deliveries was especially difficult. Labour lasted for 48 hours. She had planned to deliver at a Catholic Mission Hospital in the area, but the whole thing came as an emergency forcing her to deliver at the District Hospital. While at the hospital, she was given an injection to stop the labour pains. She relaxed, only to feel moments later something touching her thighs. This turned out to be the legs of the baby. There was no doctor at the hospital. The sister in charge and the nurse hit her to encourage her to push. She herself had no contractions. They also made a big incision. The whole process took a long time and when the already purple baby came out, she herself was unconscious. Her husband had sent for the priest to administer last rites, but fortunately she recovered.

After two years, she found she was pregnant again. She was

worried and feared she might have a similar experience, but this time she was referred to the National Hospital. The delivery was another breech, but she was operated in time. When her husband came to the hospital, he told the health workers he would never want his wife to give birth again. Before leaving the hospital, a tubal ligation was performed on her.

After this, however, whenever she got sick or something went wrong in her life, she thought she was being punished for what she had done. As a Catholic and a leader of the Catholic Women's Association, she felt guilty for doing just what her church was against.

Case four: Loose uterus

This was a chairperson of a women's group. After her seventh child, she was advised not to deliver any more children because her uterus was loose. Her husband had no objection.

The husband wanted the operation carried out at the District Hospital where she had been delivered, but she herself did not want that. When the husband insisted, she wondered whether he wanted her to die like another woman who had died in the same hospital after undergoing the same operation.

She preferred a private hospital. Private hospitals are rated high in terms of service and care. However, they are expensive and out of the reach of most rural people. The husband was against using a private hospital because of the cost. The woman therefore sold her own cow to meet the medical expenses.

The four cases discussed here, illustrate the cultural, social and economic contexts within which women use contraceptives. Fertility control, and in particular contraceptives, are directed at women who have little control over sexuality. Government rhetoric, during the numerous interaction arenas, makes it seem that contraceptives are always available and that the problem is the women. However, the service end of the programme is itself limited because of problems such as shortage of staff, supplies and lack of privacy. Furthermore, while the various agencies involved agree that fertility control is a critical need, they simultaneously disagree on the methods. Confrontation between the government and the Catholic church on the issue of contraceptives is common. But the large number of Catholic women using contraceptives seems to indicate that conditions and realities within which they live dictates what options women take, although it may mean living with a guilty conscience. Catholic contraceptive users were, not surprisingly eager to justify their actions.

CHAPTER 10

SUMMARY AND CONCLUSIONS: WOMEN'S GROUPS IN TRANSITION

1. Conceptualizing Women's Groups

This chapter draws together the major observations and attempts to discuss implications. I have analyzed the process of mobilization of women for collective action, their organizational dynamics, concerns and survival strategies from a socio-cultural and historical perspective. This has indicated the nature and major forces facilitating the continuation of mobilization of women for collective participation. It has also suggested some of the major problems and the nature of change.

Furthermore, I conceptualize women's groups in the context of the dynamic relationships between social actors and the systems or structures within which they act. As they act, they mould, modify or transform the structures (Burns, Baumgartner and Deville, 1985). The focus on women's groups as a set of actors who interact with the wider system from a subordinated position has indicated both specific and general survival strategies employed in such situations to try to transform or improve situations. From this point, I have attempted to consider some of the forces involved in social transformation and more specifically the role of conflict and tension in social transformation (Omvedt 1986, Huitzer 1979).[1] This is largely because social agents represent different and many times conflicting perspectives of what they or other social actors want. Women's groups thus operate within these conflicting environments which constrain and influence them in major ways. But at the same time, through their everyday activities and resistance in various forms, women's groups have also influenced the wider system.[2] In other words, dominated groups, and in this case women, contribute to the making and restructuring of the social system.

This work is also part of the wider concern with the welfare situation for the majority of people living in poor Third World countries and with the attempt to analyze survival strategies. In the context of improving welfare, women constitute an important resource (AAWORD, 1982). I have therefore attempted, through these two approaches, to obtain insights into the nature and forces involved in the subordination of women, and more importantly their coping strategies.

2. Women's Collective Participation in Three Historical Periods

The pre-colonial period

The pre-colonial Kikuyu society was organized around reproduction (kinship and age-grades). Similarly, Kang'ei/Nyakinyua groups into which all women were mobilized following marriage and initiation of their children were organized around marriage and reproduction.

Women's collective action during this time should be seen in the context of the sexual division of labour in a subsistence economy. Although men and women had specific roles in the agricultural subsistence economy, women had greater responsibility for food production, its disposal and the care of the family. Because of this, cooperation around food production (ngwatio) and mutual assistance during times of high demand (matega), was more frequent among women. This constituted an institutionalized strategy for dealing with overwork, time constraints and food shortages.

Contrary to what is generally accepted, Kikuyu women asserted themselves and their groups were active in the control and regulation of sex and reproduction. They in particular supervised the proper spacing of children, thus ensuring social balance which was expressed in infant and maternal survival.

The colonial period

Colonial domination, along with capitalist expansion, entailed direct exploitation of resources including human resources. To accomplish colonial economic interests, coercion as well as a civilizing ideology through missionary work were used. The results of this process on the colonized people were threefold. The majority of the people were marginalized in various ways. In particular, colonial capitalist expansion introduced new forces for subordinating women. Women's productive roles changed in two major ways. They became more overburdened because, in addition to their roles as subsistence producers, they assumed former male responsibilities. They also became providers of labour in the commercial agricultural sector. More importantly, however, they lost control over what they produced.

Colonial domination moreover implied that the thinking patterns and moral order of the colonized people were put into question. Eventually, resistance, including organized resistance, emerged as the main form of interaction. This resistance by the people shaped not only the direction through which colonial domination proceeded, but also the nature of the social organization which emerged.

The impact of the civilizing ideology on sexuality

The civilizing ideology is important from two points. It set in motion the process of change and had a far-reaching impact on sexuality in these societies. The protagonists of the civilizing ideology were the first to make systematic observations and records of the lives of the uncivilized people in general and of their sexuality in particular. Their understanding and biases form the basis of later analysis. Early anthropological and missionary work depict societies such as the Kikuyu as having been overwhelmingly under the control of taboos, magic and prohibitions, over which social actors had little control (Dumor, 1983). In this way, it is implied that these societies were static. But, even as I argue that taboos maintained social balance, my research suggests that taboos did not completely prohibit people from breaking the rules. Actors within the system did break rules. Otherwise there would have been no need for group action, such as one finds among the Kikuyu, to pressure members of the community to observe rules and maintain the expected behaviors or face punishment.

Perhaps because of the secretive nature of sexuality, sex and reproduction were regulated through a host of beliefs and taboos. In addition, group action was extensively used to effect control and punishment. In this way, people addressed sexuality and had dialogue with each other on sexuality as part of their daily life. The Kange'i/Nyakinyua women's groups effected control around sex and child spacing. Similarly, younger age-groups exerted pressure on members not engage in pre-marital sex.

But taboos and group actions were not used as regulative mechanisms just for their own sake. These societies had concrete knowledge of certain relationships between behavior and health. Practices such as examination of the weight of a baby and the concern for proper feeding of newly delivered mothers indicate knowledge of the linkage between child spacing, nutritional status and infant and maternal morbidity and mortality. This was expressed, of course, in the Kikuyu definition of health and disease. Practical experiences with high infant and maternal morbidity and mortality seem to have been a critical consideration in the area of child-spacing, and the process of reproduction in general. Rules in the form of beliefs and taboos were therefore formulated to enable social groups to deal with social problems. Kang'ei/Nyakinyua groups acted on rules to ensure the maintenance of social balance in terms of their definition of balance. But actions were also taken to achieve specific health goals. In this way, women through their corporate groups played significant roles in health maintenance.

Missionaries and colonialists perceived and depicted the Kikuyu sexual morality as one where women are sexually deprived. But at the same time, their attempts to prohibit female circumcision on the grounds that it was medically dangerous and deprived women sexual pleasure failed because of the strong resistance from the people. This forced the missionaries to allow the operation aspect of circumcision to continue within their hospitals.[3] The missionaries were, by and large, part of the colonial establishment and had a duty to promote the colonial interests. Nevertheless, as members of a distinct culture, they perceived sexuality from their own perspectives. The issue of sexual pleasure which seemed to pre-occupy the missionaries is not experienced in the same way by all social groups. As a result of deteriorating socio-economic conditions, large numbers of women are forced into prostitution and other temporary sexual relationships. In these circumstances, sexuality is, as argued in chapter twelve, utilized more for economic and survival gains than sexual pleasure. These early interactions in the area of sex and reproduction are critical and have far reaching implications to programmes which attempt to regulate sexuality and reproduction today. As the family planning and AIDS control programmes suggest, policies and plans reflect a similar use of decontextualized knowledge and incorrect assumptions.

The impact of this process of change has consequences for women in their reproductive roles. As a result of the breakdown of past control systems regulating sexuality and reproduction, women are exposed to continuous pregnancy, childbirth and child dependency. Furthermore, teenage sexuality was also transformed in ways which have led to an increase in teenage pregnancies, abortions and related complications as well as sexually transmitted diseases.

This is the context within which people's resistance or struggle in general, and in particular women's struggle, should be understood. In reaction to the mounting resistance where women played an active role, the colonial government tried to rehabilitate local community structures including women's groups and instituted indirect rule. From this period one can see the emergence of two forms of social action. Social groups act from their own perspectives based on prevailing realities but also drawing on their past experiences. In addition, they have become targets of government planning and action.

The Post-Colonial Period

The process of state targeting on women's groups intensified during the post-colonial period. The training programme and formalized women's group committees at various administrative levels facilitated interaction of women's groups from a wide geographical area. This led to what one may call a large scale women's movement. On the other hand the same process had inhibiting effects on women's groups.

This process entails getting people and in this case women's groups to implement agency plans and policies. But agency orientations and goals are, in many instances, in conflict with the needs and interests of the people. In general, planners conceive of poverty, within which most women in developing countries live, as a purely economic problem which can be overcome by carefully planned and implemented economic development programmes. This has meant for women's groups, increased focus on commercial projects, in order, it is argued, to make women economically independent. The latter is a noble ideal for which women themselves strive. But economic activities of women's groups perform poorly. Evidence suggests that groups even incur loss of their resources.

From another perspective, one may question the seriousness of governments in programmes which aim to emancipate women. It is, for example, not uncommon for women's projects to be funded without the necessary project appraisal or feasibility studies that normally precede many other programmes. At this level, one seems to be dealing with two issues. On the one hand, there is the bureaucratic incapacity to effectively handle these kinds of projects. The Women's Bureau has, for example, had a mere skeleton staff with little relevant professional qualifications to deal with the kinds of projects being planned and implemented. But more seriously, the Bureau is, since its inception in 1976, a unit in the Ministry of Culture and Social Services. Within the government hierarchy, the Ministry of Culture and Social Services has a low status. This is because it is considered to be a consuming ministry. Furthermore, as the Kenya's Five Year Development Plans (1974-1988) indicate, the Women's Bureau and therefore women's programmes have low priority in government budget allocations. This leads to a second issue, namely that there may indeed be little serious political will and commitment to programmes which would facilitate the emancipation of women. At this level, such programmes and structures simply enhance the patronizing of women by male politicians. Within the dynamics of Kenya politics, the exploitation of women's groups by male politicians is common.

Nevertheless, by tying government funding to income-generating projects, within a situation where women desperately need such funds, groups naturally start commercial projects although such projects may have little chance of survival. Commercial projects require resources including capital and skills often inaccessible to women. Participation in such projects not only deepens women's dependence on other agents, but even drains resources they already have without generating income.[4]

In turn, this affects group dynamics including their survival strategies and organizational forms. Requirements of commercial projects may for example influence the categories of women recruited into groups. In a general way, the tendency has emerged where poorer women, who may require support more than others, are excluded from the groups because they cannot afford long term contributions to these projects.

But in spite of intensified targeting and the introduction of commercial projects, the simpler mabati home improvement activities of groups still constitute the major component of women's group activities. These activities have evolved from the actual roofing of houses to the current provision of simple household items. Although they are not officially recognized, they are for women a major source of pride, in part because they offer concrete and tangible benefits.

3.   Women's Groups, Health, Sex and Reproduction

Concerning health, sex and reproduction, several contradictory tendencies were observed among women's groups. Mabati activities of women's groups are typically health promoting activities. In spite of this, women's groups considered their role in health to be minimal. Moreover, even when groups were directly involved in health activities, such activities fulfilled needs of women other than health. The Weithaga Women's Locational committee was concerned with the cleanliness of its members. But, the group was concerned with reducing nuseating odors in order to improve the image of women.

Similarly, reproductive health problems were not handled in the context of the groups. Reproduction seemed to be considered a private matter of individual couples. Groups may have been eager to show that they were actively involved and supported government fertility control programmes, but data obtained from case study groups and individual contraceptive users suggests that there is little group involvement.

At the same time, rumours about exaggerated and frightening side effects arising from contraceptive use were spontaneously discussed within the groups. The impact of such processes on acceptance of the fertility control programme was not investigated. One can nevertheless suggest some conclusions from this type of behavior.

Such behavior seems to indicate the social complexity of reproduction. More importantly, it points to the general problems of social planning and indicates the subtle mechanisms through which resistance to development plans manifest itself. Resistance in this case is more complex and hard to detect because it bears no negative undertones. It seems this is the kind of response one would expect in situations such as those I describe. Within this context, women's groups are desperate for resources. Since resources are tied to specific types of group activities, it would appear irrational for groups to accept lack of support for government programmes.

Furthermore, the nature of transformation may explain some of these discrepancies. The Kikuyu sexual moral order based on communal responsibility was transformed into one based on individuals, privatized and professionalized at the same time. When the need for population control was realized, agencies made no reference to the systems which existed before. The paradox is that, at the same time as the missionary work was dismantling the systems which controlled and regulated sex and reproduction, they initiated the process of blaming African sexuality and culture for the population explosion. Without consideration of some of the effects of the colonial capitalist expansion, including plunder and indiscriminate exploitation of resources, African population in the reserves was viewed as a major problem. Control of the African population would, it was argued, lead to social and economic development. This conceptualization has guided the planning of population control policies. However, in spite of the development of a medical technology which is considered effective, and the strong belief that population control would improve the situation of the masses of impoverished people, acceptance of family planning remains, as chapter eleven suggests marginal in Kenya. The question of regulating sexuality has become critical now with the AIDS crisis. As chapter twelve indicates, similar mistakes as those in family planning programmes are being repeated. The AIDS crisis in general, but more specifically in Africa, is a concrete example indicating complexity of human sexuality and reproduction and furthermore how unsuited agency plans and policies are in dealing with human sexuality.

4.   The Nature of Women's Struggle

Perhaps my major conclusion is that the subordination of women is a central issue against which Kikuyu women collectively struggle.[5] But the form this struggle assumes reflects the nature of the situational reality. Women's groups may avoid confrontation or openly questioning male domination. They may also refuse to consider divorce in case of marital instability. This should not be taken to imply that Kenyan or African women are conservative or still in the bondage of tradition. From a western feminist view, this may appear to be the case. But, as my study indicates, the needs of the people, their aspirations, and the strategies they employ, should be conceptualized within their situational reality including concrete material, political, cultural, moral and historical conditions.

This implies that efforts to change or improve women's paradoxical situation cannot be separated from the realities within which they act. Even in the context of women's struggle for equality in the west, countries such as Sweden and USA have followed different paths, because of the unique characteristics of the two societies as indicated in the work of Safilios-Rothschild (1979). Her comparative analysis suggests that women in Sweden and USA have used non-confrontational and confrontational approaches, respectively, in their struggle for sexual role equality. Both modes of action were instrumental for the implementation of non-sexist legislation and social policy. The Swedish model was non-confrontational because the entire movement represented a radical movement led by men and women together. In contrast, the American model, particularly at the initial stages, was characterized by emotions and hostility against men who were regarded as oppressors.

Women in Kenya struggle within a fluid social context. The Kikuyu social system is neither westernized, nor consistent with its original cultural form. The issue of subordination should therefore be seen in that context. In many cases, what is claimed to be traditional has assumed new properties becoming more oppressive to women, at the same time as new forms of oppression have emerged. A few of these may indicate the nature of change and the new situation of African women.

The commoditization of sex

The unfolding socio-economic structures have, for example, led to the commoditization of sex. This emerged from colonial conditions which disrupted the social support systems and created an unbalanced population structure in urban and other male employment centres. Besides the obvious health implications, prostitution has probably been the most powerful force in lowering the image of women, who were seen to have broken strongly regulated sexual practices. Even though prostitution involves both men and women, only women are visible in the public eye. Police and other forms of public and private harassment are applied only to women. Within the current modernization processes where masses of people, particularly women, have limited means of survival, prostitution has greatly expanded. This situation explains why women's groups are so concerned with maintaining a proper image, even though it may mean excluding from their groups women who need group support most.

Contemporary polygamy

Similarly, a practice such as polygamy has assumed properties which make it more oppressive to women. Polygamy in its cultural context played a number of functions. In the context of the economic organization, women had a heavier workload because they were responsible for food production. At the same time, husbands appropriated some of the food surplus to build their herds. It was around this issue that wives often encouraged their husbands to marry a second wife. Each wife was an independent economic entity producing on the pieces of land allotted to her. Furthermore, she owned and lived in a separate house where the husband was more or less a guest.

Polygamous marital relationships can therefore be seen from two rather opposing perspectives. In terms of the workload, polygamy was a relief for women. But at the same time, it can be argued that the system was a male mechanism for appropriation and exploitation of female labour. While this is true, even in areas where polygamy declined, women's workload was not lightened. On the contrary, women assumed former male responsibilities as a result of male migration. Moreover, because of low wages, women continued to supplement for the survival of their migrant wage earning husbands and many times also paid taxes imposed on them by the colonial administration. In this way, women's subsistence labour continued to be exploited, this time not by the husband, but for the benefit of the colonial power. In addition, other colonial policies reduced the economic independence and control women had in the past. In particular, a land tenure system where ownership rights were designated to individual male heads of households and the introduction of cash crops not only changed the properties of land, but also meant that women largely lost control and land use rights, not to mention the products of their labour.

In this context, economic arguments against polygamy have little weight. In fact, a look at the history of industrialization in the West indicates that the emergence and evolution of monogamous marriage and the family as we know it today is part of the rhythm of that process.

Polygamy has probably received most criticism as a male mechanism for sexual exploitation and control over African women. But in the context of past African sexuality and reproduction, polygamy protected women in a number of ways. It functioned as a security valve for childless women. Such women easily fitted in as part of subsistence labour and child care. With missionary condemnation of polygamy, barren women escaped into urban areas to engage in prostitution and other informal trades such as the brewing of liquor for sale. This was the beginning of prostitution among the Kikuyu people.

Polygamy played an important role in child-spacing and related fertility control as well. It should be added here that, contrary to the view often presented (Cagnolo 1933) of the African male as a sexual beast, sexuality among many African societies seems to have been secondary, at that time. As already indicated, there were numerous occasions when sexual intercourse was prohibited for both men and

women. I am not suggesting that the Kikuyu and other African societies did not recognize the individual and social needs of sexuality. Nor
am I saying that sexuality among such African societies was, as is
popularly believed, only for reproductive purposes. The practice of
Ngwiko, a type of controlled sex, was accepted among newly initiated
young men and women as well as among couples in monogamous
marital unions. Unmarried young men and women were allowed to
sleep together during many dancing and other social occasions. They
helped each other to achieve sexual satisfaction without full sexual
intercourse. Sexuality was thus accepted as an important part of being
and development and not necessarily only for reproduction.

It is therefore important to note that there was a highly developed,
internally consistent social order among many African people. I am
not implying that women were not oppressed. But compared to
European monogamous relationships, where women were more or
less toys to be loved and kept home as agents of consumption and
reproduction, African women did not live their day-to-day lives under
this contradiction of love and male domination. This implies that
women, particularly in western societies, have and continue to live
within the contradictory situation of love, romance, monogamous
marital relationships, extra-marital sexual relationships, violence and
close male domination. Male control and domination is the basis on
which monogamous marriage is founded. But, coated as it is within
love and romance, this control and related violence has until recently
been less obvious. These are some of the contradictions which have
pre-occupied western feminists, a struggle which has earned them the
title of "male haters" (Mies 1986, O'brien 1981). I therefore argue that
the oppression of African women, and indeed the oppression of
women everywhere, needs to be understood in its specific context.

Polygamy, like many customs which were prohibited by the missionaries, has survived. The 1977/78 Kenya National Demographic
Survey suggests that approximately 20% of men and 30% of women in
Kenya live in polygamous unions. But, whether living within socially
recognized polygamous or monogamous marital relationships,
growing numbers of men secretly acquire girlfriends and concubines
with whom regular sexual relationships are established. Quite often,
children are born and raised within these relationships.

The emerging sexual patterns, where a man in addition to his socially accepted polygamous or monogamous marital relationships has other secret regular and casual sexual partners, has far reaching consequences for African women. For the wife or wives, the husband is not just shared with many unknown women. This also implies that family resources are thinly distributed over a large number of women and their families. These patterns have consequences for women's health as well. Adolescent pregnancies and pregnancies outside marriage in general, which affect women adversely, have increased. Among married women, fertility per woman and related complications have increased. Within the prevailing socio-economic environment, the custom nevertheless exists out of context. In the past, each wife existed as an independent entity, producing on the pieces of land allocated to her. She also had a separate house. For the majority of the people now, these are expensive luxuries. Furthermore, whereas in the past wives and husbands made joint decisions when a new wife was married, many women now learn of their co-wives or their husband's concubines from other sources. In terms of disease control, especially of sexually transmitted diseases including AIDS, the emerging sexual patterns present major problems (see part four).

These are major problems of the custom today. Its rejection by African women should not be confused with what is commonly viewed as "women's jealousy" about other women. This is another rationalizing ideology, used even in the West to safeguard male control over women and their sexuality.

Emerging social and economic situation

From another perspective, economic exploitation of male labour has probably had much greater impact on women than has been realized. Colonial education aimed at producing male clerks. This form of education alienated men from agricultural labour. Large numbers of young men drifted into urban areas in search of monetary and preferably white collar employment, even when such work may not have been available or when productive activity based on agriculture remained a viable possibility. From this perspective, the Kikuyu men are also living in a paradoxical situation. Unlike their western counterparts, whose occupation determines the class status and lifestyle of a household regardless of whether the wife has a job outside the home, Kikuyu men are unable to fulfil those household obligations they are expected and socialized to fulfill. The psychological frustrations and other male reactions to this situation have been given little attention. What often meets the eye of, say, a western feminist or a development expert is an idle or lazy drunkard who goes home after drinking sprees only to beat his wife, often for no apparent reason.

This is a widespread phenomenon in rural Kikuyu and, although this study was not designed to investigate such problems, many cases of this kind were encountered. The likely antagonism between wives and husbands arising from migration of males from the rural areas has been reported by Roscoe (1921).[6] Furthermore, the great concern of women's groups that their achievements should not be seen to surpass those of their husbands, seem to contradict past Kikuyu concepts and values about success. Success of a Kikuyu man was directly related to the achievements of his wife or wives. If, in addition to being industrious (which mainly implied the production of surplus food), the wife demonstrated this success by being generous to visitors, the husband acquired high status. Contribution of Kikuyu women was not only recognized, but men had to negotiate with women to acquire high status. Within the current context, women's enormous contribution goes unrecognized, while the same women are forced to refrain from exposing their abilities, potentials and achievements.[7]

Movements striving for sexual equality were started among western women who, until recently, when problems of African women were analysed from a historical and structural perspective, largely depended on early mispresentations of African men.[8] Again, one can only speculate about the impact of these presentations on the struggles of Kikuyu women. While the struggle for advancement and equality of women is far from won even in western countries, the Kikuyu and other African women in similar situations have probably much wider gaps to cover. This is so, not just because of their level of impoverishment and marginalization, but also because they have to convince men that African women have real problems and are not merely under the influence of western feminists. Hence, the struggle for equality will of necessity have to focus on both men and women. Women's struggle is part of the struggle against exploitative social structures. However, given the nature of male domination over women, and the underlying prejudices and ideologies supporting that domination, it goes far beyond class struggle.

5.   The Potential of Dominated Groups

Dominated groups, such as the women's groups in rural Kenya, are an important resource for change, as this study has tried to demonstrate. In the context of Kenyan history, women have continued to exploit the power of collective action to counteract negative forces within the system even after colonial forces had disrupted their culture and collective organization. This has continued in spite of the intensified targeting process which tends to demobilize women. Secondly, women make up the majority of rural peasants, implying that collective participation and action in rural Kenya is grounded in day-to-day reality.

Women's groups were observed to help women gain self-respect and confidence to attempt changes or to resist changes in ways each individual woman could not do on her own. In the context of the groups, women were even able to develop aggressive attitudes towards outsiders, redefine their situation, and assist their members to handle a variety of problems. It is this combination of the power of collective participation and cultural continuity that makes women's groups dynamic forces.

Continued collective participation of women has not just offered a link between the past and the present, it constitutes a process of consciously selecting positive cultural traits and adapting them to meet new challenges. It is perhaps only through such dynamic participation that issues which evoke resistance can become an integral part of the collective activity and social order. An aim of this study has been to suggest not only that this is possible, but also to indicate how it may be achieved.

Perhaps use of qualitative methods, particularly those that encourage dialogue and deep interaction with subjects and communities of research as used in this study, provide an appropriate start. Group discussion as a method of data collection yielded information which could be used directly to facilitate communication among group members of varied age categories, different sexes and between the groups and the researcher. This was particularly useful in establishing a suitable climate for discussing even highly sensitive issues related to sex and reproduction. More importantly, group dynamics seemed to unfold in ways which encouraged women to question the role of researchers and that of outsiders in general.

Part Four: **Policy and Programme
Implication for Africa**

CHAPTER 11

REGULATION OF SEX AND REPRODUCTION:
THE CASE OF FAMILY PLANNING

1. Introduction

Family planning represents attempts by agencies to regulate human sexuality and reproduction. It offers yet another concrete example of problems arising when social policy and planning are not based on concrete knowledge of the local realities. This chapter reviews the family planning programmes and discusses the extent to which their goals have or have not been achieved. In spite of the growing support by local and international agencies, the impact of family planning in lowering fertility and rate of population growth, in general and more specifically in Sub-Saharan Africa, appears very limited. This is largely because assumptions and models used are not based on concrete knowledge and realities of the local situation, established practices, social networks and processes relating to sexuality in such situations.

2. The Rationale for Family Planning

Since the 1950s when the population explosion alarm was raised, population control has become a critical issue for the poor countries.[1] Whatever reasons are given -health, welfare, human rights- the ultimate goal of family planning in the poor countries is to achieve the dual goal of lowering population growth, thus ensuring improved socio-economic conditions.

Rapid population growth resulting from rising fertility and high but declining mortality characterize most poor countries and Subsahara Africa in particular. Should a decline in birth rate fail to follow the declining mortality as it did in industrialized countries, the impact on ecology, rural employment, agricultural land, family income, social welfare and political stability would as demographers and economists project, be catastrophic (Frank and McNicoll 1987, Mott and Mott 1980, Ndegwa 1985).

The general family planning model

Establishment of family planning programmes follow a rather common pattern where experts from developed countries and international agencies advise national governments on the process of instituting such programmes. In 1965, for example, a team of experts from the US Population Council visited Kenya on the invitation of the Kenya government to study the population problem and recommend a programme suitable and administratively feasible. Based on experience and knowledge derived from programmes in other countries (mainly Asian countries), the commission of experts after three weeks in Kenya made the following broad recommendations.

(1) The programme should be voluntary.

(2) It should form an integral part of, rather than alternative to social and economic development efforts.

(3) It should aim at reducing birth rate using birth control technology and should be closely linked with a national health programme.

The central emphasis was distribution of contraceptives and related information. It was assumed that availability of information would not only lower fertility, but would also change cultural values and attitudes which may otherwise hinder contraceptive acceptance.[2] But, there was little consultation with other social groups.[3] This family planning model has been instituted with little variation and has been supported by governments in Third World countries (UNFPA 1982/83, WHO 1983/84).

The growing support represents a move away from a period when many governments were suspicious and not fully convinced of the need for family planning. The history of family planning in most poor countries show a pattern where governments accepted the principles of family planning but delayed implementation. Some countries had, of course, no real need to limit population growth because they had low population compared to their resources. Zaire, for example, has low population density, abundant cultivable land and mineral wealth. Yet, according to USAID, Zaire is among the 20 developing countries having the most serious population problems and the most urgent need for assistance (Wolfson, 1978). Francophone African countries have, until recently, been under the influence of French anti-contraceptive laws instituted in 1920 (Oppong 1987, Picouet and Jones 1986). Whatever the reasons for the official reluctance in the past, a new momentum was by the mid-1970s emerging.

This should, however, be seen in the context of deteriorating economies of many poor countries of the world and Sub-saharan Africa in particular. The per capita GNP for countries in Sub-saharan Africa region range between US $ 150-600 (Shaw 1985). Secondly, and probably more seriously, agricultural food output has declined as a result of a constellation of factors such as climatic conditions and national and international economic policies which encourage production of export crops whose returns service foreign debt obligations. As a result, Africa has become a major importer of food. In this context we can understand the motivation for family planning. The question now is: what impact has family planning had in alleviating this situation?

3.   Programme Performance

The following section examines the family planning programme performance. I focus on some indicators which seem to suggest that, as a strategy for alleviating poverty in poor countries, family planning has had limited impact.

Studies and evaluations.

Knowledge, attitude and practice (KAP) studies, contraceptive prevalence and world fertility surveys are the most commonly used tools for evaluating programme impact. These studies indicate that women have gained considerable information and awareness of family planning in general and contraceptives in particular (Shepherd 1984, World Bank 1983). Dow and Werner (1983), for example, observed that in a sample of 860 Kenyan women who had some information about family planning, 92.5% had knowledge of efficient methods of contraception. Members of women's groups of this study were fully aware of family planning. In addition, a general attitude change in favour of small family size is according to Dow (1983) apparent. To the extent that one of the main goals was to make information accessible and increase levels of knowledge of modern birth control methods, family planning programmes appear to have made considerable progress.

The question however remains: has increased knowledge, awareness and information of family planning led to increased contraceptive acceptance? Emerging evidence seems to indicate that in spite of increased knowledge and stated high motivational levels for small family size, contraceptive acceptance remains low. In Zimbabwe, which is considered to have the highest rate of contraceptive prevalence in Africa, only 38% of married women of reproductive age are using either modern (27%) or traditional (11%) contraceptive methods (Boohene and Dow, 1987). After more than two decades, Kenya's family planning programme, perhaps the most expensively financed programme anywhere, still records an acceptance rate of less than 20% of the targeted population (Contraceptive Prevalence Survey 1984 and 1986, Way et al 1987).

In addition, the question of whether and to what extent family planning programmes have succeeded in fertility reduction has generated controversy because the same studies have drawn contradictory conclusions. Recent evidence suggests that the use of research designs with potential and in some cases real problems of validity have tended to inflate programme effect (Hernandez, 1984). Using a method (Interrupted Time Series Design) to develop projections of fertility levels which might have followed even without family planning programmes, Hernandez recomputed fertility performance for Taiwan, South Korea, Costa Rica and Mauritius, countries considered to have successful programmes. This design indicate that birth rate decline in these countries resulted from changes in social, economic, demographic and conditions *outside* of family planning programme consideration or influence.[4]

This suggests that those accepting contraceptives are often motivated by factors other than the programme itself. Perhaps important here is the observation that contraceptive adoption increases with educational attainment. The world fertility surveys in 38 developing countries suggest an overall pattern of decreasing fertility with increasing education (Weinberger, 1987).

Furthermore, the choice of specific contraceptive methods, in particular female sterilization, seem to be sensitive to a variety of other socio-demographic variables including age, marital status and parity. Recent research indicates that female sterilization is used more by married women in the age-group 30-45 (Ross et al 1987, Warren and Smith 1986). Although they have not indicated which contraceptive is favoured by women over 40 years, Way, Cross and Kumar (1987) observe that contraceptive acceptance in Kenya increases with age and number of children. Contraceptive users are, it seems, more interested in limiting than spacing births. It is particularly interesting to note the emerging pattern where use of female sterilization has increased in spite of some of its problems.[5] By focusing narrowly on contraceptive acceptance as the only criteria for assessing programme performance, many factors which influence fertility decisions and contraceptive use were left out. Whatever the case, the need for new approaches seems to have been realized.

New strategies and approaches

Coercive family planning programmes

Since the late 1970s, pressure for new strategies, approaches and orientations has grown. Some countries such as India, Thailand and China have introduced more forceful family planning programmes. In

China a one-child family policy, introduced in 1979, has been supported by a system of incentives and disincentives (Mies 1986). In Thailand, financial incentives in the form of village loans which were increased in size if the rate of contraceptive use also increased was reported to have led to a decline in pregnancy rate in the six villages where such incentives were introduced (Weeden, 1986). However, it is hard to state with any certainty the extent to which fertility reduction has resulted from these coercive family planning policies. This is so because, as already observed, commonly used research designs tend to inflate net programme impact. Secondly, socio-economic and demographic factors outside family planning programmes have impact on demographic change. In spite of this, some still maintain that coercive approaches have led to ,fertility decline. Caldwell and Caldwell argue, for example, that four Asian countries (India, Indonesia, Thailand and China) achieved fertility declines ranging between 29-57% through the application of coercive policies. The Asian countries are contrasted with seven African countries (Ghana, Nigeria, Kenya, Tanzania, Zambia, Senegal and Ivory Coast) where fertility has risen or remained constant. They conclude that family structures, economies and religious attitudes in Africa reduce the demand for small family size or prohibit initiation of coercive family planning policies by African governments.[6] Furthermore, although most of their data is drawn from India, they make no reference to the unintended programme-related responses such as sex determination and related termination of female foetuses known to be prevalent in that part of the world.

In addition to these coercive policies, governments and donor agencies have been experimenting with new, non-coercive approaches for motivating target subjects to accept contraceptives. There is a move from the traditional programmes based on clinics and medical professionals to approaches based on community structures and networks. Two such approaches, namely community-based distribution (CBD) and social marketing of contraceptives, are increasingly being tried out.

The community-based distribution (CBD)

The concept of Community-Based Distribution (CBD) goes back to 1970s.[7] Its main concern is to make contraceptives more accessible to the users within contexts which minimize economic as well as socio-cultural constraints. It is believed that basing family planning on local structures and networks would minimize resistance because the users and distributors have more or less similar frames of reference and are in close contact with one another in social networks. Members of the community obtain their contraceptives in their normal interaction processes, and this reduces social stigma.

I observed some of these factors in a CBD programme implemented by the Maendeleo Ya Wanawake Organization which distributes contraceptives through women's group networks in Murang'a District of Kenya. Three members from each of the women's groups involved were trained to handle non-clinical contraceptives. The three distributors were selected from various locations in the village in a way which minimized distances users had to walk. This also gave the users the possibility to choose the distributor they trust or feel most at ease with. The impact of this approach on contraceptive acceptance was not studied. There were nonetheless a number of interesting features observed. A man who needed a new supply of condoms simply and laughingly told the female distributor that his socks were worn out. Both the user and the distributor met more or less accidentally as they performed their own normal activities. Important here is the language, the mode of communication and the possibility to integrate distribution of contraceptives within normal lives and activities of the people.

The second interesting feature is the form of argument used to discourage large families. Participation in wedding ceremonies was, for example, used to illustrate problems which face women who have too many children. During a wedding ceremony which typically involves traveling far away, only women without children are selected to travel. Those with small children are usually left behind or are assigned the more tedious and boring task of preparing and serving food to visitors.

Finally, I observed that contraceptive distributors were aware of the common forms of resistance. More importantly, they were to a certain extent able to neutralize negative rumours. Training of community members to handle contraceptives moreover appears to be an important move not only in the demystification and socialization of family planning but also of health in general.

These initiatives have been observed to have improved acceptance of family planning. Increased contraceptive acceptance in the Saradidi community-based project in Kenya was attributed to the use of volunteer health helpers (VHH) who were chosen and supported by the community (Kaseje, Sempebwa and Spencer 1987). Frank and McNicoll (1987) mention Chogoria, another community-based project in Kenya, as a success story. Studies in Indonesia indicate that villages where religious and other informal leaders such as teachers, village elders and retired public servants participate in the implementation, the programme has greater success (Warwick, 1986).

The social marketing programmes

Social Marketing Programmes dispense contraceptives through existing commercial channels, thus making them more accessible to the users. It is assumed this would enhance contraceptive acceptance. These programmes also recover some programme costs (Population Reports 1985, Davies, Mitra and Schellstede 1987).

Like CBD, social marketing programmes address several of the factors known to have hindered contraceptive acceptance in the past. Dispensing contraceptives together with ordinary items reduces stigma and embarrassment on the part of the users. Particularly important, this approach encourages involvement of men. Studies in Bangladesh indicate that husbands obtain most of the contraceptives supplied through commercial channels (Davies, Mitra and Schellstede 1987, Forrest 1986). Conscious efforts on the part of family planning agencies aimed at persuading men to undertake or support family planning may have led to increased male participation. A radio advertisement programme in Bangladesh specifically addressed the male dominant position in order to encourage him to take action. From another perspective, their access and control over household cash may mean that men obtain contraceptives while purchasing other household goods. In addition to this, the condom is one of the main contraceptives distributed through social marketing. This implies also that men obtain their own supplies and are involved in their own right. This distribution channel seems a viable means for reaching men who otherwise may not like to be seen going for contraceptives in the MCH clinics. But even these new approaches are limited in a number of ways.

Limitations of the new approaches

By being based on existing social structures and networks, CBD and social marketing programmes address some of the issues which were ignored in older programmes. Apart from increasing contraceptive use, these initiatives are a step towards the socialization of family planning. But as they are now, they still omit many key areas. They, for example, still focus on married couples thus leaving adolescents out (Kigondu 1986). Given that parents strongly oppose contraceptive distribution to the young people, the problem may be more critical when programmes are community-based unless special efforts are made to address the paradoxical situation of the young people. In general these approaches do not address the more basic question of creating a sexual moral order that incorporates all key social groups.

Contraceptive seeking behaviors

Given the poor living conditions under which most people in Sub-Sahara Africa live, and further given that family planning can directly help families regulate and/or reduce the number of mouths they need to feed, clothe and educate, it is difficulty to ascertain why it is not readily accepted. Recent work indicates there are many factors prohibiting contraceptive use even when women are motivated to limit family size or postpone the next birth. Economic costs influence contraceptive availability. Contrary to bureaucratic rhetoric that contraceptives are readily available and women only need to fetch them from health facilities, supplies in rural areas of poor countries are limited and irregular. Similarly, even when contraceptives are available, it is not obvious that they are readily accessible to a majority of the poor people. On the other hand, some patterns of contraceptive seeking behaviors indicate that family planning agencies have largely failed to conceptualize reproduction in its complex social and cultural dimensions and patterns.

Unintended programme generated responses

Although family planning services are integrated into the maternal and child health (MCH), it is easy for local people to identify women who visit MCH clinics to obtain contraceptives. Therefore, women bypass facilities nearest them when seeking contraceptives in order to conceal their identity.

Secondly, target groups take actions to discourage contraceptive use. Such actions constitute resistance and are undertaken to maintain a social balance, for example, a type of problem which has been overlooked by family planning. Perhaps a most effective form of "resistance" is the resort to rumours concerning strange and frightening contraceptive side effects. According to a study in Egypt, the rumour that the pill causes weakness decreases the probability of pill acceptance (DeClerque et al, 1986). As elaborated earlier, women's groups discussed rumours in ways which discourage contraceptive use.

Equally critical are forms of resistance such as observed among women's groups. Women's groups use strategies of resistance which have far reaching implications to policies and plans, because certain aspects of their resistance are hidden and bears no negative undertones. This implies that existing contradictions between rhetoric and action by the target groups may never be understood.

Besides these forms of resistance, confrontations between target populations and family planning agencies are not uncommon. Parents and family planning agencies are often in confrontation over distribution of contraceptives to young people. Youth sexuality has on the other hand changed with far reaching health, economic and social consequences. But even as parents are aware and concerned with problems of teenage sexuality, they still uphold cultural and religious norms prohibiting premarital sex.[8]

In addition, some responses in countries where coercive policies have been introduced suggest that family planning programmes have failed to address or assess cultural values and attitudes within their changed contexts. They have also failed to assess the impact of these changes on the position of women, sexual patterns and fertility behavior. In India, sex determination and termination of female foetuses has become common (Mies 1986, Gupta 1987).[9] This constitutes a strategy reflecting social values and attitudes which support preference for male offsprings.

4.   Factors Supporting the Observed Patterns

The observations above indicate that as a strategy for achieving social and economic development in poor countries, family planning has had limited impact in many cases. There are two major underlying factors. First is the general assumption that birth control technology can solve social reproductive problems. Its introduction was therefore not conceptualized in specific social and moral contexts. Second, planners and policy makers lack concrete knowledge of the local reality. This implies little knowledge concerning the way target groups perceive their situation and the specific problems in question, their capacities or social infrastructure for action and forms and processes of resistance. From this perspective, family planning is generally poor planning because it is based on decontextualized knowledge (Burns and Dietz, 1988). The concept of decontextualized knowledge refers to the situation where planners lack knowledge about the realities of their local, everyday social setting.

Family planning for example focused on the fertility of married women. The programme thus ignored other social groups relevant to fertility and its outcome, as well as emerging sexual patterns and the authority and power structure within which sexual and fertility decisions are made. The programme further ignored reproductive problems such as infertility and sexually transmitted diseases which are of major concern to women. Lastly, plans were based on the conviction that prevailing high fertility is supported by cultural values and attitudes favouring high fertility. Donors and policy planners assumed this would, however, be overcome with information concerning modern contraceptives.

This implies that the role of cultural values and attitudes again was not considered in its concrete social context and/or the prevailing reality. My research suggests that the problem of high birth rates may derive not so much from cultural values and attitudes favouring high fertility, but rather from the breakdown of cultural systems which previously regulated and controlled sexuality and reproduction. In the pre-colonial Kikuyu fertility model, for instance, the high value of many children occurred within an elaborate social order which offered regulating and control mechanisms. Variations exist between groups and peoples in Africa. But in a general way, anthropological evidence suggests that most people in Sub-saharan Africa had strict regulating and control mechanisms (Molnos 1973, Koponen 1988, Oppong 1987). Through colonialism and ensuing modernization processes, these control and regulating systems have been eroded. Today they probably only exist in people's memory. But without understanding cultural values and attitudes within this changing context, it has not been possible to mobilize what still exists in people's memory for the support of new fertility models and more, importantly, to establish a sexual moral order.

From another perspective, there is often a genuine lack of cognitive and social infrastructure for action. Family planning depends on intimate sexual dialogue. The absence of such dialogue may therefore imply lack of support for family planning programmes from the target subjects. The extent of sexual dialogue even among married couples to whom family planning is normally targeted is unknown. Members of women's groups however dramatized how they are ordered to leave their work and put children to bed when their migrant husbands come home. Other women discussed their strategies of escaping sexual intercourse during those times which for them may be critical. Other times, women who use contraceptives employ elaborate ways of concealing this from their husbands. All this implies that there may be little dialogue between men and women in these rather intimate but strategic decisions. Little efforts have been made to understand or to address the processes of decision making and interaction patterns at the household level.

Family planning within changing sexual patterns

By focusing on married women only and emphasising technological options, family planning programmes ignored the changing sexual patterns and their impact on various social groups. Because of this, family planning has neither achieved its goal of improving women's health or their vulnerable and paradoxical situation. In fact, at the same time as the health goal is pursued, teenage pregnancies and related problems of induced abortions leading to mortality and morbidity occur in great proportions. For women in general, levels of maternal mortality and morbidity, infant and child mortality, infertility, sexually transmitted diseases and unwanted pregnancies have grown side by side with family planning programmes (Winikoff 1988).

For married women today, the problem is not just high fertility but rather the continuous and closely spaced pregnancies, childbirth and child dependency. This, combined with heavy workload and food shortages leaves women nutritionally depleted, fatigued and less resistant to many other infections. But this situation is largely a result of social and economic changes arising from colonial domination and the modernization processes which are pursued. Erosion of past sexual and fertility regulating and control systems has given rise to new sexual patterns among various social groups. Large numbers of women have, for example, been forced into temporary sexual relationships including prostitution (White 1983, Matemu 1980, Nelson 1987). These women are exposed to unwanted pregnancies, sexually transmitted diseases, single motherhood, low status and related public and private harassment.

Adolescent sexuality has changed as well. Young people become sexually active at an early age and outside marriage.[10] This has many social and medical consequences including: increased unplanned pregnancies; induced, crudely performed and illegal abortions and related complications; sexually transmitted diseases; infant "dumping"; social and psychological pressures (Sanghvi 1986, Musoke 1988, Rogo 1986, Nichols 1987). Moreover, when young girls become pregnant they are forced to drop out of school (Akuffo 1987). Without education or the possibility for skill training, these girls reproduce the poverty cycle with its related health and social problems in the future.

I found adolescent pregnancies to be a real concern for women members of groups in Murang'a District. Apart from the scale of the problem, women are forced to take over the babies of their young daughters in addition to their own large families. Furthermore, both the young girls and their mothers are blamed for lax sexual behaviors.

Men are also a social group which has until recently been ignored by the family planning programmes. This has been so despite the fact that the Kikuyu fertility model described earlier suggests, men were well integrated in the process of reproduction. Secondly, there is evidence that male participation has been central in lowering fertility in countries such as the late 18th Century France and post-second world war Japan (Gulhati, 1988).

More importantly perhaps, the failure to incorporate men within the programmes ignores male social and economic power which is often used for sexual domination over women. The family planning model has therefore ignored women's social and economic disadvantages which often imply minimal control over matters of sex. Women occupy a paradoxically vulnerable position where through sex, they hope to keep their husbands and related economic support. This often leads to many births in close succession, leaves women physically weak, and also lowers the possibility of giving their husbands the attention they require.

This situation is compounded by economic conditions where most husbands are migrant workers who come home over weekends or at the end of the month. This is a critical time and, as indicated in chapter nine, most women become pregnant during these occasions. This is so for two reasons. On the one hand, a couple may be unable to escape sexual intercourse during these short visits. On the other hand, because they are away most of the time, but more importantly, because they are not involved in family planning programmes, husbands naturally become suspicious and may not permit contraceptive use during their absence. This means that sexual intercourse takes place when women are most fertile and unprotected.

Elderly women constitute a third social group overlooked by the family planning programmes. Although their role in the control of sex and reproduction has diminished, elderly women still constitute a social pressure group which may influence acceptance of birth control methods. Elderly women, for example, advise younger women to whom family planning is targeted, not to accept being cheated. The impact of this advice on fertility behaviors of younger women is not systematically studied. But considering that the target subjects themselves may not be fully convinced, any pressure against the programme would probably justify or encourage inaction.

5.   Towards a Model for Fertility Regulation in Sub-Saharan Africa

The discussion above suggests that family planning programmes have contributed little to fertility decline, contrary to optimistic expectations and considerable investments. The programmes failed to consider fertility in its social and cultural context. In most societies including pre-colonial Sub-Sahara African societies, fertility regulation has been an integral part of the social and economic system. Fertility regulation evolved through cultural systems delineating specific mechanisms and organizing sex and reproduction so as to produce a balance between population growth and level of socio-economic development. While sex is central in fertility and reproduction, it is for all societies a complex matter (Foucault, 1976). For most societies at various levels of development, it is elaborately organized and controlled ensuring that all relevant social groups play specific roles. They do this in ways that create a specific cultural order of sexuality. This is to say that while marriage may legitimize sex and reproduction, it is inadequate to assume that married couples constitute the only social group determining sexual patterns and fertility levels. Nevertheless, this seems to have formed and continues to form the basis for family planning.

The pre-colonial Kikuyu fertility model points out that, contrary to the assumptions on which family planning is based, sexuality and fertility behavior fitted in a specific order. Moreover, this reflected the social organization and level of socio-economic development. Within this model, children were, for example, highly valued for security and status of parents, agricultural labour and continuation of the generation line. But as observed earlier, children were not just born in a continuous and closely spaced cycle, as happens to most married and unmarried women today. There were, as discussed in chapter four, social mechanisms commonly used to regulate sex in order to avoid conception and childbirth under certain circumstances.

The negative experiences with conventional family planning programmes, enhances the need to understand and base intervention programmes on people's cultural perspectives and prevailing realities. Although past cultural sexual and fertility norms have been eroded, and are therefore not functional within the present realities, they nevertheless are still in people's memory. Some of the actions observed above indicate that people often resort to these norms to resist intervention programmes. The paradox of parental opposition towards attempts to make contraceptives available to adolescents on the grounds that this would promote premarital casual sex is a case in point. In the same way, can these norms be revitalized, not only to create a sexual moral order, but, more importantly, to release people's energies and capacities to achieve higher levels of development? I am not advocating a complete return to the past. I am suggesting an alternative to technological "fixes". In other words, technology, by necessity, must fit the perspectives of the users if it is to make any impact on their lives. I am also suggesting more than simply understanding people's perspectives in order to manipulate them without fundamentally changing their conditions. Our theoretical postulate here is one of understanding the processes through which people's perspectives are shaped. Briefly stated, the prevailing material conditions, cumulative knowledge, experiences and the specific cultural order are important in the shaping of people's perspectives. It is in this context that people's past needs to be reflected.

Fertility regulation and control is thus not new among the Kikuyu and probably not among other African peoples either. It was part of the daily life of the people where the key social groups were integrated. It was organized to maintain balance between population and the well being of the community. In this way it had a specific order of discourse. Colonial economic and cultural domination generally led to the dismantling of this form of organization. This led to the situation described above where sexual and fertility behaviors are not only unchecked, but children are born within and outside marriage in close succession with considerable medical, social and economic consequences. Family planning was then introduced as a measure for reducing this fertility as though there had always been a vacuum and with disregard for the impact of colonial and neo-colonial structural formations.

Regulation and control of fertility will require involvement of all social groups based on a clear understanding of the past and prevailing sexual and fertility patterns. This suggests a more radical outlook which not only recognizes the complexity of sexual and fertility behaviors, but fits them within a social and economic model that makes sense to the users. I am therefore suggesting that a successful family planning programme will require, in addition to improving material conditions, to fit within a social moral order more understandable and acceptable to the people. Of course even if the past was understood, the problem still remains how to revitalize it especially given that younger generations who are the main victims of unwanted pregnancies and related complications may not even have it in their memory. This is where concrete knowledge of local structures and networks of relationships is vital.

Perhaps this warrants some attention to some recent processes and trends within the Kenyan context which I consider relevant in the context described above. The complexity of sexual and fertility behaviors was obvious in rural Kenya. I observed that in spite of living under the strong influence of the church, Catholic women obtain and use contraceptives including the highly controversial tubal ligation when they recognize the need. At the same time, although there is no systematic empirical evidence, parents and friends are known to secure contraceptives and in extreme cases abortion for their teenage daughters. Thus, while at the surface, parental opposition to the distribution of contraceptives and other related services to young people is strong, there may be other processes going on under the surface. An understanding of these realities is clearly necessary.

In addition, I observed that churches which have played a major role in the modernization and dismantling of past cultural sexual order seem to be undergoing some fundamental changes. In the past, adherence to the Christian church was measured by the extent to which the Africans abandoned their traditional ways of life. Church worship then strictly followed the rules of the mother churches in

Europe. Among the Catholics, church services were, for example, conducted in Latin and African followers had to memorize Latin verses. Currently this form of church worship seem to be changing even in the rural areas. Mother's Union of the Anglican Church and Catholic Women's Association (CWA) have increasingly adapted tunes from songs and dances related to past initiation ceremonies. The main purpose for adopting these tunes and dances is not just to Africanize the church but rather to make it popular in order to attract women who otherwise are not keen on church worship. Since sex education and adult life in general was imparted to the young people through these songs and dances in the past, perhaps their reappearance may be relevant in the development of sex education. In the past, the role of imparting cultural sexual values to young people was played by persons other than the parents. The concept of Christian God mother/father may here be useful. As I have indicated earlier, when I talk of sexual moral order, I do not visualize a whole order from the past. A dialogue concerning adult life in general between different sexes and across generations would probably constitute an effective start. The process of change within the church and emerging structures ca be used to demonstrate in a concrete way the possibilities worth exploring.

CHAPTER 12

AIDS IN AFRICA: PREVENTION AND CONTROL PROGRAMMES

1. Regulating Human Sexuality

The question of the regulation of human sexuality in Sub-Sahara Africa has become acute with the indications of high incidence of AIDS. AIDS is a life-threatening health problem, caused by the human immunodeficiency virus (HIV) which is primarily spread through sexual intercourse. This, and the current lack of effective, medical technological options for its control, implies that the main opportunity for control entails influencing people to change sexual behaviors which promote its spread. Control of AIDS therefore, involves dealing with human sexuality. But this is a formidable challenge, because little is known about sexuality generally and specifically in Africa. What is believed to be known is often a misconception of the reality.[1] In addition and perhaps more critical is the failure of agencies to reflect on previous experiences and mistakes. As discussed in the previous chapter, family planning programmes often fail because they are not based on concrete knowledge about sexual patterns and the regulative importance of local structures and networks. The problem is therefore not just lack of knowledge about sexuality, but the inability of the agencies to generate that knowledge and use it to facilitate prevention and control of AIDS. Given this, there is room to doubt the chances of the programmes of control now being established.

This chapter entails a discussion of HIV/AIDS and focuses on some of its main features, the problems they pose both for the understanding and control, and the nature of responses AIDS has generated. The chapter is divided into three parts. The first examines the scenario regarding information and problems of interpretation. The second deals with the AIDS situation, particularly focusing on the major characteristics and trends. Lastly, the question and patterns of agency responses are discussed.

2.   The Nature and Quality of Available Information

The current HIV/AIDS situation cannot be discussed without focusing on some of the problems affecting the nature and quality of information available. Our concern here is based on the assumption that availability of information leads to efficient planning. While it is true that the information has to be effectively applied to be useful, lack of it poses great problems to programme planning. There are two major factors which affect availability and quality of data in general but more specifically in Sub-Sahara Africa.

Resource scarcity

Keeping records and baseline data of any kind in poor countries is hampered by the inadequacy of resources including manpower, facilities and diagnostic equipment. In the case of Africa, this does not simply imply lack of information. It also means that generation of information will continue to be dominated by outside researchers whose understanding of local realities is limited by their cultural backgrounds and prejudices.[2] Mostly, such research reflects interests of the researchers rather than the needs and priorities of the local people at the same time as it reproduces distorted information.

Similarly, to ascertain prevalence and incidence of HIV/AIDS, itself an important base for control and prevention strategies, requires diagnostic and testing equipment. Supply of such equipment in most African countries is poor and testing for HIV is therefore not regular. Given this, our understanding of the magnitude of the problem in Africa remains a matter of estimation from blood samples, small-scale epidemiological and clinical studies, most of which yield varying estimates.

Because of the social stigma and fear associated with HIV/AIDS, testing requires proper counseling services and care. Such services are similarly inadequate or non-existent in these countries. As a result, even where tests are taken, results are not made available as a matter of routine. This way, those testing positive may never know their status and may continue to transmit the virus unknowingly.

Nature of the disease

In addition, the nature of the disease creates other problems. As a sexually transmitted disease, perhaps the major problem is the general lack of information on sexual behavior. Partly because of its association with sexuality, but also because of its threat to life, HIV/AIDS has generated a great deal of fear and stigma at individual, national and international levels, further distorting the available information.

I am not implying that increased knowledge about HIV/AIDS and its causation would automatically influence sexual behavior. There are indications that while considerable knowledge has been gained recently, sexual behavior promoting transmission continues.[3] The observation in family planning programmes disputing the assumption of a linear relationship between information and behavior apply to HIV/AIDS as well. The question of how to effectively use existing and newly generated information still remains.

In view of the short period of the existence of HIV/AIDS, a great deal of information has been gained from epidemiological and clinical studies. However, many uncertainties still surround HIV/AIDS, mainly because even when available, medical tests often give inaccurate results (Roberts et al 1988, Lancet, August 26, 1989, Eales 1988). This problem is particularly acute among individuals whose immunity may already be lowered by other infections such as malaria or drug use.

In the case of perinatal transmission, existing medical tests are not sensitive enough to determine whether infection occurs during pregnancy, at birth or during breast-feeding (Ryder et al, 1989). As a result, the rate of perinatal transmission remains unknown. This has implications for African mothers and infants especially now, when the campaign promoting breast-feeding on account of its role in strengthening an infant's immune system is hardly won. At the same time, it has raised ethical questions because seropositive mothers in western countries are now given information about HIV/AIDS and are left to make the decision whether to breast-feed or not. Mostly they decide not to breast-feed. The impact of such a move for the poor countries, where the choice is between infant death from diarrhoea or HIV infection, raises great concern (Munyakho, 1988). Medical ambiguities and uncertainties are furthermore complicated by other characteristic features of HIV/AIDS.

3.   Some Characteristic Features of HIV/AIDS

Clinical manifestations of AIDS

Clinical studies suggest that while, the onset of AIDS is characterized by persistent, generalized swelling of lymph nodes, fever and night-sweats followed by what is commonly known as AIDS-related complex (ARC) developing later into full-blown AIDS (Lefrere et al 1988), the complications manifest themselves differently in different populations. This created a need for different criteria for defining and diagnosing AIDS. The case definition criteria developed at the Centre for Disease Control in USA could, for example, not be applied in Africa. WHO therefore developed a clinical case definition criteria specific for Africa in 1985. But, as new information is gained, it has become necessary to modify the criteria for diagnosing AIDS.[4]

The incubation period

It is not certain precisely how long the incubation period is, but WHO (1988) estimates that HIV-infected persons develop AIDS within 10-15 years.[5] Once the infection has developed into full-blown syndrome fatality is certain. The period from diagnosis of AIDS to death vary in different populations as well. In developed countries, the period varies between 18 and 36 months, although emerging evidence indicate, the period may be shorter among the intravenous drug users in the same regions (Rieder and Ruppelt 1989).

In Africa, survival time appears shorter (Mann et al, 1988). This may be attributed to a number of factors, the overriding being the poor socio-economic situation of most African countries, which is reflected in the poor state of health among its population, lack of health facilities, manpower and diagnostic equipment. However, it is not yet clear which and when different individuals and social groups develop the disease.

The distribution patterns

WHO has described, three broad, epidemiological patterns of distribution of HIV/AIDS. These patterns reflect levels of incidence and the social groups or population mostly affected in different regions. Of importance here are the patterns emerging in western industrialized countries and the Sub-Sahara African region. In both regions, HIV/AIDS is widespread. In Western Europe and North America HIV/AIDS has primarily been observed among homosexual males. The male/female ratio ranges between 10:1 to 15:1.

This pattern may, however, be changing due to increasing HIV prevalence and incidence among intravenous drug users.[6] Apart from transmission of the AIDS virus through needle sharing, drug users are also in heterosexual relationships. Furthermore, women drug users often engage in prostitution not just for survival but to maintain their habit as well. Given this, heterosexual and perinatal transmission in these regions may be higher than so far recorded. Reider and Ruppelt (1989) suggest that heterosexual and perinatal transmission has been underestimated because, being largely a disadvantaged social group in many ways, drug users are less likely to present themselves for testing or medical care even when this could help. Moreover, because of their poor state of health prior to infection, they are likely to die early in the course of the disease before AIDS is diagnosed. Such deaths, according to Reider and Ruppelt (1989), are often recorded as caused by drug overdose.

In contrast, HIV/AIDS is observed to affect sexually active heterosexuals in Sub-Saharan Africa. The ratio between men and women is 1:1 (WHO 1988, Quinn et al 1986, Gachihi and others, 1989). This pattern implies that perinatal transmission is high.

But even for Africa, epidemiological studies suggest that specific social groups and areas have much higher prevalence rates. The problem appears to be concentrated in urban areas, long highway commercial routes, mining and plantation centres (WHO 1988, Diwan and Nordberg 1988). Incidence figures in African cities may compare well with those in USA and some European countries. The annual incidence of AIDS among adults in Kinshasa has been estimated at 55-100 of AIDS per 100,000 population. By comparison, annual incidence for adults in New York city in 1986 was 110 per 100,000 for men and 12 per 100,000 for women (Sabatier and Mariasy 1988). While this may be so, the problem is more critical in Africa not just because of the inadequacy of resources, but because of the impact this has on survival strategies and population movement between urban centres and the countryside. I have discussed in part three above the process of colonial domination and its role in transforming or restructuring the Kikuyu social structure in general and sexual patterns in particular. The separation of husbands and wives and the growing rate of prostitution and other loose forms of sexual relationships that develop, as part of the survival strategies for large numbers of women creates suitable environment for transmission of HIV/AIDS in urban areas.

Prevalence in the rural areas of Africa is generally low. But given the high rate of increase indicated by the figures below, and the existing socio-economic structure where migrant husbands move between the urban centres and the rural areas, prevalence levels are likely to increase in the rural areas. As in the case of drug users (who are an important link in heterosexual and perinatal transmission), wage earning husbands link urban and rural areas in areas where such socio-economic structures exist. But so far, transmission through this route remains a matter of estimation for the reasons of resource inadequacy discussed above.

Because of these problems and uncertainties, available information should be critically assessed and used cautiously.

Nevertheless, available figures give some indication of the HIV/AIDS situation and the rate of transmission in general and more specifically in parts of Africa.

By the beginning of 1988, 77,266 AIDS cases were reported to WHO worldwide. In December 1988, the figure reported by 143 countries rose to 132,000, while by June 1989, the world total cases of AIDS was 157,191. By August 1989, 177,965 cases were reported by 177 countries (WHO, 1989). WHO however estimates that by late 1988, the world total AIDS cases occurring since the start of the pandemic was over 350,000 (Chin and Mann, 1989). According to this estimate, the rate of transmission may be higher than available

Table 20: Reported cases of AIDS in selected Sub-Saharan African countries

Country	March 1988	March 1990
Congo	1250	1250
Burundi	960	2355
Uganda	2369	7375
Rwanda	901	1806
Centr Afr Rep	254	662
Malawi	583	2586
Zambia	536	2709
Tanzania	1608	5627
Kenya	1304	6004
Zimbabwe	380	1632
Zaire	335	4636

Source: WHO Weekly Epidemiological Reports March 1988 and 1990.

figures show. Figures from some countries of Sub-Saharan Africa show similar trends. Table 20 presents figures from those countries of Central, East and Southern Africa, regions known to have high prevalence rates of HIV/AIDS. According to WHO Weekly Epidemiological Reports (1988-1990), most countries, had by the end of 1988 nearly or more than doubled the March 1988 caseload recorded in table 20. By the end of 1988, Kenya had 4,295 while Tanzania had 4,158 confirmed cases of AIDS. In March 1989, confirmed cases of AIDS in Kenya had risen to 5,949. In January 1989, Uganda had 6,772 confirmed cases of AIDS, and by March 1990 the figure had risen to 7,375. In June 1990, 12,444 cases of AIDS were reported to WHO by the Uganda Government. Zaire reported 11,732 cases during the same month.

4.   Agency Responses to the Problem

Given the scenario described above, particularly the problems of data on sexuality, it is disquieting to note that the prevention and control programmes in Africa are repeating many of the errors of family planning. With few medical options for its control, the only other meaningful option is changing social behavior including sexual behaviors which promote the spread of HIV/AIDS. This therefore requires above other things a clear understanding of sexuality in its changing context. But, as the following section suggests, these programmes are typically not based on concrete knowledge of the local reality. Secondly, some of the agency targeted options are inappropriate because their regular availability cannot be ascertained.

Condom promotion and related problems

So far the main option advocated on a large scale is safe sex including condom use and the practice of monogamous sexual relationships. This is implemented through mass campaigns the impact of which is evaluated through knowledge, attitude and practice (KAP) studies.

Because of the poor resource base of most Sub-Saharan African countries, the supply of condoms will probably not be large and regular. Some countries such as Uganda are already experiencing problems of supply. Okware argues that a donation of two million condoms may look enormous, but if all Ugandans use them, this is the supply for only one night. Furthermore, major donor agencies such as

USAID have already indicated they cannot ascertain a regular supply either (Watson 1988, The Lancet, May 20, 1989). Faced with resource problems of great magnitude, the Uganda government chose to promote monogamous sexual relationships (Republic of Uganda AIDS Control Programme 1987-1991). While lack of resources is a problem limiting what can be done, there are other factors which have far reaching implications for the control of HIV/AIDS. In the context of condom use, the problem is not just availability, but more importantly also the ability to ensure effective use of what is available.

Although the potential for condom use both as a contraceptive and for protection against sexually transmitted diseases including HIV/AIDS is high, its actual use remains low. Part of the problem, as has been discussed is that agencies encouraged this option without concrete knowledge of the prevailing power relationships, sexual patterns and the context within which sexual and reproductive decisions are made. But it is not simply lack of concrete knowledge of the social and cultural context that is the reason condoms are not widely used. The agencies involved in these programmes present contradictory messages to the users. Some agencies promote condoms while others such as the Catholic Church forbid its use. The precise impact of contradictory messages is not yet clear. Perhaps this may, as the case of Zambian Christian women indicates, even evoke open confrontation in addition to the silent resistance. Christian women in Zambia were recently in confrontation with the government over a message in a pamphlet which advised young people to use a condom if they have sex with more than one partner. The women argued that the message condoned casual premarital sex. This case in particular, but also the general resistance to use the condom as a preventive option in the face of a life threatening problem, seem also to underline the failure of agencies to critically use experiences from previous programmes. In the context of the family planning programmes, few efforts were made to involve the men, even though the condom is a male contraceptive. The level of condom acceptance among men has therefore remained low. At the same time, negative attitudes about it have been generated. Furthermore, as a contraceptive, the forms of resistance generated against the family planning programmes apply also to the condom. Such resistance especially precludes condom use among the young people.

In view of the low rates of condom use, interesting changes are taking place. During the fifth International AIDS Conference in Montreal, the female condom was one of the technological devices demonstrated (Leeper, 1989). Two arguments in support of this device were advanced. A female condom would give women more control over their sexuality. Furthermore, the condom is accordingly designed to enhance sexual pleasure for women. There are two types of problems. Developing technological options for women only reinforces the view of an easy technical solution to social problems, including the complex sphere of sexuality. This technological development attempts to address the question of women's powerlessness and sexual pleasure. While the idea and aim of empowering women is critical, a technological solution of this nature still discourages addressing the problems of involvement of men and women in sexual issues. Moreover, contrary to views from feminists suggesting that sexual pleasure is complex and that little is known about female sexual desire (Segal 1983), it is here assumed that sexual pleasure is the same among all categories of women. In the context of the emerging sexual patterns in Sub-Saharan African countries, a technological option aimed at enhancing sexual pleasure would still not solve problems facing certain categories of women. Within the sexual relationships such as the ones entailed in the newly evolved but growing "sugar daddy" phenomenon, women are likely to derive little sexual pleasure. The concept of sugar daddy describes both the sexual relationships and the social and material conditions under which such relationships develop. This is a sexual relationship between elderly wealthy men and young, often poor unmarried women, including school girls. In addition to an official wife or wives wealthy, powerful men exploit a situation that forces growing numbers of women into prostitution and other temporary sexual relationships. For women who use sex as a saleable commodity, it should not be assumed that sexual pleasure is experienced the same way as for those women who have choices. Furthermore, in the case of women who experience sex during the early years of growth, even if supplies of female condom were sufficient and regular, the possibility of sexual pleasure is still remote.

Mass campaigns and related problems

Mass campaigns appear to have generated considerable awareness about HIV/AIDS, although in many cases the information is inaccurate. But, there is little evidence of changes in sexual behavior and attitudes in the intended forms (Bertrand et al, 1989). As indicated earlier, AIDS prevention and control programmes are organized around the models and assumptions of family planning. They, therefore, inherit problems inherent in those assumptions. In addition, due to the nature of HIV/AIDS new problems are experienced. As in family planning, AIDS programmes are organized around the assumption of a linear relationship between available information and behavior. But lack of such a relationship is, in the case of AIDS, not just because the information is transmitted through mass media to a passive public. As pointed out above, contradictory messages are presented to the public through these campaigns. Moreover, AIDS campaigns themselves fluctuate. They started aggressively but lost momentum after some time. The campaigns seem to have generated fear instead of disseminating knowledge which persuade people to change their risky sexual behavior.[7] During periods when campaigns are strong, such fears may increase. When the campaign tides are low, people may resume their usual high risk behavior. Apart from fluctuation of the campaigns, new knowledge about the disease is constantly acquired. This means changing the type of information disseminated.

Problems related to evaluation methods

While behavior change, including condom use, may be minimal, part of the problem may be the methods used to evaluate the impact of AIDS campaigns. Unlike family planning, HIV/AIDS involves intervening in more intimate issues including numbers of sexual partners per given time period and techniques used during sexual intercourse. This is information which cannot be generated through KAP surveys commonly used for evaluation.[8]

Evidence suggests that KAP studies miss various programme-related changes in sexual behavior and the everyday life of the people as well. There are indications that condom use has increased. Already in 1984, a community-based primary health care programme in Kawangware, a slum area in Nairobi, reported condoms to be popular. Of course, a rise in condom sales does not imply widespread use among all social groups and categories of people who need them. It was, for example, indicated in the Kawangware programme that condoms were being used in extra-marital sex as protection against sexually transmitted diseases.[9] Similar observations indicating that condoms are largely used in extra-marital sex have come from Uganda (Forster and Furley 1988). This implies that condom use is largely associated with forms of sexual relationships which are less socially acceptable. My observations among women in Kenya in April 1989 suggest that the condom is partly stigmatized. The mere request for condom use during sexual intercourse, particularly within more steady relationships, is now interpreted to mean either the presence of a sexually transmitted disease or mistrust of a sexual partner. This situation naturally affects women more negatively. But, even assuming, for instance, that condoms were widely available and were used in all current extra-marital sexual contacts, the wives of husbands already infected prior to condom use would nevertheless remain unprotected.

The case of Ugandan women suggests that married women are increasingly refusing sexual intercourse if they suspect their husbands to be involved in extra-marital sex (Kisekka and Otesanya 1988). But given their vulnerability and powerlessness, women who can question their husbands or enforce condom use are in the minority. KAP studies do not generate this type of knowledge. Such knowledge is therefore inaccessible to planners, policy makers and foreign donor agencies.

Interpreting the changing sexual patterns

The twin problem of basing and organizing programmes on inappropriate models and assumptions, and at the same time doing little to understand or gain the concrete knowledge of the social and cultural context, is common in both fertility and AIDS control programmes. The family planning programme assumed that high fertility is maintained by cultural values favouring large numbers of children (Caldwell and Caldwell 1988). But little was done to address the concrete contexts and patterns within which such values exist, whether past or contemporary. It was only assumed that these values would change as women used contraceptives and realized the benefits of family planning.

Similarly, it is now assumed that promiscuous behavior which promotes transmission of HIV/AIDS is largely a consequence of African cultures. This view has recently been supported by Caldwell et al (1989) who argue that in spite of the attempts by missionaries and colonial administrators to civilize or more specifically westernize Africa, sexuality there has remained permissive. According to them, the fear of AIDS will accomplish what colonial administrators and missionaries were unable to. The assumption that promiscuity is culturally supported reinforced the suggestion dominating the early 1980s, that HIV/AIDS originated in Central Africa.[10]

But as discussed above, even for Sub-Saharan Africa, the epidemiology of HIV/AIDS suggests concentration in specific areas which have large male migrant labour. These are also centres of rapid social and economic changes, where as a result of erosion of control systems, new sexual patterns have emerged. Even for the Lake Victoria region including Kagera which, according to Udarvady (1988), has historically and culturally freer sexual behaviors, it is difficult to determine the extent to which sexual behaviors are still culturally regulated given the upheavals and war situation of the past decade or two. Furthermore, what is often claimed to be open sex took place in contexts where in fact many control mechanisms existed.

Early anthropologists had limited understanding of the concrete context of sexuality in Africa, mainly because of their political interests, arrogance and cultural backgrounds. Observations made by Leakey (1977), a missionary who lived all his life among the Kikuyu, help to elaborate this point. Among the Kikuyu people, there were many occasions when sexual intercourse among married couples took place as part of ritual. At the same time, there were many taboos prohibiting sex during ritual occasions. But since the ritual had to be performed in order to ascertain the well-being of the community, the wife could have ritual sex with a man other than her husband, but mostly an age-mate of the husband. Leakey, whose records refer to the Kikuyu life before 1903, attempted to find out the feelings of Kikuyu women about having sex with a man they probably did not love. To a missionary like Leakey at that time, monogamy and romantic love were perhaps the only acceptable forms of marriage and sexual practice. For the Kikuyu women, ritual sex was a social responsibility and duty which had to be performed for the good of the community. Failure to perform it could be catastrophic. The idea of romantic love as a prerequisite for sex did not arise in that case. A practice such as the one described here is what is often referred to as open sex. Sex was open in the sense that it was socially acceptable for men and women to have sexual intercourse outside their marriage under certain conditions. In most cases however, this was public knowledge and had no negative connotation. In this way, it differs from the victorian sexual model, where extra-marital sex is socially prohibited, but nonetheless widely practised secretly.

According to the Kikuyu sexual model presented earlier, promiscuity is new and needs to be addressed within that context. The Ngwiko or limited sexual play among initiated young people was interpreted by the missionaries as open sexuality. There is no denial because as just indicated, sex in most African cultures was open. But, at the same time, sex took place within strict rules of conduct. In the case of Ngwiko, young men and women were allowed to sleep together and to achieve sexual satisfaction without full sexual intercourse. Sleeping together without sexual intercourse however, required strong discipline on the part of the young people concerned. This discipline did not developed naturally. It was socially instilled through the long process of education which culminated in initiation ceremonies. Without these control mechanisms and processes which instilled discipline and social responsibility, sexuality among the various social groups has changed. As discussed above, large numbers of people have sex with many different people secretly. In the past, when sex occurred outside marriage, those involved were at least known to their age-groups, both men and women. Sexual contact tracing within the emerging sexual patterns is overtly difficult and is a major factor limiting the control of sexually transmitted diseases. For HIV/AIDS, the risks of anonymity and secrecy are even more critical because of its long incubation period.

This notwithstanding, there is a striking paradox in the kinds of programmes being implemented. It is assumed on the one hand, that African societies have sexual customs peculiar to themselves. On the other hand, AIDS prevention and control programmes have so far been designed as though sexual practices are the same everywhere. This implies, for example, that the programmes have not considered promiscuity and analysed it in its concrete context. Promiscuity among gay men in USA, as described by Shilts (1987), has features and patterns different from female prostitutes and promiscuous males in Africa. Homosexual males have larger numbers of sexual partners per given time. Anal sex is moreover a practice more commonly used by homosexual males. Evidence seem to indicate that anal sex and having large numbers of sexual partners are high-risk practices. Although according to the Kinsey Institute, anal sex is prevalent among heterosexuals as well (Lorian 1988), there is little evidence of its existence, particularly in rural areas of Sub-Sahara Africa. In spite of this, anal sex is one of the questions WHO (KAP) surveys have tried to determine. The demand for such knowledge in the control of AIDS is no doubt great. But it has to be generated by methods other than KAP surveys. The following section demonstrates the limitations of KAP surveys especially in the sensitive issue of sexuality.

KAP surveys generally provide only surface patterns. They have little potential, for example, in generating a deep understanding of the realities and ongoing but less obvious processes. If we take, for example, the practice of anal sex, the question would attempt to establish whether or not women, say, in a rural area practice anal sex. A number of responses are likely. Most probably the response will be negative. The fact that the response is negative does not say much. Nevertheless, in communities where forms of sex other than the normal are taboo, such a question is highly decontextualized. Moreover, the usual practice in such surveys is to employ young educated interviewers. The main motivation here is communication considerations, not between the interviewers and their respondents, but between the researchers and the interviewers. For many rural communities in Africa, there are rules governing who interacts with whom especially in matters of sexuality, including asking questions. It is particularly embarrassing for young people to question men and women who are older than themselves about sexuality. In this context, to question people on sexual matters which are considered taboo would seem to be a lack of respect for and an affront to the community.

It is often argued that people answer these questions anyway. The problem here is not whether people agree to answer questions or not. And it is true that most rural people in Africa have a positive outlook and are not likely to refuse answering questions. But as I have argued before, this positive posture is many times also used for resisting what does not fit into the ideals of the people. The women's groups of this book, for example, resist fertility control without any negative undertones. When they are questioned about their role in encouraging fertility control, their response is positive. But intensive observations of their activities and interactions indicate that, contrary to their response, in fact they discourage the use of contraceptives. In other situations, where communities have been exposed to numerous research activities, respondents may answer questions primarily to get rid of the interviewer. This fits within the form of resistance just mentioned. The concern in view of these methodological problems is the nature of information obtained and more importantly the relevance of the conclusions to policy and planning. In my view, control of HIV/AIDS requires methods and strategies carefully based on knowledge and realities of the local situation, including the nature and patterns of change, and processes relating to sexuality.

5.   Summary and Conclusions

This chapter has focused on HIV/AIDS and discussed it from the point of view of the major features, distribution patterns and responses that it has generated. Available epidemiological evidence indicate that HIV/AIDS is widespread, but there are variations in populations affected in different regions.

Control programmes are largely based on campaigns similar to those of family planning. This means they share many of the problems inherent in the assumptions of family planning. There are however unique problems arising because of the nature of HIV/AIDS.

The main emphasis of the programme at present is to promote safe sex including condom use and monogamous sexual relationships through mass campaigns. The impact is evaluated mainly through KAP surveys. From these observations, one can draw a number of conclusions. HIV/AIDS has many ambiguities and uncertainties which limit the possibilities for its control. No attempts have been made to base the control programmes on an understanding of the concrete or contextualized knowledge of actual practices, power relationships, network of relationships and ongoing processes. In the recent past, however, the need for a better understanding of the communities where programmes are introduced has gained momentum. But what is the nature of this understanding? Is it an understanding of the local cultures that only enables development agencies to manipulate the communities and entice their co-operation in programmes planned by such agencies. I am concerned with an understanding that encourages the local people to unleash their potentials say to mobilize and organize themselves; empowers them to question outsiders and programmes which are irrelevant to their needs and priorities; enables them to make choices and to selectively adapt technological innovations suited to their environment and needs. Such an understanding therefore implies formulating and designing models whose priority include mobilizing capacities of affected communities to better cope with their problems.

Appendix A

A letter from District CDO to all locational CDAs, in June 1979.

Re: Government assistance to women's groups

There are specified procedures in allocation of any government grants-in-aid of whichever nature especially to projects related to development.

This applies also to aid given to women groups. Initially, the group's main objective is to improve the living conditions for every member with group cash contribution. While they have not fulfilled this objective and if they do not start any other project such as piggery, poultry or building shops; they are not likely to be considered for aid.

(1) If they are to be considered for Aid, their application should follow through the Committees on Locational or Divisional levels. This is for consideration by District Community Development Committee (Self-Help) or District Development Committees.

(2) If any group is considered for aid through the Women Bureau, the Locational and Divisional CDAs have to be consulted first so that project analysis and report is available.

227

(3) Other than through these two procedures, any group may benefit from government aid through direct contact with any officer who is capable of contributing a personal donation to individual group. Even then, the CDAs are required to indicate such in their reports.

The purpose of writing these details is to enlighten you on what information you have to give to Ndikwe Women Group.

You are aware of their case and that somehow this office was committed at their fund raising in 1977. This office may not be able to accept the commitment because other than the procedures indicated in this letter, there is no other way to help them. When they start economic oriented project, then they are advised to apply for aid .

I have also mentioned this to the two officers who made this mistake that the office has no liability to the commitment.

Appendix B

To All Divisional CDAs Murang'a District (with enough copies to Locational CDAs)

Re: Election of women committees

This is to remind you of the above underlined subject. According to the District constitution, the exercise should commence in this month (Oct. 1978) as appended.

1) Groups committee in October
2) Locational committee in November
3) Divisional and District committee in December

Please advise women to elect learned members who are:

a) able to read and write
b) Have sense of development.

After the Divisional elections please send the three names to the Districts office as usual.

District Community Development Officer, Murang'a

Appendix C

Kihara Mixed Self-Help Group: Rules Governing the Group

1) Members should attend general meetings. Failure will result in a fine of Ksh 5 if no proper reason is given.

2) Decision reached or passed by committee should be accepted by members of the group. A proper reason may however be given to why the decision cannot be accepted.

3) Any member of the group who is deemed to be drunk or taken drugs which affects ones mind (Kurefia) is not allowed to speak in any meeting.

4) No member is allowed to use abusive language in any meeting.

5) No two members can speak at one time, one member at a time is allowed by the speaker.

6) Failing to contribute towards your share twice no fine if all amount due is paid on the next turn. Failing next turn is liable to a fine of Ksh 5 per turn.

7) Harvesting month every member will pay an addition of Ksh 10 in order to increase the share then Shs 20.

8) Failing to continue with contributions no refund is allowed unless one sells his shares to an incoming member together with all contributions and fines due will be met by the new member.

9) General meetings will be starting at 09.00 a.m. to 01.00 p.m.

10) Contribution of shares will be taking place on 7th day of every month from 9.00 hrs to 11.00 hrs. If 7th day follows on Saturday, Sunday or public holidays payment collection will be the following week day.

11) General election of the members of the committee can take place whenever the group members and existing committee members deem it necessary (1 year).

12) Withdrawal of any member of the committee, a general election should take place. Members of the committee cannot nominate a member in order to be a member of the committee.

These rules will be approved by the C.D.A. & the sub-chief on 7th December, 1982. Any changes or amendments made by the above will be accepted and if any additions will also be accepted by the members of the group. Both committee and governing rules of the group as indicated above after being approved will become effective immediately.

Secretary

Appendix D

Minutes of the Divisional Women's Committee Meeting at Kahuro on 6th February 1976

Present: Nine locational women's representatives. Seven government officers (the divisional and locational CDAs).

Absent: Two representatives from Gikindu Location with apology. Three representatives from Mbiri Location without apology.

Min 1/76: The meeting started with a prayer led by one of the committee members at 11.30 AM.

Min 2/76: The Divisional CDA thanked all the members for having attended the meeting. She also introduced the Divisional Officer (D.O).

The DO welcomed the members to the Divisional Centre and said they should be free to discuss their ideas. He encouraged the members by saying that they had done alot of good work. Millions of shillings had been achieved through self-help work. He singled out Mugoiri and said it had the most groups in the Kiharu Division, and would soon celebrate its achievement. The DO reminded women that caring of group funds is most important. One or two groups in the Division were affected by this and he settled the matter by changing group leaders.

He further gave an example of Kandara groups which were planning to keep cows, poultry etc and over 50 grade cows had been given.

The CDA reported that some groups in Kiharu had already started keeping poultry, pigs and goats which is a step forward, even though some of the group members fail to continue with the group soon after receiving their share. They don't either refund the money given by the group. Some of the affected members are the converted ones. Another member appealed to the DO to follow up the groups' progress. Also requested for were the field officers in the Department of Agriculture etc, to be visiting these newly started projects as we are almost connected with the work we do in keeping the animals by the groups. Those giving help should be thanked for the nice work they have done. The D.O responded that any person who refused to pay what is required to be paid will be reported to his office for advice and then he will take further action. He is also ready to visit any group in need of help of keeping proper accounts if he is informed in time and when necessary.

Min 3/76: Election 1, Chairlady 2, Vice chairlady 3, Secretary 4, Treasurer

Min 4/76: Divisional representatives to the District committee from Weithaga, Mugoiri and Gikindu Locations.

Min 5/76: Any other business.

The committee noted that there were sewing machines given to various groups in the Division and they are not utilized. They will therefore be traced and reclaimed to be given to more active groups.

The committee agreed to start contributing food to the areas affected by drought. Whatever they contribute will be handed over to the locational CDAs, who will report to the Divisional CDA for further forwarding by the district Community Development Office.

All the participants were given lunch at three shilling.

The meeting ended with a short prayer at 3.30 PM.

Notes

Chapter 1

1. There is a tendency to confuse women's groups, Women's Bureau and Maendeleo Ya Wanawake Organization. We have defined women's groups as small grassroot structures concentrated in a small geographical area. The other organizations are national, Women's Bureau being a government agency while the other is a voluntary agency. Both target their programmes through women's groups.

2. Carman, the colonial medical officer in the 1920s has given a vivid description of the process of establishing western medicine in Kenya.

3. Development Plan 1984-1988. The section dealing with health.

4. According to World Bank estimates, 83% of all occupied dwellings were in 1979 without water supply, 70% of rural population are poor smallholders while a conservative figure of 11% of all households is reported to be landless. The majority of the people are therefore subject to malnutrition, poor sanitary conditions and subsequently disease, ill-health and death.

5. The number of medical personnel is shown to have increased. But the majority of all the available doctors for example work in the urban areas. Furthermore, a large proportion of qualified medical doctors instead of practicing in hospitals, are deployed as administrative heads of various departments of the Ministry of Health headquarters in Nairobi.

6. Response to government population control programme is generally poor. During fieldwork in early 1985, preliminary results from a contraceptive prevalence study showed a 14% acceptance rate. A director of the study was depressed by these results (CBS -Personal Communication 1985).

Chapter 2

1. Soil erosion in the African reserves was regarded to be a growing problem. The problem was blamed on the increasing African population and their animals rather than the indiscriminate exploitation and plunder of resources during colonial domination process.

2. See chapter 5, for a discussion of how white settlers acquired land in the White Highlands.

3. This is important in the context of reproductive health problems such as sexually transmitted diseases and related complications. More groups in Gikindu and Mbiri the two locations bordering Makuyu Division had recruited childless women. It is likely that the presence of single males creates problems of prostitution similar to those experienced in urban areas, resulting in high rates of sexually transmitted diseases and related complications. My key informants indicated the area has a high prevalence of sexually transmitted diseases.

4. Vivid accounts of actual battles fought in this particular area between Mau mau and the colonial government forces have been given by Mau Mau fighters. These written accounts tally with information gathered through interviews during this study. The Kayahwe River which borders Kiharu to the south, is still referred to as the slaughter area by the local people. They recalled an extensive battle between government forces and the Mau Mau fighters.

5. Rural people have mainly been exposed to research methods where their role is just to answer questions.

6. Here the researcher gets immediate feedback which is then applied to draw more information. This is considered to be an aspect of the Participative Research Method, which is increasingly being used for both research and development programmes.

7. This is the power of collective participation which gives rural women confidence to confront outsiders.

8. This is also considered to be part of the direct feedback from use of participative research methods.

Chapter 3

1. From this point of view, what Molyneux says is relevant to what is being advocated here that:-

   "The recent growth in the study of social movements, which combines "history from below" with the sociology of dominated groups, represents an attempt to redress a bias inherent in many conventional interpretations of social phenomena. Such interpretations have been preoccupied with those who have power and the institutions through which it is mediated, to the exclusion of those who oppose it and who, in so doing, may be decisive factors in promoting social change."

2. In this view, social actors are invisible. The dependency school of thought falls into this category.

3. Hyden's premise is that, what he calls "economies of affection" (African support systems) have prohibited the development of capitalism in Kenya and socialism in Tanzania.

4. Hutton and Cohen furthermore maintain that who resists whom is a question that needs to be determined because even those who show extreme conservatism and resistance to change, act in coherent and consistent patterns.

5. The historical materialist analysis of the development of capitalism has shown this. Mies has discussed witch hunting in Europe as one period in the development of the capitalist system when women were violently forced to abandon their control of medicine.

6. The German delegation to the 1863 Congress of the International Workingmen's Association, for example, demanded among others, liberation from forced celibacy through formation of families.

7. Some of the cosmetics and beauty products, particularly those meant for lightening dark skins are hazardous to the health of millions of African women because they contain mercury and hydroquinone which are used as active ingredients. Barrett states that, within the apartheid system in South Africa, about R30 million is spent each year on skin lightening creams.

8. Weber's analysis of the conditions necessary for the development of western capitalism is interesting. To Weber, capitalism did not develop in China and India the latter of which was a British colony because of:

(i)   Failure to break the kinship bonds and the traditional way of life particularly the belief in ancestralcult and magic.

(ii)   Lack of overseas colonies.

(iii)   Lack of rational warfare or even armed peace during which time several competing autonomous states constantly prepare for war.

To insinuate as has been the case that, the same western capitalism would through transfer of capital, or even through ex-colonies starting simply from the scratch as western countries did, seems to avoid the very role played, and continue to be played by capitalist expansion in stifling the necessary conditions for its development, not to mention conditions for developing alternative approaches to human development. Hyden for example still concludes that capitalist mode has to precede socialism in these social systems.

9. Prostitution in Kenya has been facilitated by the presence of tourists and soldiers serving the American and British naval bases. On controversy between the British and Kenya governments, over the issue of prostitution and AIDs, see Weekly Review January 16th 1987. On the scale of prostitution, see Matemu (1980). Using court cases in Mombasa where a monthly average of 70 arrests occur, he tries to estimate the extent of prostitution in Kenya.

Chapter 4

1. For a comparative analysis of cultural practices among societies in East Africa, see Molnos (1973) and Koponen (1988).

2. This practice was later strongly condemned and prohibited by the missionaries who could not believe that young men and women could sleep together without engaging in full sexual intercourse.

3. Compare this with women's resistance in other societies such as Sande women in Sierra Leon as described by MacCormack, (1975), and the the Aba riots of 1929 among Ibo women in Nigeria described by Onwuteaka (1965).

4. These were elders in the fourth age-grade described by Leakey.

Chapter 5

1. Weber had seen the existence of overseas colonies as one of the factors contributing to the development of capitalism in the west.

2. Ross (1927) has shown that during times of labour shortage, forced labour was extended to women and children. But, when wives visited their working husbands, they had to remain hiding from European employers for weeks.

3. White (1983) has described the various forms of prostitution in Nairobi during the late 1930s indicating the process and patterns of acquiring property, and the ways prostitution benefited and was encouraged by the colonial administration .

4. Missionary Medical doctors had probably the best chance to encounter female patients and therefore be acquainted with the physical nature of circumcision. Between 1920-1925, Dr Philp had performed 44 operations on circumcised Kikuyu women at Tumutumu Mission Hospital.

5. This pattern, where the missionaries prohibited the ceremonial and ritual aspects of the Kikuyu customs was not only limited to female circumcision. Strayer (1978) reports of similar approach with regards to the Ituika ceremony of handing over the government from one generation to the other. Elders were forced to eat the ceremonial goats without the accompanying ritual ceremonies.

6. Many groups including international women's organizations are still concerned with the issue of female circumcision (Hosken, 1979). WHO estimates that 70 million women in Africa are still affected. (The Zimbabwe Herald, September 25 1987). Many other practices continue but in new contexts and forms. One such custom is the inheritance of a widow. In the past, this ensured that a widow and her children remained within the confines of the clan land which she continued using. She could marry if she wanted but this also meant renouncing her rights on the clan land. Today, male relatives expropriate the property without concern of the welfare of the woman or her children.

7. Dougall (1938), has described colonial education as "a little clerkly instruction in individualism" while schools as "merely reading centres which have failed to do much to promote health, industrial skills and agricultural progressiveness among the people."

8. For a detailed account of this phenomenon, see Welbourn (1961) These independent churches and schools were recognized by the colonial government and were given grant-in-aid. They were however banned at the outbreak of Mau Mau confrontation.

9. The absence of women in church committees is probably due to the fact that except in special circumstances, religious and ritual ceremonies were in general performed by elderly men.

10. According to the Colonial Office Advisory Committee on education, mass education was recognized as necessary. However, it had to be directed to loyal Africans and those who had helped Britain fight her wars which had thus exposed them to civilization. For the education of women, see Janisch (1955).

11. According to Horn (1933), large native hospitals were built and fitted with the most modern lines and up-to-date operating theatres, and all medical equipment including laboratory facilities.

12. One should note here that women and girls did not feature in the medical training programme which was started as a result of African protests.

13. For an account of how liberation movements in Zimbabwe exploited indigenous medicine and religion as a resource to fight, see Ranger (1985).

14. Lord Attricham, the governor of Kenya 1925-1931 for example states that Mau Mau was founded on witch doctors, old women and young tribesmen all who had come to realize that a civilized Africa held nothing for them equal to their ancient worth.

15. The trials and burning of witches in Europe has been shown to be part of this process. According to Mies (1986):-

    "The persecution and burning of the midwives as witches was directly connected with the emergence of modern society: the professionalization of medicine, the rise of medicine as a natural science, the rise of science and modern economy. The torture chambers of witch-hunters were the laboratories where the texture, the anatomy, the resistance of the human body-mainly the female body was studied."

16. Among them were the well known and controversial Dr. Arthur of Kikuyu and Dr. Philp of Tumutumu Mission Stations.

17. Culwick (1944) also mentions some of the dangers of the nutritional propaganda. Nutritional education put emphasis on the virtues of animal foods thus encouraging sophistication. This also led to despising the traditional foods and traditional food preparation like soaking grains which had been replaced by the less nutritious milled maize flour.

18. For an official view of the villagization scheme (see Hughes 1955 pp 170-174, and Masefield 1955). Depressing conditions in the colonial villages to which the philanthropists could no longer close their eyes are described by Shannon (1954 and 1955). A typical village in the then Fort Hall District was according to my personal experience close to the following:-

     At five o'clock in the evening, women were released from one or the other of the forced communal labour to go and fetch food, firewood and water. If they were late coming back after one hour, their foodstuff was not only confiscated by home guards, but they were beaten and forced to spend the night in a cell, whose floor was kept wet from water or human waste. Being late was more or less obvious because at that time, land was still scattered and distances covered were prohibitive. Secondly, even if they managed to get to the farms, there was little food to gather as they had not had time to cultivate. During the many days, women were detained, children were forced not only to be on their own, but were starving and sick. The village then was characterized with hunger and widespread malnutrition, chronic wounds, scabies, jiggers, plague epidemics, dysentery, venereal diseases and prostitution, rape and other forms of sexual harassment especially by the notorious home guards and other colonial officials. See also Gikonyo (1972), pp 226-229.

19. Soil conservation in the reserves had been recognized as an important programme for improving agriculture and conditions of life.

20. At the time of writing, Maendeleo leadership has been dissolved by the government and incorporated into the ruling party KANU as the women's wing of the party.

21. The abhorring conditions in the African reserves during the emergency and the period preceding it could not have escaped the attention of social welfare organizations.

22. Lamb (1974) for example shows how peasants in Murang'a District avoided and fought against restrictions imposed on them by the market forces, the political and administrative bureaucracy, to produce coffee, pp83-109.

23. For more details on the family planning programme, its rationale and procedures for instituting it, and its impact on fertility reduction, see chapter 11.

Chapter 6

1. During the same time, portions of food were given to labourers. In the 1950s, the government was feeding large numbers of prisoners and detainees.

2. The government of Kenya has recently dissolved the Kenya Coffee Growers' Association. This is part of the process where the state has taken actions to reduce the influence of mass-based autonomous organizations thus ensuring government control.

3. Many development agents concentrate their efforts in income-generating or commercial activities of women's groups. The main aim is to make women economically independent. But as chapter nine indicates, income-generating projects have many shortcomings (Pala 1975, SIDA 1984, Mwagiru, 1985).

4. This problem is not unique to self-help water supplies. Harambee projects are increasingly patronized by political heavy weights who compete in terms of who contributes most. In the context of the Kenyan politics, these harambee projects have been turned into a political yardstick for measuring which politician is what is popularly called "development conscious." This has in turn encouraged extortion of community members and women's groups in particular for the support of specific harambee projects and political patrons. The concept "from me and my friends" is increasingly used by politicians to denote that their large contributions have been acquired from other sources.

Chapter 7

1. Group meetings are also forums where members of a group interact with each other and spontaneously discuss a wide range of issues including local gossip. During one of many such discussions, a small group of elderly women discussed while waiting for the group meeting, various things ranging from local gossip to food preparation. An elderly woman told about her problem with collards, the vegetable widely grown and used as relish. This particular woman had suffered from a bloody diarrhoea

two months back. Though not sure, she suspected collards to be the cause. The impact of such a message was not systematically investigated. But in a situation where people hold different beliefs about disease causation, experiences told by a peer may be more convincing than that of other agents.

2. Gaturi locational files on women's groups. The specific letters were written in May 1981 and January 1985

3. Mbiri locational files on women's groups.

4. Mugoiri locational files. The guest of honour was the member of parliament from the area. Invited guests were expected to contribute towards the party

5. Gaturi files. These parties were organized in May 1982 and March 1983. The CDA was in both occasions invited as the guest of honour.

6. See minutes of the Divisional women's committee meeting, on 1st February 1985, held at the Divisional CDAs office. The main issue discussed at the meeting was the visit to the old men's home.

7. This may explain the conclusion reached by McCormack, Walsh and Nelson (1986) that women's groups at the Coast Province of Kenya are not based on past cultural background of the people at the Coast. Instead, they have developed as a result of targeting by government and donor organizations. While such studies may be limited because of their narrow focus on economic activities of the groups, and the need to justify continued activities by donor organizations, they nevertheless indicate the impact of the targeting process.

8. This information is based on available minutes of five Divisional women's committee meetings. (see also Appendix D).

9. Available records show that nine such presentation ceremonies took place in the study area between 1978 and 1982.

10. Public barazas, are frequently organized at the village, location, division and district administrative levels.

11. Locational files. Similar advise is contained in a letter, written in 1978 by the district CDO concerning committee elections See appendix B.

12. Key informants and participants of this particular seminar indicated that most emphasis was on family planning. Records in the locational files, further show that in January-February 1983 a family planning motivational seminar had been organized by Maendeleo.

13. Like Muita, Kihara self-help group started collective cultivation on an adjoining plot. With Ksh 9000 in its bank account Kihara mixed group planned to start a kerosin kiosk, to provide lighting and energy, which is otherwise not readily available in the area. Contacts had been made with various oil companies. But, because the price is controlled by the government, kerosin is not a profitable product, and few companies wish to invest in it. Oil companies were instead closing some of their kerosin pumps in the country.

14. The readiness to capture external resources was obvious. A form of competition among the two mixed groups was apparent. When for example I visited one of the groups, the other one was anxious to receive a similar visit. I was regarded as a resource and in this way both groups aimed at getting this resource.

15. These are local committees which evaluate and recommend projects to the divisional and district development committees, for funding.

16. The ornaments used during the previous dance group had been sold. These elderly members were however not sure who had sold them or to whom they had been sold. Some thought the CDA had taken them.

Chapter 8

1. This gave ample time to inform the local people about government plans. And given the nature of advertising of government support to women's groups, the period was probably used for this.

2. See chapter four.

3. Gaturi location files on women's groups.

4. ibid.

5. See Kihara mixed group, by-law number 3 (Appendix C).

6. The problems and limitations of the family planning programmes are discussed in chapter 11

7. The experts even assumed that these values would change rapidly with increased information on modern contraceptives and as women realized the benefits of family planning.

8. It is however strictly wrong to say that women's groups are not concerned with reproductive health problems. Their stand against what they refer to as loose morals particularly indiscriminate sexual relationships and prostitution reflects their concerns.

9.   The Kikuyu fertility model described in chapter four suggests this clearly.

10. Specific groups had a large number of widows. A third 18(33%) of the 54 members of Nyakio Women's Group were, for instance, widows.

11. This particular group was mixed. The registration officer asked women separately, whether they would be able to handle men. According to the women, those men in the group did not pose any threat (Hau niwona hari na mundu wa bata). The women maintained this even though the dominant position of men was evident. During the group meeting, all men present were provided with proper chairs to sit on, under a shade, while women sat wherever they could secure a clean place on the floor. Similar observations were made on Kihara mixed group discussed in chapter 9.

12. In 1983, Gitumbi Women's Group (discussed in chapter 9), suddenly dropped its membership from 150 to 65 when the pig project was added to its ongoing home improvement activities. Apart from not being a priority for most members, the project became too expensive for most of them.

13. In the pre-colonial context, the Kang'ei/Nyakinyua women's groups played the important role of imparting social values and rules to the youth through dances and songs. During the colonial period, cultural dances and songs were used as a resource to politicize African masses and mobilize them to resist colonial rule. Currently, while only giving lip service and many times discouraging cultural life of the people, the post-colonial government has used women's groups, as channel for imparting the virtues of its leadership and policies. Many groups which were formed in the 1960s and early 1970s had been involved in dancing and had traveled to Nairobi and Gatundu, the home of the first president for that purpose. During this time, women's groups were referred to as Nyakinyua with a slightly derogatory inclination.

Chapter 9

1.   See chapter five.

2.   Shining iron roofed houses raised the status of an area.

3. In some cases, groups save contributions over a period of time or until it is enough for all the members. It is then shared in a big ceremony. However, because of the pressing needs of most women, this method is not used frequently and it is limited to wealthier groups. In 1971, Weithaga Mission Women's Group mobilized and pooled together funds enough for all the members. Members were then asked to choose a household item they wished to have. All the items chosen were purchased and presented to group members in a grand ceremony presided over by the local councillor.

4. Targeting through community structures, particularly rural women, is in Kenya a historical process. The use of community structures started during the colonial period mainly as a form of control. See the establishment of Maendeleo clubs discussed in chapter five.

5. The interaction patterns are discussed in chapter seven.

6. Similar observations were made in the Mwea Rice Irrigation Scheme. A number of women's groups had been encouraged to produce fish. In spite of a large number of people living within the scheme, no attempts had been made to encourage consumption of fish in the area. Consequently, the groups were confronted with problems of fish harvesting, and securing market outlets in Nairobi some 200 kilometres away.

7. Male key informants on the other hand accused women of lack of interest in contraceptives. One of the Chiefs in the study area had just become the father of eleven living children. The chief and his wife were only children in their respective families. As children are named after relatives, the chief and his wife each had reason to reproduce and name all those their parents had not named. The chief however blamed his wife for the large family.

8. The critical inadequacy in personnel and supplies in this hospital has been discussed in chapter two.

Chapter 10

1. Comparing women's movements in India and Thailand, Omvedt argues that the atrocities within the Indian system has provided impetus for organizing and dynamism of women's movements in India in a way that is not found in Thailand pp 50.

2. Their active role in liberation movement led the colonial government to intervene by instituting indirect rule in general and Maendeleo women's clubs in particular.

3. This Kikuyu resistance should however be seen in the context of resistance against colonial domination, and not as has often been implied as merely a tool for male domination over women.

4. This is probably a general problem in Africa and Third World Countries where available scarce resources have been wasted thus forcing these countries into deeper poverty and dependency. Development Alternatives with Women (DAWN, 1985), for instance suggests that

    the Basic Needs Strategy arose from the realization by mid-1970s that, the gap between survival needs and their fulfilment was growing and that growth had failed to trickle down to the poor. Similarly, evaluation of some aid programmes for example SIDA's Rural Water Supply in Kenya indicate that, the programme has not reached the poorest category of people it was intended for. On the contrary, it may even be creating wider gaps.

5. Roscoe reports about a devastating famine among the Busoga of Uganda. The famine was not just because of natural factors, but the changes which had occurred in the division of labour as a result of colonial domination. Men who were in the Busoga tradition responsible for digging and tilling the land were withdrawn for government work. In the absence of men, women did not till the land as a result of which they could not produce any food. On their return, men who had been taken against their will, found women, unwilling to provide them with food.

6. These are even stronger controls than taboos could ever be. (see Dumor, 1983).

7. Cagnolo, a catholic priest working among the Kikuyu people, was, as late as 1930s, when colonial domination had clearly forced the Kikuyu into the periphery, still condemning Kikuyu men for having no regard for women.

    "Among the savage people a woman is merely a chattel... And the Kikuyu people whose acquaintance we have now made, what does he think of his womankind. A woman is made to conceive, to serve him, and to work hard in cultivating the fields; to take her beyond that, in his opinion, would be taking her out of her province and making her a useless thing."

    Similarly, the East African Women's League, believed during the emergency period that Kikuyu girls could only be entrusted to European nuns and not Kikuyu male teachers.

Chapter 11

1. Kenya Governor's Colonial Dispatch 1951. By the 1930s, resistance to colonial domination was mounting in Kenya. Although colonial domination had displaced the Africans in many ways, rapid population growth was seen as the basic problem needing immediate attention. Most efforts then were directed to agricultural improvement but by 1950s, the Family Planning Association of Kenya was distributing contraceptives in Nairobi and Mombasa.

2. Kenya National Family planning 1967. Of particular importance to the experts were value systems which assign women a subservient status, favour high fertility and maintain extended family relations.

3. Warwick (1988) states that members of parliament, religious leaders and the Ministry of Health which was to become the major implementing institution were not consulted.

4. This work moreover suggests that when validity in research designs is improved, the net impact of the programmes, whether expressed in contraceptive use or fertility reduction, may even be lower or non-existent.

5. Female sterilization has generated controversy and opposition from various social groups particularly the Catholic Church. In Kenya, Catholic Bishops described tubal ligation as "mutilation of women" (Weekly Review, November 16, 1984). But church opposition aside, female sterilization is an irreversible method. It constitutes a radical decision on the part of women opting for it. This may explain why some women in El Salvador who used sterilization took a long time between the making of the decision and the operation (Bertrand et al, 1986).

6. They have discussed the impact of kinship, lineage family structures and religious beliefs on the economic life and fertility without mentioning that the concerned societies are since the turn of the century in a flux of change.

7. In 1975, a CBD department was created within the International Planned Parenthood Federation (IPPF).

8. In 1985, Kenyan parents for example strongly opposed a proposal by IPPF to supply contraceptives to girls from the age of ten years. Those opposed argued that supplying contraceptives to teenagers would legitimize premarital casual sex. This opposition forced the Family Planning Association of Kenya (FPAK) to disassociate itself from the IPPF's plan (Weekly Review, June 20, 1986).

9. Between 1978-1983, 78 000 female foetuses were aborted after sex determination tests.

10. Studies being carried out in parts of Machakos in Kenya, indicate that the average age when adolescents become sexually active is 12 years, but cases of even six years have been observed (Maggwa-Department of Obstetrics and Gyneacology-Personal communication, 1989).

Chapter 12

1. Caldwell and others (1989) have for exampled argued that African sexuality (implying one sexual model in the entire Africa) has resisted change and remained intact in spite of the colonial attempts to civilize it.

2. The prejudices are evidently well established. In a recent article, Rushton and Bogaert (1989) have tried to argue although unconvincingly, using a gene-based evolutionary theory, that populations of African ancestry are inclined to a greater frequency of uninhibited disorders such as rape, unintended pregnancy and sexually transmitted diseases including AIDS. The 84 sources referred to in their article include only materials that support their theory. These problems of perception and prejudices lead to gathering of distorted information.

3. One would expect that information and knowledge on the transmission patterns of HIV, would, discourage HIV-infected people from having unprotected sex. But in USA, Shilts (1986) describes how gay men continued, to frequent gay bath houses and to have unprotected sex even when they were diagnosed to have AIDS. They argued that somebody had infected them and they in turn would do the same. Kisekka and Otesanya (1988) report of similar behaviors in Uganda.

In addition, there is bureaucratic insensitivity which has caused delay in taking actions to enhance control of the disease. The Public Health Department in USA, for example, closed gay bath houses many years after the infection was well established and considerable numbers of gay men had died from AIDS. Similarly, testing of blood and blood products as a measure of control was instituted only after considerable numbers of haemophiliacs and others needing blood transfusion were infected (Shilts, 1986). Panem (1988) documents how the lack of bureaucratic co-ordination at Federal level left the US government totally unequipped to deal with the medical emergency of Aids and concludes that bureaucracies can be a co-factor in the spread of AIDS.

4. Persistent cough and lymphadenopathy are, for example, also common to patients with tuberculosis (Harries, 1989). Its use for defining AIDS cases may lead to inflation in areas where tuberculosis is endemic.

5. There is evidence suggesting that this characteristic feature of HIV/AIDS facilitated its spread during the early part when little was known. The role of sex clubs and bath houses in San Francisco and New York in the spread of HIV/AIDS is documented (Shilts, 1986). At the Lake Region in Uganda, fishermen and their spouses were by 1983, dying from a disease which was not responding to treatment whether hospital or indigenous. In accordance with the belief system about disease causation, the local people believed the new disease was caused by witchcraft from Tanzania as reprisal for unfair trade and smuggling transactions. Because of its foreign nature, it was believed that Ugandan healers had no healing power over Tanzanian witchcraft. This led to large scale migration from the fishing towns to other areas of Uganda as a last resort. This possibly facilitated the spread of HIV/AIDS to the new areas (Serwadde et al, 1985).

6. Intravenous drug use constitute, according to studies conducted in USA and Europe, the second most frequent risk behavior for AIDS and constitutes the primary source for heterosexual and perinatal transmission in the same regions. According to cases reported to the Centre for Disease Control (CDC) in USA, 19 139 or 26.4% of the first 72 223 cases of AIDS were from intravenous drug users. Figures reported to WHO indicate similar pattern where 2 165 or 21.8% of the first 9 930 cases in Europe were from drug users (Des Jarlais et al, 1989).

7. The fear of casual non-sexual contact with HIV-infected and people with AIDS is strong everywhere. In her book, Kübler-Ross (1987) describes her long battle with the people of Highland County in USA. Her plan to establish home care for babies with AIDS was opposed by residents arguing that such children would bring AIDS to their county. She also records incidents where burial firms refused to bury bodies of AIDS victims.

8. The WHO KAP survey questionnaire administered in a number of countries has among others asked whether anal sex is practised even in rural areas where such practices may be taboo.

9. Personal communication with the programme director, in 1984.

10. During this early part, Central Africa was like Haiti, and homosexuals presented in the world map as a risk zone.

Bibliography

Adams, J. 1989 AIDS: *The HIV Myth*. MacMillan, London.

Ahlberg, B. M. 1982 *Drugs and Beauty: The Case of Low Income Women*. Paper Presented to the Fourth International Congress on the Prevention of Alcoholism and Drug Dependency. Nairobi.

Ahlberg, B. M. 1983 *The Rural Water Supply (RWS) Programme in Kenya: Its Impact on Women*. SIDA, Stockholm.

Ahlberg, B. M. 1984 Beliefs and practices related to measles and acute diarrhoea. In Van Ginneken, J. K. and Muller, A. S. *Maternal and child health in rural Kenya: an epidemiological study*.

Akuffo, F. O. Teenage Pregnancies and School Drop-outs: The Relevance of Family Life Education and Vocational Training to Girls' Employment Opportunities. In Oppong, C. (ed), *Sex Roles, Population and Development in West Africa: Policy-Related Studies on Work and demographic Issues*. Heinemann, London, 1987:154-164.

Association of African Women for Research and Development AAWORD. *Development Dialogue*, 1982: 1-2, Dag Hammarskjld Foundation, Uppsala.

Barrett et al *South African Women on the Move*. Zed Books Ltd, London, 1985, p 165-168.

Baumgaartner.et al *The Shaping of Socio-economic Systems: The Application of the Theory of Actor-Systems Dynamics to Conflict, Social Power, and Institutional Innovation in Economic Life*. Gordon and Breach Science Publishers, New York, 1985.

Beck, A. *A History of the British Medical Administration of East Africa, 1900-1950*. Harvard University Press, 1970.

Bertrand, J. T, Landry, E. G and Araya, Z. J. D Is Female Sterilization Voluntary in El Salvador. *International family planning perspectives, 12(2) June 1986.*

Bertrand, J.T., Bakutuvwidi Makani, Kinavwidi Lemu Niwembo and Balowa Djunghu *Knowledge of AIDS, Sexual Behavior and Condom Use in the context of AIDS Prevention. Results of the 1988 Survey of Contraceptive Prevalence and K-A-P for AIDS in Kinshasa, Zaire*. February 1989.

251

Bifan, P , Adagala, K. Kariuki, P. W. *The Impact of Development on Women in Kenya: A Methodological Approach*, UNICEF/University of Nairobi, 1982.

Boohene, E. and Dow, T. E. contraceptive Prevalence and Family Planning Program Effort in Zimbabwe. *International Family Planning Perspectives 13(1):1-6, March* 1987.

Boserup, E. *Women's Role in Economic Development.* London, 1970.

Bottignole, S. *Kikuyu Traditional Culture and Christianity.* Heinemann Nairobi, 1984.

Boyes, J. *John Boyes the King of Wa-Kikuyu.* Frank Cass & Co. Ltd, London, 1926

Browne, G. *Witchcraft and British Colonial Law. Africa*, 8(4):481-493, October 1935.

Bunche, R. J. The Irua Ceremony Among the Kikuyu of Kiambu District, Kenya. *Journal of Negro History*, vol 26:46-65, 1941.

Burns, et al, *Man, Decisions, Society: The Theory of Actor-system Dynamics for Social Scientists.* Gordon and Breach Science Publishers, New York, 1986.

Burns, T and Dietz, T. Towards a Theory of Socio-Cultural Evolution. SCASSS, Uppsala, 1988.

Burns, T. R. and Flam, H. *The Shaping of Social Organization: Social Rule Systems Theory with Application.* Sage, 1987.

Cagnolo, C. *The Akikuyu: Their Customs, Traditions and Folklores.* Torino, 1933.

Caldwell, J. C and Caldwell, P. Is the Asian Family Planning Program Model Suited to Africa? *Studies in Family Planning.* 19(1):19-28, January/February 1988.

Carman, J. A. *A Medical History of Kenya: A Personal Memoir.* Rex Collington, London, 1976.

Caulfield, M. D. Equality, sex and Mode of Production. In Berreman, (ed) *Social Inequality Comparative Development Approaches*, Academic Press Inc, 1981.

Chambers, R. *Rural Development: Putting the Last First.* Longman, London, 1983.

Chirimuuta, R. C. and Chirimuuta, R. J. *AIDS, Africa and Racism.* London, 1987.

Chodorow, N. Family Structure and Feminine Personality. In Rosaldo, M. Z. and Lamphere, L. (eds), *Women, Culture and Society.* Stanford University Press, 1974.

Ciancanelli, P. Exchange, Reproduction and Sex Subordination Among the Kikuyu of East Africa. *The Review of Radical Political Economics*, 12:2:25-36, Summer 1980.

Clark, C. M. Land and Food, Women and Power in the Nineteenth Century Kikuyu. *Journal of International African Institute*, 50(4):357-369, 1980.

Collins, R. *Conflict Sociology: Towards an Explanatory Science.* Academic Press, New York, 1971.

Collins, R. *Max Weber a Skeleton Key.* Sage, Beverly Hills, 1986.

Colonial Annual Reports 1957-1962.

Colonial Office Advisory Committee on Education. *Mass Education in African Society.* Colonial No. 186, London, 1944.

Colony and Protectorate of Kenya. *Report of the Commissioner Appointed to Enquire into the Methods for Selection of African Representatives to the Legislative Council.* Nairobi, 1955.

Culwick, G. M. Nutrition in East Africa. *Africa,* 14(7), July 1944:401-410.

Daily Nation, Reviving Morals to Fight AIDS. February 1, 1989.

Davies, J., Mitra, S. N. and Schellstede, W. P. Oral Contraception in Bangladesh: Social Marketing and the Importance of Husbands. *Studies in Family Planning, 18(3),* May 1987.

DeClerque, J, Tsui, A. O, Abu-Ata, M. F and Barcelona, D. Rumor, Misinformation and Oral Contraceptive Use in Egypt. *Soc Sci. Med. 23(1),* 1986.

Deere, C. D. Rural Women's Subsistence Production in the Capitalist Periphery. In Cohen, R. Gutkind, P. C. W. and Brazier, P. (eds) *Peasants and Proletarians: The Struggles of Third World Workers.* Hutchinson University Library, 1979.

Des Jarlais, D. C. HIV-1 Infection among Intravenous Drug Users in Manhattan, New York City, from 1977 through 1987. *Jama,* 261(7), February 17 1989.

Diwan, V. K. and Nordberg, E. AIDS in an African Perspective: Epidemiology and Control. In Sterky, G. and Krantz, I. ed *Society and HIV/AIDS.* Stockholm: IHCAR, 1988:7-23.

Dobson, B. Woman's Place in East Africa. *Corona,* December 1954:454-457.

Dougall, J. W. The Development of Education of the African in Relation to Western contact. *Africa,* 11(3):312-323, July 1938.

Dow, T. E. and Werner, L. H. Perceptions of Family Planning among Rural Kenyan Women. *Studies in Family Planning 14(2),* February 1983.

Doyal, L. *The Political Economy of Health.* Pluto Press, London, 1979.

Dumor, E. Women in Rural Development in Ghana. *Rural Africana*, 17, Fall 1983.

Eales, L-J. Nye, K. E. and Pinching A. J. Group-Specific Component and AIDS: Erroneous Data. *The Lancet*, April, p 937.

East African Women's League. *Newsletter Nos 1-13*, 1953.

Eliot, C. *The East African Protectorate 1905.* Frank Cass and Co. Ltd, London, 1966.

Ehrenreich, B. Hess, E. Jacobs, G. *Re-making Love: The Feminization of Sex.* Anchor Press/Doubleday, USA, 1986.

Engels, F. *The Origin of the Family, Private Property and the State*, 1891.

Engels, F. *The Conditions of the Working class in England.* Progress Publishers, 1973.

Essex, M. and Kanki, P. J. The origin of the AIDS Virus. *Scientific America*, October 1988:64-71.

Feldman, D. A , Friedman, S. R and Des Jarlais, D, C. Public Awareness of Aids in Rwanda. *Soc Sci Med, 24(2),* 1987.

Feldman, D. A. and Johnson, T. M. (ed) *The Social Dimensions of AIDS: Methods and Theory.* Praeger Publishers, 1986.

Feldman, R. Rural Women in Kenya. *The Review of African Political Economy*, No. 27/28:67-85, 1984.

Fisher, J. *The Anatomy of Kikuyu Domesticity and Husbandry.* Nairobi and London, Department of Technical Co- operation, 1954.

Forrest, C. Giving Clinics Man Appeal. *People 13(1)*:6-7, 1986.

Forster, G. M. *Traditional Cultures and the Impact of Technological Change,* 1962.

Forster, S. and Furley, K. *Public Awareness Survey on AIDS and Condoms in Uganda.* Queens' College, Cambridge, 1988.

Frank, O. and McNicoll, G. An Interpretation of Fertility and Population Policy in Kenya. *Population and Development Review*, 13(2):210-243,June 1987.

Foucault, M. *The History of Sexuality Vol 1: An Introduction.* Penguin Books, 1976.

Furedi, F. The African Crowd in Nairobi; Popular Movements and Elite Politics. *Journal of African History* 14(2):275-290, 1973.

Furedi, F. The Social Composition of the Mau Mau Movement in the White Highlands. *The Journal of Peasant Studies*, 1(4):487-505, July 1974.

Giddens, T. *The Constitution of Society.* Oxford Polity Press, 1984.

Gikonyo, G. G. *We fought for freedom - Tulipigania Uhuru.* East African Publishing House, Nairobi, 1972.

Godfrey, E. M. and Mutiso, G. C. M. The Political Economy of Self-help: Kenya's Institute of Technology. *Canadian Journal of African Studies,* 8(1), 1973.

Gulhati, K. In the Hands of Men. *People* 13(1):3-4, 1986.

Gupta, M. D. Selective Discrimination Against Female Children in Rural Punjab, India. *Population Development Review,* 13(1):77-100, 1987.

Haavic-Mannila et al, *Unfinished Democracy: Women in Nordic Countries.* Pergamon Press, Oxford, 1985.

Hafkin, N. and Bay, E. Women, Production and Capitalism, Colonialism and Women's Roles. In Allen, C. and Williams, E. (eds) *Sociology of Developing Societies in Sub-Saharan Africa,* 1982.

Hanger, J. and Moris, J. R. Women in Household Economy. In Chambers and Moris (eds) *Mwea, an Irrigated Rice Settlement in Kenya.* Afrika-Studien, No. 83, Munich, 1973.

Harries, A. The Clinical Spectrum of HIV Infection in Africa. *Africa Health,* June/July 1989:35-39.

Hernandez D. J. *Success or Failure? Family Planning Programs in the Third World.* Greenwood Press, 1984.

Hobley, C. W. *Bantu Beliefs and Magic with Particular Reference to the Kikuyu and Kamba Tribes of Kenya Colony: Together with Some Reflections on East Africa After the War.* London, 1922

Holding, M. Some Preliminary Notes on Meru Age Grades. *Man* Nos. 30-31:58-65, May-June 1942.

Holmquist, F. Implementing Rural Development. In Hyden, G. Jackson, R. and Okumu, J. (eds) *Development Administration-The Kenya Experience,* Nairobi, chap 10:202-229, 1970.

Homan, F. D. Consolidation, Enclosure and Registration of Titles in Kenya. *Journal of Local Administration Overseas,* 1(1), January 1962:4-14.

Horn, A. E. The Control of Disease in Tropical Africa. *Journal of the African Society,* 31(126), January 1933:20-30.

Hosken, P. F. *The Hosken Report: Genital and Sexual Mutilation of Females.* Lexington Mass, 1979.

Hughes, O. E. B. Villages in the Kikuyu Country. *Journal of African Administration* 7(4):170-174, October 1955.

Huizer, G. *Peasant Movements and Women's Liberation: Some Questions on Action Research Strategies.* Third World Centre, Occasional Paper, No. 7, Nijmegen, 1979.

Huizer, G. and Mannheim, B. *The Politics of Anthropology: From Colonialism and Sexism. Towards a View From Below.* Mounton Publishers, 1979.

Hutton, C. and Cohen, R. African Peasants and Resistance to Change: A Reconsideration of the Sociological Approaches. In Oxaal et al, *Beyond the Sociology of Development*, 1975.

Huxley, E. The Menace of Soil Erosion. *Journal of the Royal African Society* 36(144):357-370, July 1937.

Hyden, G. *No Shortcut to Progress: African Development Management in Perspective.* Heinemann, London, 1983.

Illich, I. *Medical Nemesis: The Expropriation of Health.* Calder & Boyars, 1975.

ILO, *Employment, Income and Equality; A Strategy for Increasing Productive Employment in Kenya.* Geneva, 1972.

Janisch, M. Reinforcement for African Girl's Education in Kenya. *Overseas Education*, London, January 1955:152-169.

Kandiyoti, D. *Women in Rural Production Systems: Problems and Policies.* UNESCO, 1985.

Kanongo, T. *The Kikuyu Squarter Phenomenon in the Nakuru District of the Rift Valley- An Interpretation.* University of Nairobi, Department of History, Seminar paper No. 21, 1977.

Kaseje, D. C, Sempebwa, E K , Spencer, H. C. Community-Based Distribution of Family Planning Services in Saradidi, Kenya. *Annals of Tropical Medicine parasitology. Suppl 1*, April 1987.

Kayongo-Male, D. *Evaluation of the Women's Bureau Training Programme for Leaders.* Women's Bureau, Nairobi, 1981.

Kayongo-Male, D. Helping Self-help Groups Help Themselves: Training of Leaders of Women's groups. *Journal of Eastern African Research and Development*, 13, 1983:88-103.

Kenyatta, J. *Facing Mount Kenya.* London, 1938.

Kershaw, G. The Changing Roles of Men and Women in the Kikuyu Family by Socio-Economic Strata. *Rural Africana* Winter 1975-1976:173-194.

Kessler, E. S. *Women - An Anthropological View.* Holt, Rinehart and Winston, USA, 1976.

Kigondu, J. G. The Organization of Family Planning Services for Adolescents in Kenya. In Rogo, K. O. *Kwale Workshop on Adolescent Fertility,* Kenya Medical Ass/ Ministry of Health, 1986.

Kilson, M. L. Land and the Kikuyu: A Study of the Relationship Between Land and the Kikuyu Political Movements. *Journal of Negro History*, 40(2):103-153, April 1955.

Kinoti, H. W. *Aspects of Gikuyu Traditional Morality*. Doctoral Thesis, University of Nairobi, 1983.

Kisekka, M. and Otesanya, B. *Sexually Transmitted Diseases as a gender issue: Examples from Nigeria and Uganda.* Paper presented to AAWORD- Third General Assembly, 1988.

Koponen, J. *People and Production in Late Precolonial Tanzania: History and Structures.* Finninsh Society for Development Studies, 1988.

Krige, E.J Girls' Puberty Songs and their Relation to Fertility, Health, Morality and Religion among the Zulu. *Africa*:38(2):173-200, 1968.

Krueger, R.A. *Focus Groups: A Practical Guide to Applied Research.* Sage Publications Inc. California, 1988.

Kübler-Ross, E. *AIDS the Ultimate Challenge*. Macmillan Publishing Company, New York, 1987.

Lamb, G. *Peasant Politics: Conflict and Development in Murang'a.* Julian Friedmann Publishers Ltd, Sussex, 1974.

Lambert, H. E. *The Use of Indigenous Authorities in Tribal Administration: Studies of the Meru in Kenya Colony.* University of Cape Town, 1947.

Lambert, H. E. *Kikuyu Social and Political Institutions.* Oxford University Press, London, 1956.

Leacock, E. B. *Myths of Male Dominance, Collected Articles on Women Cross-Culturally*. Monthly Review Press, 1981.

Leakey, L. S. B. *The Southern Kikuyu Before 1903. vol. 1-3*, Academic Press, London, 1977.

Leeper, M. Evaluation of WPC-333. Female Condom Barrier. *Book of Abstracts. Fifth International Conference on AIDS*. Montreal, 4-9 June 1989.

Lefrere, J. J et al Evolution towards AIDS in HIV-Infected Individuals. *The Lancet*, April 28 1988.

Levy, M. J.*The structure of Society*. Princeton, 1952.

Leys, C. *Underdevelopment in Kenya: The Political Economy of Neo-colonialism 1964-1971*. Heinemann, London, 1975.

Likimani, M. *Passbok Number F.47927: Women and Mau Mau in Kenya.* MacMillan Publishers Ltd, London, 1985.

Livingston, I. "Experimentation in Rural Development: Kenya's Special Rural Development Programme." In Killick, T. (ed) *Papers on the Economy: Performance, Problems and Policies.* Heinemann, Nairobi, chap 3:320-328, 1981.

Lorian, V. AIDS, Anal Sex, and Heterosexuals. *The Lancet*, May 14 1988:1110.

Mabey, D. The Impact of Other Sexually Transmitted Diseases on HIV Transmission. *Africa Health* June/July 1989:21.

MacCormack, C. P. Sande Women and Political Power in Sierra Leon. *The West African Journal of Sociology and Political Science*, 1(1), October 1975.

Majdalany, F. *State of Emergency: The Full Story of Mau Mau.* Longmans, London, 1962.

Mann, J. M. A Global Strategy For a Global Challenge. *The Magazine of the WHO*, March 1988.

Marx, K. *Capital. vol 1*, International Publishers, New York, 1967.

Masefield, G. B. A Comparison Between Settlement in Villages and Isolated Homesteads. *Journal of African Administration*, 7(2):64-68, 1955.

Matemu, M. *Prostitution and Law in Kenya: A Socio-legal Inquiry.* LLB, Nairobi University, 1988.

Mbithi, P. and Rasmusson, R. *Self-Reliance in Kenya- The Case of Harambee.* The Scandinavian Institute of African Studies, Uppsala. vol V11, No. 2, 1977.

Mboya, P. Maendeleo Ya Wanawake in South Nyanza. *African Woman* 2(1):14-16, 1956.

Middleton, J. *The Central Tribes of the North-Eastern Bantu (The Kikuyu, Including Embu, Mbere, Chuka, Mwimbi, Tharaka and the Kamba of Kenya).* International African Institute, London, 1953.

Middleton, J. Kenya: Administration and changes in the African Life 1912-45. In Harlow, V. and Oliver, E. M. (eds) *History of East Africa.* Oxford University Press, London, 1965.

Mies, M. *Patriarchy and Accumulation on a World Scale Women in the International Division of Labour.* Zed Books Ltd, 1986.

Milligan, A. The Forgotten Men of Kenya. Interview with Mbugua, I. of AMREF. *People* 13(1), 1986.

Mitchell, P. E, Land and Population in East Africa. *Colonial* No. 290, London, 1952.

Molnos, A. *Cultural Source Materials for Population Planning in East Africa, Vol 3, Beliefs and Practices.* East African Publishing House, 1973.

Monsted, M. *Women's Groups in Rural Kenya and Their Role in Development,* CDR Paper A 78. 2, Copenhagen, 1978.

Moto No. 73 February 1989. Unique AIDS Support in Uganda.

Mott, F. L. and Mott, S. H. Kenyas Record Population Growth: A Dilemma of Development. *Population Bulletin* 35/3/80, 1980.

Munyakho, D. Breast Feeding and HIV Infection. *The Lancet*, June 18, 1988:1394-1395.

Muriuki, G. The Kikuyu in the Pre-colonial Period. In Ogot, B. A. (ed) *Kenya Before 1900.* East African Publishing House, Nairobi, 1976.

Murray, J. M. *The Kikuyu Female Circumcision Controversy, With Special Reference to the Church Missionary Society's Sphere of Influence.* University of California, 1974.

Musoke, R. Abandoned Babies in Kenyatta National Hospital. *Journal of Obstetrics and Gynaecology of Eastern and Central Africa,* 7(1):15-17, 1988.

Mwagiru, W. *Rural Women's Mutual Aid System in Kenya: A Case Study of Central Province.* University of Nairobi, 1985.

Nag, M. Why People Desiring Birth Control Still Do not Use Contraception. *Populi,* 13 (2), 1986.

Ndegwa, P. *Africa's Development Crisis and Related International Issues.* Heinemann Educational Books, 1985.

Nelson, N. Selling her Kiosk: Kikuyu Notions of Sexuality and Sex for Sale in Mathare Valley, Kenya. In Caplan, P. ed. *The Cultural Construction of Sexuality.* London: Tavistock, 1987.

Ng'ethe, N. Politics, Ideology and the Underprivileged. The Origins and Nature of the Harambee Phenomenon in Kenya. *Journal of Eastern African Research and Development*, 13:150-170, 1983.

Ngugi Wa Thiong'o, *Decolonizing the Mind- the Politics of Language in African Literature.* Zimbabwe Publishing House, Harare, 1987.

Nichols, D, Woods, E.T, Gates, D. S, Sherman, J. Sexuality, Contraceptive Practice, and Reproductive Health Among Liberian Adolescents. *Studies in Family Planning*, 18(3):169-176, 1987.

Obbo, C. Dominant Male Ideology and Female Options: Three East African Case Studies. *Africa* 46 1976.

Oboler, R. S. *Women, Power and Economic Change*. Stanford University Press, California, 1985.

O'brien, M. *The Politics of Reproduction*. Routledge & Kegan Paul, London, 1981.

Okoth-Ogendo, H. W. O. Land Ownership and Land Distribution in Kenya's Large- Farm Areas. In Killick, T. (ed) *Papers on the Kenyan Economy Performance, problems and policies*. Heinemann, Nairobi, chap 4:329-338, 1981.

Omvedt, G. *Women in Popular Movements: India and Thailand During the Decade of Women*. UNRISD, Participation Programme, Report No. 86.9, 1986.

Onwuteaka, V. C. The Aba Riots of 1929 and its Relation to the System of Indirect Rule. *The Nigerian Journal of Economic and Social Studies* 7(3), 1965.

Oppong, C. (ed). *Sex Roles, Population and Development in West Africa: Policy-Related Studies on Work and Demographic Issues*. Heinemann, 1987.

Ortner, S. B. Is Female to Male as Nature is to Culture. In Rosaldo, M. Z. and Lamphere, L. *Women, Culture and Society*. Stanford University Press, 1974.

Pala, A. O. *The Women's Group Programme in the SRDP*. Second Overall Evaluation of the SRDP, University of Nairobi, 1975.

Panem, S. Planning for the Next Health Emergency: We must Learn from the AIDS History, or be Condemned to Repeat it. *Issues in Science and Technology*, Spring 1988:59-64.1988

Parsons, T. *The Social System*. Glencoe, 1951.

Pedraza, G. J. W. Land Consolidation in the Kikuyu Areas of Kenya. *Journal of African Administration*, vol 8:82-87, 1956.

Peil, M. Female Roles in West African Towns. In Goody, J. (ed). *Changing Social Structures in Ghana: Essays in Comparative Sociology of a New State and an Old Tradition*. International African Institute, London, 1975.

Phillips, A. *Divided Loyalties: Dilemmas of Sex and Class*. Virago Press, 1987.

Philp, H. R. A. Artificial Atresia in Kikuyu Women. *Kenya Medical Journal*, 2(3):86-94, June 1925.

Picouet, M. and Jones, N. A New Wave of Understanding. *People* 13(3), 1986.

Pinchbeck, I. *Women Workers and the Industrial Revolution 1750-1850*. Virago Press Ltd, London, 1930.

Population Reports Family Planning Programs. *Contraceptive Social Marketing: Lessons from Experience*. No. 30, 1985.

Presley, A.C. The Mau Mau Rebellion, Kikuyu Women, and Social Change. *Canadian Journal of African Studies*, 22(3):503-526, 1988.

Quinn, T.C, Mann, J.M, Curran, J.W, Piot, P. AIDS in Africa: An Epidemiological Paradigm. *Science* Nov 1986.

Ranger, T. *Peasant Consciousness and Guerrilla War in Zimbabwe: A Comparative Study*. Zimbabwe Publishing House, 1985.

Republic of Kenya, *Development Plan 1984-1988*.

Republic of Kenya, *Economic Survey 1978 and 1985*.

Republic of Kenya, *Fertility Survey 1977-78*.

Republic of Kenya, *Population Census 1979*.

Republic of Kenya, *Women of Kenya, Review and Evaluation of Progress, End of Decade*. Nairobi, 1985.

Republic of Kenya, *Contraceptive Prevalence Survey 1984 and 1986*

Republic of Uganda, *AIDS Control Programme 1987-1991*.

Rice, J. H. Soil Conservation Organization in Fort Hall District as Adapted From the Indigenous Ngwatio Systems. *The East African Agricultural Journal*, April 1947:200-201.

Rieder, I. and Ruppelt, P. *Matters of Life and Death: Women Speak about AIDS*. Virago Press Ltd, London, 1989.

Roberts, C. A. Berrisford, C. H. and Duncan, R. J. S. 1988 False Positive Anti-HIV Tests with Wellcome Kits. *The Lancet*, April 30, 1988:996-997.

Roberts, C. C. Witchcraft and Colonial Legislation. *Africa*, 8(4), October 1935.

Rodney, W. *How Europe Underdeveloped Africa*. Bogle-L'Ouverture Publications, London, 1972.

Rogers, B. *The Domestication of Women: Discrimination in Developing Countries*. Tavistock Publication, New York, 1980.

Rosberg, C. and Nottingham, J. *The Myth of Mau Mau*. New York, 1966.

Roscoe, J. *Twenty-Five Years in East Africa*. Cambridge University Press, 1921.

Ross, J. A , Wardlaw, T. M and Huber, D. H. Cohort trends in Sterilization: Some International comparisons. *International family Planning perspectives* 13(2), June 1987.

Ross, W. M. *Kenya From Within, a Short Political History*. London, 1927.

Routledge, W. S and Routledge, K. *With a Prehistoric People. The Akikuyu of British East Africa.* London, 1910.

Rushton, J. P. and Bogaert, A. F. Population Differences in Susceptibility to AIDS: An Evolutionary Analysis. *Social Science and Medicine,* 28(12), 1989.

Ryder et al, Perinatal Transmission of the Human Immunodeficiency Virus Type 1 to Infants of Seropositive Women in Zaire. *The New England Journal of Medicine.* 320:1637-1642, June 22 1989.

Sabatier, R. AIDS in Developing World. *International Family Planning Perspectives,* 13(3), September 1987.

Sabatier, R. *Blaming Others: Prejudices, race and worldwide AIDS.* The Panos Institute, London, 1988.

Sabatier, S. and Mariasy, J. AIDS in Africa: Mobilizing Scarce Resources. *Christianity and Crisis.* July 1988.

Sacks, K. Engels Revisited. In Rosaldo, M. Z. and Lamphere, L. (eds) *Women, Culture and Society.* Stanford University Press, 1974.

Safilios-Rothschild, C. Women as Change Agents: Towards Conflict Theoretical Model of Sex Role Change. In Lipman- Blumen, J. and Bernard, J. (eds) *Sex Roles and Social Policy: A Complex Science Equation.* chap 13:287-301, Sage, 1979.

Sarsby,J. *Romantic Love and Society: Its Place in Modern World.* Penguin Books Ltd, Britain, 1983.

Sanghvi, H. C. G. Medical Consequences of Adolescent Fertility in Kenya. In Rogo, K.O. (ed) *A Manual of Clinical Family Planning Practice.* Medical Ass./Ministry of Health, Nairobi, 1986.

Schlegel, A. (ed) *Sexual Stratification: A Cross-cultural View.* Columbia University Press, 1971.

Segal, L. Sensual Uncertainty, or Why the Clitoris is not enough. In Cartledge, S. and Ryan, J. (ed) *Sex and Love: New Thoughts on Old Contradictions.* The Women's Press, London, 1983.

Sen, G. The Sexual Division of Labour and the Working Class Family: Towards a conceptual Synthesis of Class Relations and the Subordination of Women. *The Review of Radical Political Economics.* 12:2 Summer 1980.

Sen, G. and Grown, C. *Development Alternatives with Women for a New Era.* DAWN, 1985

Serwadde, D. et al Slim Disease in Uganda and its Association with the HTLV-111 Infection. *The Lancet* 11, 1985.

Shannon, M. Rehabilitating the Kikuyu. *African Affairs,* 54(215):129-137, April 1955.

Shannon, M. Women's Place in Kikuyu Society. Impact of Modern Ideas on Tribal Life- A long-term Plan for Female Education. *African World*. September 1954:7-10.

Shannon, M. Social Revolution in Kikuyuland. Rehabilitation and Welfare Work in Kenya's New Village Communities. *African World,* September 1955:7-9.

Shannon, M. Rebuilding the Social Life of the Kikuyu. *African Affairs.* 56(225):276-284, October 1957.

Shaw, T. M. *Towards a political Economy for Africa : The Dialectics of Dependence.* MacMillan, London, 1985.

Shepherd, G. *Responding to the Contraceptive needs of rural people.* A Report to OXFAM on Kenya. Part 1 & 2, 1984.

Shilts, R. *And the Band Played On: Politics, People and the AIDS Epidemic.* Penguin Books, London, 1987.

SIDA, *Study on the Production and Marketing of Women's Group Products in Kenya.* Business and Economic Research Co. Ltd, Nairobi, 1984.

Sindiga, I. The Persistence of High Fertility in Kenya. *Social Science and Medicine,* 20(1), 1985.

Sokoloff, N. J. *Between Money and Love: The Dialectics of Women's Home and Market Work.* Praeger Publishers, New York, 1980.

Sorrenson, M. P. K. *Land Reform in the Kikuyu Country.* Oxford University Press, 1967.

Sorrenson, M. P. K. *Origin of European Settlement in Kenya.* Oxford University Press, 1968.

Stamp, P. Perception of Change and Economic Strategy Among the Kikuyu of Mitero, Kenya. *Rural Africana,* No. 29, Winter 1975-1976:19-43.

Sterky, G. Towards Another Development in Health. *Development Dialogue,* Dag Hammarskjld Foundation, Uppsala, 1978.

Stichter, S. *Migrant Labour in Kenya; Capitalism and African Response, 1895-1975.* Longman, London, 1982.

Stoneham, C. T. *Mau Mau.* Museum Press, London, 1953.

Strayer. R. W. *The Making of Mission Communities in East Africa: Anglican and Africans in Colonial Kenya 1875-1935.* Heinemann, London, 1978.

The Lancent, August 26, 1989. *Indeterminate Western Blots and HIV.*

The World Development Report 1984. *UNFPA Inventory of Population Projects in Developing Countries Around the World 1982/83.*

Thiam, A. *Black Women Speak Out: Feminism and Oppression in Black Africa.* Pluto Press, 1986.

Tiger, L. *Men in Groups.* Vintage, New York, 1970.

UNICEF/CBS, *Situational Analysis of Children and Women in Kenya.* Vol. 1-4, 1984.

USAID/Kenya Office of Population and Health, *USAID Analysis and Strategy for Assistance in Family Planning and Fertility Reduction in Kenya,* 1985.

Wainwright, R.E. Womens' Clubs in the Central Nyanza District of Kenya. *Community Development Bulletin,* 4(4):77-80, Sept 1953.

Ward, E. H, Kenya's Greatest Problem. *Journal of the Royal African Society* 38(151):370-380, July 1953.

Warren, C. W. and Smith, J. C. Contraceptive Use and the Need for Family planning in Puerto Rico. *International Family Planning perspectives,* 12(4), Dec 1986.

Warwick, D. P. Culture and the Management of Family Planning Programs. *Studies in Family Planning,* 19(1), January/February 1988.

Watson, C. Uganda: An Open Approach to AIDS. *Africa Report,* November-December 1988.

Way, A. A , Cross A. R and kumar, S. Family Planning in Botswana and Zimbabwe. *International Family planning Perspectives* 13(1), March 1987.

Weeden, D., Bennett, A. and Lauro, D. An Incentive Programme to Increase Contraceptive Prevalence in Rural Thailand. *International Family Planning Perspectives,* 12(1), March 1986.

Weekly Review September 21st 1984, November 16, 1984, June 20th 1986, January 16th 1987, February 17, 1989.

Weinberger, M. B. The Relationship Between Women's Education and Fertility: Selected Findings from the World Fertility Surveys. *International Family Planning Perspectives,* 13(2), June 1987.

Welbourn, F. B. *East African Rebels, a Study of Independent Churches.* SCM Press Ltd, London, 1961.

White, L. A Colonial State and an African Petty Bourgeoisie: Prostitution, Property and Class Struggle in Nairobi, 1936-1940. In Cooper, F. (ed) *Struggle for the City: Migrant Labour, Capital, and the State in Urban Africa.* Sage, Beverly Hills, 1983.

WHO A Global Response to AIDS. *Africa Report,* Non-Dec 1988.

WHO The work of WHO in the African Region 1983-1984: *Biennial Report of the Regional Director.*

WHO *Weekly Epidemiological Record.* 1988, 1989, 1990.

WHO, *Health for All Series.* No. 3, 1981.

Whyte, M. K. *The Status of Women in Preindustrial Societies.* Princeton University Press, 1978.

Whyte, W. F. *Street Corner Society: The Social Structure of an Italian Slum.* The University of Chicago Press, 1943.

Wilson, M. B. E. Land Consolidation in the Fort Hall District of Kenya. *Journal of African Administration,* 7(3):144-151, July 1956.

Winikoff, B. Women's Health: An Alternative Perspective for Choosing Interventions. *Studies in Family Planning,* 19(4):197-214, July/August 1988.

Wipper, A. The Maendeleo Ya Wanawake Organization: The Co-optation of Leadership. *The African Studies Review,* 18(3):99-120, December 1975.

Wipper, A. The Maendeleo Ya Wanawake Movement in the Colonial Period: The Canadian Connection, Mau Mau, Embroidery and Agriculture. *Rural Africana,* No. 29:195-214, Winter 1975- 1976.

Wolfson, M. *Changing Approaches to Population Problems.* Development Centre Studies of the OECD in Co-operation with The World Bank, 1978.

Women Action Group. *Speak Out* No 5, Oct-Dec 1988.

Worthman,C.M.and Whiting,J.W.M Social Change in Adolescent Sexual Behavior, Mate Selection, and Premarital Pregnancy Rates in a Kikuyu Community. *Ethnos* 15(2):145-165, 1987.

World Bank, *Kenya Growth and Structural Change.* vol. 1 & 2, 1983.

Zeitlin, I. M. *Rethinking Sociology. A Critique of Contemporary Theory.* Meredith Corporation, New York, 1973.

Index

Social formation 4, 6,
   50
   agents 18, 35,
   93, 173
   actors 4, 32-33
   173, 177, 237
   distance 19
   order 3, 33, 129
   149 184, 187
   organization 33,
   41, 59-60, 62-63
   125, 175
   structures 32,
   119 186, 214
   system 32-33, 36,
   42-43, 56, 59,
   71, 74, 130, 176,
   181-2, 241
   stigma 8, 127,
   169, 173, 197,
   211
   transformation 4,
   33, 173,
Sorrenson MPK. 71, 83
Strategies survival
   53, 138, 146,
   173, 176 181
Stratification 34, 35
Struggle women 35,
   138, 177, 181,
   186,
Subordination 4-5, 35
   -37, 39-42, 47,
   52, 56, 138, 174,
   181-2
Subsistence 15, 42,
   44, 46, 63, 88 89
   93 136 174-5, 183

Survey 18

T

Targeting 103, 104-5,
   116-7, 119, 122,
   128, 140, 143,
   145, 153, 177,
   187, 204, 216,
   243, 246
Teenage pregnancy 168,
   177, 203
Third World 35
Traditional medicine
   25, 29
   healers 25-27,
   153
   birth attendants
   26-27 155
Transactions 14, 53

U

Unemployment 29, 83,
   127, 136, 150,
   155

V

   Violence 46 184

W

Wainwright RE. 86
Weber M. 40